THE BORDERS OF RACE

THE BORDERS OF RACE

Patrolling "Multiracial" Identities

Melinda Mills

FIRST**FORUM**PRESS

A DIVISION OF LYNNE RIENNER PUBLISHERS, INC. • BOULDER & LONDON

Published in the United States of America in 2017 by
FirstForumPress
A division of Lynne Rienner Publishers, Inc.
1800 30th Street, Boulder, Colorado 80301
www.firstforumpress.com

and in the United Kingdom by
FirstForumPress
A division of Lynne Rienner Publishers, Inc.
Gray's Inn House, Clerkenwell Road, London EC1 5DB

© 2017 by Lynne Rienner Publishers, Inc. All rights reserved

ISBN: 978-1-62637-582-6

Library of Congress Cataloging-in-Publication Data
A Cataloging-in-Publication record for this book
is available from the Library of Congress.

British Cataloguing in Publication Data
A Cataloguing in Publication record for this book
is available from the British Library.

Printed and bound in the United States of America

 The paper used in this publication meets the requirements
of the American National Standard for Permanence of
Paper for Printed Library Materials Z39.48-1992.

5 4 3 2 1

To my Mom and Dad,
for encouraging me to chase my wildest dreams

Contents

Preface

Consider this. It is early 2010 and a U.S. Census form arrives in the mail for me. I pause for a moment, reflecting on how excited I was for the last Census, when for the first time there was an option for me and others like me to check two or more races, if we so desired. I recall with delight my eagerness to choose all that applied to my racial identity. Despite how important and refreshing the choice seemed at the time, I realize I cannot recall exactly what choice I made. I wonder to myself, "Did I write in 'biracial' under the 'some other race' option? Or check 'white' and 'black' as I usually identify?" Then, with the new form sitting in my hands, I puzzle for a moment over how to identify in this particular moment. How will I choose?

I think about and reflect on the range of experiences I have had in the space and time between these surveys. From all appearances and including what I know and/or have been told, I have white and black parentage. Because I grew up in the generation between the Civil Rights Movement and the Multiracial Movement, I did not have the chance to grow up enjoying all of the fruits of the Multiracial Movement's labor that are available to multiracial people these days. Still, I continue to choose the racial identity I prefer and can easily see that more and more people have the freedom to choose. I know it has not always been this way. I celebrate the increased freedom to assert my agency and embrace these increased choices.

While I remain grateful for these choices, made possible not only by the Multiracial Movement but also the broader collective efforts of the Civil Rights Era that laid the foundation for the movements that followed, I also know that these choices can sometimes feel like constraints. Given that I have lived in some of the largest metropolitan areas in the country, I have friends who identify with almost all of the possible choices available on the Census as well as friends who choose identities that they created by and for themselves.

Among these friends and people I know, some of them, like me, identify as biracial. That is, their known birth parentage is of different racial groups. Some of these people may refer to themselves as multiracial, often oscillating between biracial and multiracial to capture their two or more races. While both biracial and multiracial refer to at least two races, "biracial" refers to exactly two races and "multiracial" refers to two or more races. Because biracial is a more specific term and multiracial is a bit broader, I began to default to multiracial in order to be more expansive and inclusive. Still other friends and acquaintances *only* use the term "multiracial" because they identify with more than two racial groups.

Over the course of years, through my daily and varied experiences from early childhood to the present, I learned that "biracial" is more than "black and white." I grew up with some biracial peers who have no known black ancestry. I learned to use the term to describe people who are biracial in a variety of ways including, but not limited to, the following: white and Asian, black and Native American, black and Asian, or any two races. I learned that, prior to the most recent Census, even Hispanic was constructed as a racial group and not an ethnic category. And yet, I know plenty of Hispanic people of various racial backgrounds.

I have met people who identify as three or more races, and this social fact challenges the "two-and-only-two" race logic to which many people subscribe. This system was somewhat prevalent in some of my childhood memories and then again amplified in my experiences in the mainland United States. I now know that the "two-and-only-two" racial classification system no longer suffices. I believe that new words are needed to describe people's current racial realities, beyond the ones formalized by the Census. Since I affiliate with lots of different people, I know that biracial and multiracial people of any combination create names for themselves, or "names we call home," as Becky Thompson and Sangeeta Tyagi (1996) say. These names speak to the specificities of people's mixtures, combining and conflating race and ethnicity, like "Blaxican" for black and Mexican, or "Cubarican" for Cuban and Puerto Rican. These racial equations allow multiracial people to mash up and remix their heritage into recognizable affirmations, and to signal the many racial groups that blend in them.

These "new" terms tend to replace outmoded ones, like "mulatto" or "mutt." Sometimes I even call myself by names I create, even though all others do not have permission to use them. These names take on new meanings depending on the speaker. Names can affirm and empower but they can also injure. I know this because I have been the target of name-calling. Sometimes strangers refer to me as the incorrect racial group, or sometimes with the wrong epithet in angrier instances. This confuses me, because I am not those names. I know that no one deserves to be called an epithet. I am white and black yet some people see me as "some other race." I know exactly who I am but still people think I "look, well, (fill-in-the-blank race)." This dynamic reminds me of sociologist Ronald Takaki's *A Different Mirror* (1993) and writer Jess Row's *Your Face in Mine* (2015), because both of them speak to the reflections of ourselves we see in others and vice versa.

It is almost as if multiracial people really do have superpowers, or at least the ability to loosely resemble everyone while not looking exactly like anyone, though I do not buy those notions of hyper-beauty and hybrid vigor. Nevertheless, I am amazed by how many different ethnicities and nationalities people see reflected in my face, my "oh-so-beautiful face," as they say. Perhaps this partially explains why people really do see (a part of) themselves in me, in my face.

The comments and perceptions of others prompt me to think about sociologist F. James Davis's (1991) point that the majority of the people living in the United States are racially mixed. I puzzle over this statistic, then wonder if this "Generation E.A" (Ethnically Ambiguous) is real, even though I know that race is not real, biologically speaking. I know that being born multiracial is not a choice, or a trend, even though some people regard it as both. I know that race is imagined as biological realness in part because people rely on biological or physical appearances including skin color, hair color and texture, and other features to determine a person's race. I know that looks can be deceiving, that seeing is not always believing, because despite how many times I insist that as far as I know I am only black and white, others will insist that their knowledge of me trumps my own. I think, "Do they see something that I don't see? Do they know something that I don't know?" I spent time in my childhood thinking of clever ways to respond to this quintessential question, "What are you?" but I was shy and easily shaken by the imposition and insistence of others. I learned to doubt that I know what I am talking about because others express such great certainty about who I am. Again, I think, "How is this possible?"

I entered adulthood still nagged by these questions, and eventually encountered some wonderful mentors, who saw that I was smart and curious but struggling to make sense of the seemingly disparate parts of my heritage. These mentors shared their library of books on multiracial identity and more. They informed my decision to pursue doctoral research on multiracial identities and interracial relationships, nurturing the inception of my professional life as a feminist social scientist. Yet I now realize, all of these years later, that I sometimes still have no good answers to that "What are you?" question—the one that used to confuse and annoy me and now amuses me. I wonder why I can effortlessly slip into so many "other" racial categories but encounter so much resistance when I attempt to claim my known heritage. I make racial fluidity and flexibility look so easy, and yet so difficult at once. In my "black+white=brown body," I find it ironic that I can seldom claim whiteness without contestation. I know that the current racial hierarchy and history of determining racial locations makes this so. Nevertheless, I celebrate my brown body, its ability to be so racially malleable.

Like many other multiracial people, my brown body allows me to be something of an interlocutor, not maliciously trespassing but a visitor among other racial groups all the same. Since friendships and other relationships have a funny way of influencing people's racial sense of selves, and I am no different, these deep and meaningful connections to others, to their respective racial groups, may grant me temporary "honorary membership" into them. This happens when people with ambiguous faces like mine are mistaken for races often outside of those we claim as our own family heritage.

I have learned that I have a face, both like and unlike the one that appeared on *Time* magazine in 1993; alike in its racial ambiguity but different in its darker complexion. To strangers, my face suggests a "global mixed race," meaning that I could be from anywhere, even though I am from a specific somewhere, a particular small place I call home: St. Thomas. No matter the place, strangers stop to ask me *the* question, or its twin, "Where are you from?" When people casually observe, "You're not from around here, are you?" I automatically feel "Othered," not native to this nation; yet I am, but in a different sort of way, because I was born on a U.S. territory. I rehearse my responses to observations like this one because I feel a rush of emotions, a sensation that follows me, that reminds me that I am "out of place," or maybe just "out of category." I have all the claims to citizenship, yet, because of my racial ambiguity and multiplicity, am still sometimes made to feel this longing to belong, or a belonging nowhere and everywhere. I realize that I am crossing all sorts of borders that most people have learned not to cross.

This book, *The Borders of Race*, is an examination of the experiences of 60 individuals who have also learned various lessons in negotiating racial borders. Their stories speak to the ways that multiracial people have shared and divergent experiences in discovering and crossing racial borders. My hope is that the book summarizes their experiences in interesting and accurate ways, while challenging and inspiring readers to reexamine race.

Acknowledgments

I am grateful to all of the people who made this book possible. The 60 respondents who willingly offered their time to this project pushed me to new understandings of what it means to be racially mixed in the United States and in a global context as well. I appreciate the honesty, courage, care, and compassion each and every respondent expressed as they thoughtfully reflected on my questions. They narrated stories about their experiences that enrich our collective sense of multiracial lives. I am honored that they trusted me to amplify their voices throughout the pages of this book.

When I first entered the Ph.D. program in sociology at Georgia State University, I was quickly introduced by a friend to a professor identified as an expert educator and researcher on race and ethnicity. This professor, Charles Gallagher, guided me through the process of researching and writing about racially mixed people. He affirmed my interest in studying multiracial identities and interracial relationships, offering support and insight throughout the process. I am also appreciative of my other mentors, Wendy Simonds and Ralph LaRossa. Both Wendy and Ralph shaped my scholarship with their thoughtful insight and enhanced my own thinking with their wisdom. Together, all three professors exemplified the kind of professor and writer I strive to be, and for their example, guidance, and inspiration, I am grateful.

I want to thank the faculty, staff, and students at Castleton University, especially those in my home department of Sociology, Social Work, and Criminal Justice. I also want to thank my colleagues in the Women's and Gender Studies Program for creating a space to engage each other, discuss our ideas critically and amiably, and share our scholarly work. Thanks also to my wonderful editor, Carrie Broadwell-Tkach, and copyeditor, Joanne Moorehead, for their careful attention to detail.

This book would not have been possible without the love and support of family, friends, and communities I call home. I am especially grateful to my parents, Carolyn and Mel, my sister, Maria, and my community of friends near and far. I am especially thankful to Eric for our friendship and for supporting me throughout this book project, particularly during the final stretch.

1

The Borders of Race

Although she was born in a northern city in the U.S. into an interracial family, Bobbi, a black white multiracial woman, soon moved with her family to a European city. Growing up in a military family meant that she and her family moved around a lot, living in different cities and towns in the United States and Europe. Bobbi would later come to realize that these migrations were as much geographic moves as they were racial ones. Depending on the geographic location, Bobbi felt like she moved between racial categories, even though her racial composition stayed the same. Bobbi shared that she sensed her race shifted from one racial group to another, depending on where she was in a particular part of the country, and even in a particular part of a city. The social landscape and demographic of places and spaces shape the way people perceive Bobbi, and multiracial people like her. These perceptions are also based on how she looks, or appears to others. Except that Bobbi's appearance is what scholars call "racially ambiguous." Having a racially ambiguous appearance is not synonymous with multiracial identity, but many people with racially mixed heritage do identify as such (see Brunsma and Rockquemore 2001). The term, "racially ambiguous," suggests that the racial composition or heritage of the individual in question is difficult to determine. In addition, it is important to keep in mind that one's racial mixture is not always discernible to the naked eye. Thus, a person with a racially ambiguous appearance may look "clearly mixed" but is no more or less so than the majority of people in the nation's population. That is, a white person and a multiracial person may be more racially similar than not, despite phenotypic or physical appearances to the contrary.

According to F. James Davis (1991), much of the nation's population could claim a multiracial identity or at least acknowledge a multiracial heritage. However, the vast majority of people reject this racial reality, given the country's history of a sexually violent past. This sexual violence remains a persistent stain on the nation, a perpetual embarrassment from which most people want to keep their distance. However, because of this sexual violence, racial groups as we now know them reflect this forced racial mixture. Increasingly, that racial mixture is now chosen, as are the many ways people who are multiracial choose to identify. Next, I will discuss what is multiracial and who is multiracial now. Then, I will discuss historical and contemporary mixture.

What is Multiracial? Who is Multiracial Now?

Like the 9 million people who checked two or more races on the U.S. Census form in 2010, or the 6 million who did so in 2000, when the choice first formally became available, Bobbi is multiracial in that she claims two or more races (see Jones and Bullock 2012; Jones and Smith 2001). She could be consider a part of what writer Danzy Senna (2004) dubbed, "the mullato millennium," a moment in time literally and figuratively birthing multiracials. At some point during our interview conversation, Bobbi proudly beamed, "I'm always multiracial in social groups." She reveled in the opportunity to embrace her racial sense of self and share that publicly with others. What exactly did Bobbi mean when she described herself in this way? In part, Bobbi is speaking to her public racial identity, or the identity that she asserts in public. This may or may not contrast with her private identity, or that which she asserts at home.

Bobbi's way of being multiracial is both like and unlike the millions of people who identified as multiracial on the most recent Census form. Here's how: Bobbi chooses "multiracial" as her preferred racial identity; a preferred racial identity means the identity a person prefers or chooses freely, rather than that which is imposed upon them, or s/he feel forced to choose. However, she also admits that she sometimes simplifies her life by choosing blackness, or "opting for black." When Bobbi does this, she is often guided by a feeling that she is not being given the space, socially and/or formally, to acknowledge her racially mixed parentage. In social situations, this means that she often senses people's reluctance to embrace or even accommodate her multiple races, or they explicitly refuse to allow her to choose. In formal circumstances, such as on surveys including the U.S. Census, the space now exists for people to identify the composite parts of their racial identity; however, this has not always been the case. Despite federal government mandates to create opportunities for people to identify as part of the multiple-race population, many agencies and institutions lag behind in these efforts to provide forms allowing individuals to check all races that apply.

The Census refers to members of this population as the multiple-race population or the two or more races population. Bobbi's black and white parentage is typical for this population, with this particular combination being one of the most common (see Jones and Bullock 2012). More specifically, black men and white women partner with far greater frequency than black women and white men. Research indicates that the particular racial combinations of parents in interracial families shape the racial identities of multiracial children (see Stone 2009). Arguably, parents' racial identities, as well as their gender identities, impact how multiracial children learn to racially identify and arrive at their preferred racial self-identity.

But Bobbi is also multiracial in another way. This way is something I want to call "more than multiracial," for lack of a better term. Bobbi was born into a black and white interracial family that blended into a different kind of mixture when her father remarried her Asian stepmother. During our interview conversation, Bobbi explained to me that she knew she was multiracial because she has a white biological mother and a black biological father. In this way, she is like the almost 2 million individuals in the U.S. who reported this racial combination. According to a report on the two or more races population by Jones and Bullock (2012), the number of people reporting exactly two races, specifically white and black, increased considerably from 2000. This white and black population grew by over 1 million people, to 1.8 million, with this category growing the most in size in comparison to other multiple race groups.

Bobbi was less sure about how to account for the important role her stepmother plays in her life. What terms might describe her way of being multiracial that recognized the complexity of her biological and blended family's composition? How might Bobbi convey or account for the important social, ethnic, and cultural influences of her Asian stepmom? Perhaps Bobbi came looking for answers to those questions in our interview conversation together; while she searched for some answers to her own questions about race, identity, and family, she provided asnwers and insight to the questions I posed to her.

While Bobbi's experience is not altogether common, it is not exactly unique either. The U.S. Census data indicate considerable growth in the number of interracial households in the country. By 2010, interracial heterosexual marriages constituted about 10% of all households in America (see U.S. Census 2012). What is less clear is how many of those unions are blended ones, where the racial composition of families has shifted as family members move in and out of these family structures.

Among interracial families that have not blended, individuals begin to understand one another racially. Speculatively, much the same can be said for interracial families that are blended structurally. Scholars including France Winddance Twine (2011) who have studied interracial families have found that members can form "honorary memberships" as a result of the sustained exposure to and meaningful intimacy with family members located in different racial groups. Following Twine, one could suggest, as I do in Chapter 6, that Bobbi, as well as her siblings, enjoy "honorary Asian" membership in their stepmother's racial and ethnic group. That an increasing number of people identify as part of the multiple-race population also reflects another pattern: an increasing number of interracial unions.

As this shifting and restructuring of the family unit occurs, family members may endure or experience similar shifts in how they identify. This begins to explain why a black and white biracial woman like Bobbi would describe a close connection to her Asian stepmom, and feel that she is all three, not just black and white. In part, her feeling this way captures the contours of race, or the way that people can cross racial borders not solely their own, when they feel like they have respectfully become a part of those racial groups. That Bobbi feels multiracial in many different ways also illustrates both the social construction of race, and the porosity of racial categories.

Bobbi noted that she is often mistaken as her stepmother's biological daughter; the two women do not make a distinction otherwise, so Bobbi could be seen as "passing" as Asian. That she slips into the racial and ethnic group of her stepmother shows how slippery racial locations are, and how easily being racially misread can be. Her entrance or slippage into another racial category also shows that her racial location is not fixed, or rather that there are no exact coordinates to locate a black and white multiracial person squarely in any one group. The racial rules of the past might work to place parameters around the choices that Bobbi makes. That is, the history of slavery and the practice of hypodescent largely dictated how people with any known black ancestry would have to identify (see Gallagher 2006). However, as more and more people ask themselves and others questions about race, the more these choices ostensibly open up. Or do they? I will revisit this momentarily.

Crossing Racial Borders

Along with all of the other individuals I interviewed for this book, Bobbi exemplifies an individual who crosses the borders of race. She does this by claiming a black white biracial or multiracial identity in public, as well as a singularly black identity formally (most of the time). If she had the words to describe her particular kind of mixture, including the aforementioned Filipina identity of her stepmom, Bobbi would acknowledge that dimension of her identity as well. Instead, when she has the "'What are you?' experience" (see Rockquemore 1998), Bobbi says "I always say 'American.'...I tell them I am mixed with black and white."

I begin with Bobbi's example because she was one of the first people I interviewed who observed not only how she crossed racial borders, but how she discovered them as well. Sociologist Heather Dalmage (2000) describes this process of "discovering racial borders" in her book, *Tripping on the Color Line*. People typically discover racial borders when they cross them, as Bobbi noted here: "There are always people that come up to me and ask, 'What are you?' That was when I first moved here. That's when I first kind of realized, 'Okay, there's definitely a difference and I kind of need to decide, I guess, which one (race) I'm gonna be.'" In my estimation, Bobbi's realization relates to the borders of race and to the "geographies of race." As she indicates, she discovers differences in the way people see her, and she notices that others' perceptions of her shift, depending on the geographic location of the social interactions she has with strangers, school peers, or others. While the composition of her racial parentage does not change, her racial location, or the perception of that location, does. In Europe, in what she describes as a close-knit military family and community, race did not matter much. In contrast to the prevailing colorblind narratives that dominate discussions of race or the lack thereof, the tight-knit and strong ties formed in the military unit where she and her family lived for almost a decade in sum (with breaks in between), people may not have made much of any racial differences that they *did* notice. They did not deny these differences but also did not allow them to be divisive or counterproductive to the operations of military life.

In particular, her arrival to the American South signaled a difference, to her and to others. More and more people conveyed to her the idea that they knew that she was not "just black," with some even thinking she is Asian like her stepmom. This "like mother, like daughter" effect hints at the racial logic that can occasionally buffer multiracial people like Bobbi from racial border patrolling. When people do encounter this racial border patrolling, they often note that it can surface in the form of curious looks or glances, to what Amy Steinbugler (2012) calls, "visual dislocation." This dislocation happens when members of interracial families do not "sufficiently" resemble one another or when strangers fail to recognize their familial ties given the racially disparate or different appearances of the family members.

Bobbi moves more easily through situations where she accompanies her stepmom because of her "Asian by proxy" identity and aforementioned honorary Asian membership. The two are seen as sharing the requisite racial resemblance or look convincingly like one another to avoid eliciting any contestations or much suspicion. Bobbi unintentionally yet effectively "passes as Asian," blending the borders of her own multiracial parentage and blending into an altogether different racial category, as race and family blend together. Because of their family's racial composition and their own ostensibly ambiguous appearance, Bobbi and her siblings often negotiate the borders of race. Based on her accounts, strangers ask Bobbi questions about her racial identity. They are seeking to clarify her racial location or where she resides in the racial scheme of things. Strangers may not know that Bobbi, like so many other multiracial people, inhabits an interstitial space between races. This book details these and other experiences among multiracial individuals who have learned to navigate the borders of race.

Shifting Categories of Race and Studying the Shifting Nature of Race

Every decade, the Office of Management and Budget administers a survey in an attempt to enumerate the national population. Since its inception, the US Census form has changed in one way or another. These changes illustrate the social construction of race. They speak to changes in the social landscape, the changing face of the population, and people's racial literacy and consciousness. These changes reflect the shifting nature of race. If race were static, the categories introduced in that first survey would have stayed exactly the same over the course of time. That they have been modified and updated shows how race changes, sometimes in name, and in other ways.

The survey administered by the U.S. Census in 2000 was the first formal opportunity for any individuals completing the form to check all races that apply, or officially choose "two or more races," as desired. This opportunity partially stemmed from the collective efforts of advocates and activists who converged in the form of the Multiracial

Movement; the success of the movement culminating in the expansive racial identification options (see Dalmage 2004a) provided on the 2000 Census survey. These increased choices allowed people to formally identify as multiracial where applicable, and generally to decide how to racially represent themselves and members of their household.

The 2000 survey presented people with six race categories: White, Black, African American, or Negro, American Indian and Alaska Native, Asian, Native Hawaiian and Other Pacific Islander, or Some Other Race. The data survey initially revealed that almost 7 million people reported two or more races, although a report by Jones and Bullock (2012) offer a correction in response to a population overestimate; a more accurate picture of the two or more races population puts the number closer to 6 million people.

The changes to the Census, and the broader efforts of the Multiracial Movement, partially prompted my interest in the multiracial population and inspired my formal investigation of the topic of multiracial identity. I turned to the Census to get a better sense of the national population. Comparing data across decades provides a "then and now" sense of the multiracial population. Then, population estimates speculated that 7 million people would check two or more races. Due to overestimates, however, the actual number of people in what the Census refers to as the multiple-race or "two or more races" population was closer to 6 million. Now, a decade later, that number has grown to 9.0 million people (see Jones and Bullock 2012). Most people reporting more than one race reported exactly two races, as reflected in the data and presented in the 2010 Census Briefs (Jones and Bullock 2012).

The Census observed an 87 percent change between 2000 and 2010, with 1.6 million people claiming a white and Asian racial combination. Almost 2 million people, or 1.7 million, reported white and some other race, and 1.4 million people reported white and American Indian and Alaska Native combinations (see Jones and Bullock 2012). Since the number of individuals reporting more than one race escalated in the decade between the 2000 and 2010 surveys, the 2010 enumeration of the multiracial population reflects the prevailing pattern of the 2000 survey, but to a larger degree. In both Census surveys, these four groups have the largest number of people reporting those particular racial combinations. Cultivating a curiosity for anyone who reflected any of the 57 racial combinations made possible in the Census survey, I maintained a broader focus than the top four multiple-race groups.

By 2010, the contemporary multiracial population had changed by 32%, not adjusting for the data error in overstatement of the percentage of people in the 2000 "two or more races" population. In the 2010 U.S.

Census, people were prompted to "mark one or more boxes" in response to Question 6, which asks: "What is this person's race?" The racial categorical options include the following: White; Black, African American, or Negro; American Indian or Alaska Native; Asian Indian, Japanese, Chinese, Korean, Filipino, Vietnamese, Other Asian, Native Hawaiian, Guamanian or Chamorro, Samoan, or Other Pacific Islander; or Some Other Race. Of the 9.0 million people who constitute this population, about 92% of them formally reported exactly two races (see the Census Briefs 2012:4).

Despite the initial overestimation in this portion of the population, the changes in the 2000 Census did something interesting. By allowing people to choose more than one race, this Census made multiracial people appear from behind the veil of singularity that imposed itself on the "two or more races population" in previous surveys. In their daily lives, they could share their racial multiplicity, as desired, but formally, this option had been denied until the 2000 Census. This explains why the survey presents the "two or more races" population as incipient and emergent, thereby effectively reinventing multiracial people as "something new," rather than as an always already existing portion of the population (Morning 2000; Rockquemore 1998; Williamson 1980; Turner 2013). Thus, categorical comparisons then, between 1990 and 2000, of the multiracial population prove cumbersome, as people of "some other race" were hiding in plain sight—their racial mixture concealed within single race options. Providing people with the opportunity to formally claim or recognize racial mixture drew attention to members of this population. Some of the attention remains oppositional, as people acknowledge and debate this ostensible "first generation" of multiracial people (Daniel 2002). [1]

In effect, the option to choose two or more races was a victory celebrated and applauded by members of the Multiracial Movement, and beyond, who supported this idea and its coming into fruition (see Dalmage 2004a). One ostensible downside to the option to identify as two or more races was the absence of a "comparison other" or a preexisting reference point. That is, there was no U.S. Census data collection on the multiple-race population prior to 2000. In its absence, multiracial people appeared to emerge from the Census 2000 as if entirely new members of the population. This is not the case. Instead, it is a hiccup in how racial data was collected; this hiccup proved a small interruption to the otherwise celebrated victory of being able to choose more than one race. Because individuals were not given the opportunity to choose two or more races in the 1990 survey, they were effectively blending into the single race categories and/or choosing them as their preferred racial identity anyway. Statistically, the survey disappeared those multiracial people who would have wanted to claim two or more races in any applicable surveys prior to 2000. Those who choose to identify as a single race, but might otherwise have preferred to check all that apply, effectively (re)appeared in the data as multiracial in 2000.

Any multiracial people claiming a single race would continue to show up as such from survey to survey. However, given the racial identity options possible, multiracial people may consistently choose the same singular racial identity, or shift from one racial group to any others that constitute their racially mixed background. (This shifting should not be seen as whimsical or arbitrary, but rather should be understood as one reason why studying race is complicated.) In either case, opting for a singular racial identity (either the same at every turn, or different singular racial identities across time and space) would technically disappear them from the multiple-race population. That is, if they claim membership in a single racial group, they would show up as belonging to that which they indicated. They would not be counted as a member of the multiple-race population. Making this move effectively erases any mixture they could otherwise claim. This is why it is hard to close the gap between the 1990 and 2000 Census surveys, and/or that of 2010 even, because race and racial identity are not static. Some multiracial people may always, sometimes, seldom, or never choose to racially identify a certain way. These options, this flexibility, explain why studying shifting mixture is messy and fraught with nuances and contingencies. These qualities of race underscore the importance of this study.

The changing nature of race makes measuring race challenging at best. That multiracial people may assert a multidimensional identity that changes over time and place, or a singular racial identity, or some combination thereof means that they have a lot to consider in how they assert their racial identities. It is important to value and explore the experiences of multiracial people, to more fully grasp some of the slipperiness of race, and their ways of managing the borders of race. This may be particularly so for multiracial individuals who choose a wide variety of racial identity options, their identity alternately between the different racial groups of their parentage and/or heritage, or some combination thereof, or something altogether different.

As my opening example of Bobbi illustrates, multiracial identity reflects the racial parentage and heritage of multiracial individuals, but little research has yet to more fully address the influence of family members who blend into interracial families. All of these social forces rearrange the structure of families and change the face of families that are interracial and multiracial in many different ways. These changes capture the shifting nature of race, as well as any shifting mixture that exists in individuals and that individuals experience as members of these families. As families blend structurally and racially, multiracial individuals may opt for different racial identities, to acknowledge and respect the role of new family members woven into their existing family units.

The possibility exists, in a postmodern society, for anyone to enjoy the fluidity and flexibility of racial subjectivities. Across time, place, and space, multiracial people may assert or express their racial selves differently, depending on a variety of push and pull factors (see Rockquemore and Brunsma 2002). The increase in the number of people reporting more than one race partially constitutes this multiracial population. Because many people with racially mixed parentage and heritage continue to claim singular races, they ostensibly "disappear" themselves or potentially veil their racial mixture (see Somerville 2000). I discuss this in terms of "invisible mixture," a problem that complicates recognizing who counts as multiracial (see also Lewis 2006). From the standpoint of a researcher trying to identify multiracial people for a study, I found both shifting and in/visible mixture made identifying racially mixed people a challenge of this study. I address some of these dynamics and the research design in the chapter that follows. Next, I describe some of the important foundation work on racial identity formation, as it helps explain the many dimensions of multiracial identity and the many racial identity options that exist; this work complements my discussion of the difficulties of studying shifting mixture.

Shifting mixture captures any fluidity or flexibility in a multiracial person's preferred racial identity expression. Shifting mixture complicates the way we understand race. It troubles a racial classification system that historically necessitated multiracial people to fit into "one-and-only-one" racial category. Much of my work is centered on this concept of shifting mixture, a concept I use to describe the fluid and flexible nature of race. Shifting mixture gets expressed by multiracial people in any multitude of ways, including when they formally indicate one race at one moment in time, and then another or other races at other moments; or choose a single race at one moment or claim all of the composite parts of their heritage. Shifting mixture reflects racial fluidity as opposed to a static position within a racial group. Shifting mixture underscores the extent to which people cross racial borders, or find racial borders crossing them.

In general, surveys cannot capture shifting mixture or the very racial fluidity and liminality I described above. Nor can they capture the growing number of identity options that many multiracial people choose to assert in their lived experiences. Based on research by Kerry Ann Rockquemore and David Brunsma (2002), people with racially mixed parentage and heritage express a number of racial identity options. They may opt for any and/or all of the following: singular, border (validated and invalidated), blended, protean, and transcendent. These identity options respectively speak to multiracial people choosing to identify as members of a single racial group; claiming their two or more races, and having that choice affirmed and validated, or contested and invalidated; claiming the sum of their parts; synthesizing these parts into a whole rather than fragmented or fractional identity (i.e.,"half and half"); and opting not to claim a racial identity. The border identity can locate multiracial people in the "borderlands," or that liminal space across the color line, a term which feminist mixed race and heritage woman of color Gloria Anzaldua (1987) introduced in her work. Some multiracial people who assert a border identity describe themselves using terms such as "biracial," "multiracial," or "mixed." When biracial people assert a border identity that others support and affirm, that marks a validated identity; when others reject or contest that identity, they invalidate, sometimes with expressions such as, "Well, I don't think of you as biracial." (see Rockquemore and Brunsma 2002).

Alternately, multiracial people can assert a protean identity, in which they claim any and all of the races that constitute their racial heritage, or they might choose a transcendent identity, eschewing race by regarding it as irrelevant to their (racial) identity. The latter allows them to maintain a raceless identity, by refusing to choose, or otherwise opting not to racially identify with any of the socially constructed and available categories. Many people do not know that these racial identity options exist, including some multiracial people. These identity options are not mutually exclusive and can be incorporated into a blended identity, in which the multiracial person may have a tendency to emphasize one race but not necessarily at the exclusive of any others in her background. Throughout this work, I explore how people of various racial combinations work to assert their multiracial parentage and to consider what informs their racial identity choices.

Shifting mixture emphasizes the potential protean identities that many multiracial people assert. The word, "protean," speaks to diversity, versatility and fluidity. According to Merriam-Webster's dictionary (2016), the term denotes an ability to "change into many different forms" or "do many different things." Rockquemore and Brunsma

(2002) introduced the term, protean identity, to capture this changeability in multiracial people's racial identity. The term also reflects the racial composition of a person's parentage. Among members of the "two or more races" population, that might mean that someone who is Asian and white chooses to assert multiracial, White, and/or Asian identities, or someone Black and American Indian or Native American opting for biracial, Black, and/or Native American racial identities.

Books by Rockquemore and Brunsma (2002) and Rockquemore and Laszloffy (2005) detail these multiracial identity options in greater detail. Their work, and that of many others, pushes the collective and current understanding of the complexity and dimensionality of multiracial identity (see Khanna 2011). Their work illustrates the variations made possible in a racially mixed person's heritage, with the options to choose any and all of the above, some of the above, and/or none of the above. These pioneering works created a pathway for understanding shifting mixture and the many different ways that multiracial people might move (or be moved) in and out of racial categories in a racially divisive society. The term, shifting mixture, then also speaks to these migrations and movement of multiracial people which are often voluntary and intentional, but can also be involuntary or imposed from the outside.

Understanding The Borders of Race: Racial Mixture within the Racial Hierarchy

Given the current racial hierarchy that cleaves the national population into three broad categories of whites, honorary whites, and collective blacks, multiracial people can cross color lines in intentional and accidental ways. Feeling that they primarily identify with one part of their parentage, some multiracial people choose a singular racial identity; increasing evidence indicates that more and more people who are multiracial (white and some other race besides black) are "opting for white" (see Rockquemore and Arend 2002). Some scholars argue that darker skinned or black multiracials experience a more limited range of options or less freedom to choose (see Chang 2015; Gallagher 2004).

Consider the research of Charles Gallagher (2004). In his article, "Racial Redistricting: Expanding the Boundaries of Whiteness," Gallagher provides evidence of the white racial category expanding to incorporate white multiracial people, with the exception of white black biracial people. He found that parents of multiracial children were likely to choose a white identification for their children, unless they were black multiracial children. This occurs because multiracial people—of racial combinations including white and some other race/s (except black)—are seen as culturally, socially, and economically similar to white people. The selective inclusion of white multiracial people into categorical whiteness enables them to enjoy white privilege and to opt for white or at least make claims to whiteness without facing contestation from others (see McIntosh 1998). Their inclusion contrasts with the general exclusion of white black biracial people, or multiracial people with any known black ancestry, who are largely denied similar opportunities for inclusion in the white category. Their exclusion typically occurs as a result of a persistent anti-black racism observable in society and well documented in the social scientific literature.

Much of the literature to date provides evidence to suggest that Asian and Latino multiracials enjoy more freedom to choose their preferred racial identity, in comparison to black multiracials (see Gallagher 2004; Lee and Bean 2007; Xie and Goyette 1997). Constraining the choice of black multiracials (Lee and Bean 2007) denies them the same range of racial identity options otherwise available and accessible to multiracial people of racial combinations "beyond black." For multiracial people with any known black ancestry, these choices show up more as constraints, a dynamic that reflects racial inequality and a persistent antiblackness in this country. George Yancey (2003) makes this point in his book, *Who is White?* He addresses the persistent black/nonblack divide in American society. Glenn Loury (2002) reiterates this point, focusing on the devaluation and stigmatization of blackness that remains.

The research of Lee and Bean (2007) echoes Gallagher's findings, indicating that Asian and Latino multiracials increasingly opt for white as well. They may also symbolically claim their ethnic heritage but do so in ways that contrast with black multiracials. Lee and Bean (2007:19) posit:

> Experiences with multiraciality among Latinos and Asians are closer to those of whites than to blacks. Furthermore, that racial and ethnic affiliations and identities are much less matters of choice for multiracial blacks indicate that black remains a significant racial category.... The findings thus suggest that a black-nonblack divide is taking shape, in which Asians and Latinos are not only closer to whites than blacks are to whites, but also closer to whites than to blacks at this point in time.... In essence, rather than erasing racial boundaries, the country may simply be reinventing a color line that continues to separate blacks from other racial/ethnic groups.

While I agree with Lee and Bean's assertion that the shifting color line continues to deny black multiracials the same range of racial identity options, I would also argue that the presence of multiple color lines means that black multiracials are increasingly mixed with more than white. They may not opt for white if their racial parentage combines blackness and nonwhiteness. The U.S. Census data clearly indicates that the numbers of multiracial people will likely continue to increase (see U.S. Census 2010). Given that data set, it is also likely that the particular combinations of multiracial people will continue to diversify, such that even more color lines emerge or that the existing color lines will prove harder to maintain.

Despite the potential blurring of racial borders and the dissolving of color lines, the racial hierarchy persists as people maintain their place in society, in part by maintaining the logic of race. Why does the aforementioned racial inclusion and exclusion happen? Why does it matter? Based on the current racial hierarchy, one's racial location positions them closer to or further away from access to various resources (Bonilla-Silva 2003a, b; Gallagher 2006, 2004). For people who approximate whiteness, their social location is closer to whites and they enjoy privileges accordingly. For darker-skinned multiracials and people of colors (a term I borrow from Reanae McNeal in Keating 2013), their social location is typically much further away from whiteness and its attendant privileges. For multiracial people, negotiating racial identity likely involves the negotiation of this social location and the proximity to racial privilege. This negotiation may not be consciously or publicly acknowledged in a society that encourages colorblindness precisely to protect this system of inequality. Some scholars argue that even the category "multiracial" serves as a strategy of keeping white racial privilege intact, reserving it for those putatively deserving individuals (whites and honorary whites), and denying it to those people (collective blacks) who are not (Bonilla-Silva 2003a).

Many of the accounts of multiracial people reveal that their racial fluidity and multiplicity make them aware of where they belong and where they do not. For white-looking multiracial people with invisible mixture, they arguably "enjoy" many of the white privileges afforded people who, as Ta-Nehisi Coates (2015) puts it, believe themselves to be white. As Peggy McIntosh (1998) describes, these privileges accrue and allow white(-looking) people to move through life without much resistance from others. They do not encounter the weight of oppression or become targets of racial discrimination in ways that so many darker-skinned people do (see Almaguer 2008; Ferber 1998). Conversely, for darker-skinned multiracial people, they are denied any privilege that knowledge of their familial claims to other categories (white or honorary white) might otherwise generate. They are not bestowed with the same racial privileges as their multiracial counterparts with whiter or lighter skin color. Instead, they likely inherit the social, economic, and political disadvantages attached to collective blackness, as constructed in a society fractured by race and structured by racism. These disadvantages reflect how much racism is internalized by everyone and maintained through this racial sorting mechanism and the overall racial organization of society.

Navigating the Borders of Race and Clarifying Multiracial Borders

Historically, the color line has divided the national population into two racial groups: whites and blacks. This racial binary attempts to reign in the racial variation observed in the population; the binary negates this racial variation by funneling people primarily into two-and-only-two categories. Nevertheless, this color line has persisted, in part because of anti-black racism whereby society was structured to create a different quality of life for blacks than whites.

Within the past decade or so, scholars have begun to contend that the white/black binary no longer (or ever did) sufficiently characterizes the national population. They argue that the color line continues to evolve, so much so that it has developed into multiple color lines. According to Jennifer Lee and Frank Bean (2007), these multiple color lines have emerged to form new racial hierarchies. This explains why people are often categorized into three broad categories introduced by sociologist Eduardo Bonilla Silva (2003a,b): "whites," "honorary whites," and "collective blacks." These three categories point to the problem (or limitations) of the previous color line, as they hint at a new racial hierarchy emergent at the start of the 21st century.

Lee and Bean (2007:3) contend, "If the problem of the 20th century was the color line, the question of the 21st century could be one of multiple color *lines*" (italics theirs). This question, "Are multiple color lines emerging?," invites consideration of how multiracial people brighten or blend racial lines through their racial identity choices. Brightening racial lines is a way of clarifying race or amplifying the divisions between groups socially constructed and perceived as different. Blending racial lines speaks to the way many multiracial people inhabit interstitial spaces between racial groups while also moving to the center of the racial groups of their parentage and heritage.

This movement within and between racial groups blurs racial boundaries.

Increasingly, some multiracial people permeate racial lines or boundaries not their own; they have an appearance that approximates any number of racial and ethnic groups and their ambiguity allows them to effectively take advantage of the porous nature of racial borders and float into racial groups that are outside of their known parentage or heritage without much resistance or contestation. This movement, however, can also reveal how rigid racial borders can be, for example, when multiracial people are blocked or impeded from entry or membership into certain racial groups. These rigid racial lines may be inflexible to them based on their known racial composition or their phenotypic (physical) appearance. That racial lines can be either rigid and inflexible or porous and permeable speaks to the shifting nature of race. These characteristics of racial lines also highlight the ways in which people protect or defend them, a point I will return to momentarily.

Lee and Bean (2007:3) argue, "Multiracial identification thus provides an important analytical lens through which to gauge the placement, strength and shifts of America's color line." Their research shows that racial categories curiously expand and contract depending upon the individuals being considered for inclusion or exclusion. The expansion and contraction of racial categories occurs in part to ensure that certain racial groups maintain their positions of power, privilege, and dominance (whites), while others (honorary whites) who approximate whiteness enjoy some, but not all, of the advantages of whiteness; while others still (those considered to be part of the collective black category) are generally denied a good quality of life and much of the resources, privileges, and power of the dominant racial group. The scholarship on the current racial hierarchy speaks to this point, as does much of the literature on racial inequalities.

The matter of inclusion and exclusion factor in to this discussion of the expansion and contraction of racial groups because some scholarship suggests that members of racial groups previously excluded from full membership or citizenship in this country, now arguably enjoy greater rates of inclusion and enjoyment of racial privileges because of their closer position to the dominant group. This largely explains why, for example, many people consider Asians (especially some of their larger ethnic groups in the U.S., including Japanese, Chinese, and Filipinos) to be "honorary whites."

Use of the term "honorary white" to describe the racial location of Asians remains a dubious distinction that is not without contestation, as scholars, including Anthony Ocampo (2016) and Brenda Gambol (2016), demonstrate. In their respective work, they contend that Filipinos inhabit a more complicated racial location, one that is not always already "honorary white" or closer to whiteness than blackness or any other race. I mention their work here as it also relates to my above example of Bobbi and her interracial family that is white and black by her parentage and Asian by remarriage. These scholars invite us to consider the close connections and feelings of racial solidarity and kinship between Filipinos and racial and ethnic minority groups, including blacks and Latinos, in the U.S.

Ocampo's discussion of Filipinos as the "Latinos of Asia" alongside Gambol's discussion of Filipinos as "honorary blacks" invites readers to consider the multiple color lines that people cross in their daily lives. Crossing color lines can be both celebrated and contested. These color lines can be blurred such that people considered "outsiders" to certain racial groups can still experience a sense of belonging somewhere rather than nowhere (see Deters 1997); color lines can also be "brightened," such that the socially constructed distinctions between racial groups become more apparent. Their scholarship challenges some of these distinctions and the taken-for-granted nature of race and ethnicity; such research also reveals some of the complexities within categories previously perceived as simpler or more cohesive.

The work of Ocampo, Gambol, Deters, and others shows that racial and ethnic categories can sometimes fail to adequately capture these complexities or the connections people form within a racial hierarchy and across racial and ethnic groups. That a Filipina may consider herself both Asian *and* Latina speaks to these increasingly changing color lines, or existing color lines that have always already been blurred. A Filipina who describes feeling like she has more in common with black people in this country (and therefore embraces her "honorary black" membership) is asserting an identity similar to a black white biracial woman like Bobbi (who embraces her "honorary Asian" membership as she makes claims to her Filipina stepmother's familial influence on her identity).

Much of the recent and emergent scholarship provides evidence that racial categories constructed as singular have the residue of racial mixture. This research reminds us that racial groups expand and contract, contingent upon which individuals want entry into them. It partially explains why both whiteness and blackness expand as racial categories, the former opening up for those considered desirable and deserving, the latter broadly inclusive of those largely rejected or excluded from categorical whiteness.

I will note here that other scholars continue to demonstrate how blackness is broadly defined. Take sociologist Nikki Khanna (2011:155) who notes, "Multiraciality is nothing new in the African American community, and for many black Americans it may seem senseless to begin now differentiating biracial people from blacks (since many so-called blacks are actually multiracial)." Similar understandings of other single race categories as always already mixed (much like the black category) fail to exist. Blackness seems to envelop or incorporate mixture into its folds, while other racial categories maintain illusions of purity, particularly whiteness. Curiously, there is a greater specificity with which we understand who is white, Asian, Latino, and Native American, and yet, blackness remains a seemingly more inclusive category, even as black people remain the most excluded from social opportunities, access to privilege and power, and a good quality of life in society.

Why is "black" such an expansive category while the other racial groups remain ostensibly more exclusive and closely guarded? Consider the "one drop rule." This specific mechanism was introduced to ensure that the black slave population maintained its size. The "one drop rule," or hypodescent, pressures people with any known blackness to claim a black identity (Davis 1991; Gallagher 2006; Khanna 2010; and Lee and Bean 2007), while allowing people with ancestry from other racial and ethnic groups, such as Asian and Latino heritage, to choose from a wider range of options.

The construction and perception of white purity and black contamination guides much of the felt inclusion and exclusion in society. The "problem" with the persistence of even multiple color lines is in their failure to adequately capture these complexities and ostensible contradictions, as well as the racial migrations within and across racial locations or lines. Multiple color lines neglect or deny people multiple places at once; typically, people's racial location is envisioned as a coordinate, or a dot on a map, not an intersectional point converging or moving along multiple lines, across time and space.

Let's return to Ocampo's work for a moment, as his focus on Filipinos introduces interesting questions about the racial location of this ethnic group and challenges or complicates current conceptualizations of Asians and/or Latinos as members of seemingly separate groups. In turning the title of Ocampo's book, *The Latinos of Asia*, into a question, readers can consider the multiple locations that people inhabit and the many racial migrations or moves that multiracial and multiethnic people make. These migrations reflect multiracial people in motion, sometimes literally moving from one country to another or one region of this country to another, and sometimes figuratively moving between racial categories socially constructed as discrete or distinct, innately different from one another. These distinctions falter when we consider anthropological evidence of humans sharing more genetic similarities than differences even amidst what appears to be quite visible racial human variation (see Bliss 2012).

That Ocampo and others open up the space for these discussions of racial and ethnic multiplicity, racial migrations and translations, and the fluidity and ambiguity of identity acknowledges how society can and does open up space for people to embrace these multiple racial locations for themselves and others (see also Roth 2012; Hochschild 2014). My work attempts to accomplish this goal as well, while acknowledging that the same hierarchy that sorts people into their respective racial locations also imposes different kinds of constraints on multiracial individuals depending on their racial composition.

Revisiting Race

Lee and Bean (2007), among others, speculate that within the next three decades, 1 in 5 people in the U.S. will identify as multiracial (see also Farley 2001; Smith and Edmonston 1997). This contention raises a number of issues. The first issue that arises is that this rising population data makes the multiracial population appear amplified or suddenly birthed into our national population, when it has existed from the nation's very foundation. This amplification occurs in part because of the changes in race reporting in the Census survey. Prior to 2000, people could not formally choose more than one race. In the 2000 Census, for the first time, people were allowed to choose more than one race, or all that applied. And, nearly 6 million people did so. Because many of those people lived during the 1990 Census, and therefore only checked one race, in many ways, the US Census (2000) metaphorically birthed the "two or more races" population, making them appear rather instantaneously, as opposed to people always already in existence.

Another issue with the above claim about population estimates of multiracial people relates to terminology. Not everyone employs the existing terminology about race in the same way. Instead, given variations or differences in people's racial consciousness and racial literacy, people attach different meanings to racial terminology. Furthermore, as I discussed earlier, not all people with racially mixed parentage or heritage call themselves multiracial. They opt for a variety of names to refer to their racial multiplicity, sometimes simply by preferring to name their racial identity in singular terms. People should have the space to claim their preferred racial identity, or use their own terms (of race) on their own terms, as a matter of agency or expressed choice, free of societal constraint. Social scientist researchers need more nuanced ways of exploring and measuring multiracial identity (a topic I turn to more centrally in Chapter 2).

As Rockquemore (2005:18) posits, "[m]ost people do not have the cognitive schema for 'biracial.'" Instead, people often make that term ("biracial") or "multiracial" synonymous with or equivalent to "mixed with white." Interpreting these terms in such limited ways reveals patterns in the way people are thought to think about race, and encouraged to both center whiteness and perpetuate the invisibility of whiteness at the same time. While it is important to acknowledge members of the "two or more races" population who are mixed with white, it is equally important not to ignore or erase other types of mixture, particularly that which *excludes* whiteness.

Making the term "multiracial" always already equivalent to "white and some other race(s)" centers whiteness at the core of multiracial identities, rather than simply a possible part of them. In some ways, whiteness becomes synecdoche, where the part becomes the whole, or "multiracial" becomes metonymy for presumed whiteness (see Dawkins 2012). In either case, this association of multiracial identity with some whiteness creates a hegemonic kind of mixture, proving troublesome in its erasure of mixtures that do not involve whiteness (see Gambol 2016). Associating mixture with whiteness ignores or makes invisible or illegible other racial combinations and mixtures. This association potentially intensifies what is always already "invisible mixture," in that multiracial people of "two or more races," but none of which is white, may not be seen or recognized as "multiracial."

To my mind, many race scholars have made similar moves, working to acknowledge mixture, but in so doing have basically erased its existence prior to the 2000 Census. This erasure also occurs, casually and informally, in social situations where multiracial people's preferred racial identities are illegible or invalidated. Take, for example, the work of George Yancey (2003). In his discussions about "thin" and "thick" racial identities and interracial relationships, he neglects to fully consider that some people might already assert a multiracial identity. In other words, if multiracial people have felt denied the choice to assert and embrace their racial multiplicity, they may likely be hiding in plain sight. They are not necessarily "passing" as a member of a singular racial group but researchers may read them as such, or through a singular racial frame. In these cases, multiracial people remain "clearly invisible" (Dawkins 2012), rather than what I call "clearly mixed."

In part, this practice of presuming racial singularity in people who do not look "clearly mixed" reinforces racial categories as racially singular, cohesive, and homogeneous; the same presumption often occurs with ethnicity as well, with the presumption suggestive of a purity in ethnic categories. This move also ignores the fact that prior to the 2000 Census multiracial people were sorted into (and formally sorted themselves into) singular categories. However, we cannot be clear whether they did so for enumeration purposes only (asserting a formal identity different than their instrumental one) because of an absence of choices (being able to "check all that apply"), or because they intentionally chose to locate themselves in a single racial location or category.

To that end, consider the example of multiracial people who could be said to embody what I call "invisible mixture." These are individuals who do not look "clearly mixed," but based on physical appearance alone appear to belong to one-and-only-one racial category. This appearance, or its logic, can be contested but for purposes of this example, I will continue. For any multiracial people with invisible mixture, and based on research by F. James Davis, this could likely be about 80–90% of the population, they likely fall into the racial group in which they look like they belong. This way of sorting people out reflects the logic of what Eduardo Bonilla Silva (2003a,b) and Edward Telles (2014) call a "pigmentocracy." This term calls out the patterns of racial discrimination reflected in preferential treatment of whites and the persistent devaluation of black lives, or colorism, despite claims to the contrary.

Based on racial hierarchical practices in this country, people who identify with any of the many racial group options presented in the U.S. Census are distilled into one of these three groups, regardless of how many boxes are checked. Herbert Gans and others suggest that multiracial people may float between categories contingent on a variety of factors. Bonilla Silva (2003a,b) would argue that skin color most heavily informs where multiracial people get sorted, such that a white-looking multiracial person would enjoy residence in the white or honorary categories, while a darker-skinned multiracial would likely reside in the collective black category.

What complicates many people's lack of such a cognitive schema is twofold: 1) multiracial people both fit and do not fit into singular race categories; and, 2) society seems unable to understand that someone who looks "clearly mixed" may or may not identify that way (as mixed or multiracial). That is, "multiraciality" is not always legible or visible to everyone, or at all times, nor is it always claimed. For people with racial ambiguity, they may also appear "clearly ambiguous," which may make racially categorizing them more difficult to some.

Looking clearly ambiguous or having an appearance incongruent with one's identity creates a dilemma for those who rely on phenotype, or physical appearance, to decipher/determine race. In this society, people expect continuity or congruence between individuals' appearances, and their asserted identities (see Buchanan and Acevedo 2004). For example, when Rockquemore (2005) writes that she is "black by self-definition, white by phenotype, and biracial by parentage" (2005:17), she is highlighting how her appearance proves ambiguous enough to be read racially different by different groups, in different contexts, for different reasons. In part, she argues, and I would agree, that people in the U.S. are quite ill-equipped and unwilling to deal with this racial ambiguity, as expressed by the generalized anxiety with ambiguity we observe regarding multiracial individuals (see also Streeter 2003, 1996). In general, others often expect that their perceptions of a racially ambiguous person will align with the latter's appearance and identity. When this proves not to be the case, the likely results are cognitive dissonance and border patrolling; the border patrolling, which get expressed as questions (such as "What are you?") that are designed to clarify racial lines, helps people resolve any experienced cognitive dissonance (see also Gaskins 1999).

Multiracial Border Patrolling

Throughout this book, I discuss what happens as people fit into and fall out of racial categories, or blend multiple racial categories as a result of their racially mixed parentage and heritage. This movement of multiracial people over and across and within racial borders often prompts others to pose the ubiquitous question, "What are you?" People ask this question and related ones to figure out the exact racial coordinates of the multiracial person's location. However, as sociologist Heather Dalmage (2000:4) asks in her book about interracial families and multiracial people, "How do any of us know what to call ourselves racially?" This question helps us to reflect on the history of racial categories and the social construction of race in America, as discussed above (see also Davis 1991; Omi and Winant 2014).

Because many multiracial individuals like Bobbi (from the beginning of the chapter), serve as "the nation's racial Rorschach tests," they may find managing their racial multiplicity complicated at best or confusing (for others) at worst. As Dalmage (2000:106) explains, "Human bodies are interpreted and explained as they might be with a

Rorschach test. Some bodies easily match a category's description and appear simple to interpret; others are more ambiguous.... When people encounter a racially ambiguous person, they conduct a flurry of analyses to determine how the individual should be categorized. This is a racial Rorschach test, taken in a society that creates and accepts racial stereotypes. Interpretations develop within a cultural, social, and historical context and, like all interpretations, depend on the language available to frame ideas."

Dalmage's discussion explains why Bobbi, like other multiracial people, faces a lot of inquiries about her racially ambiguous appearance. That she is "clearly mixed" seems to invite others into conversation so that they might explore the borders of race with her to better figure her out racially. Bobbi is one of these tests because what Dalmage makes clear is that racially ambiguous people, like Bobbi, are likely to be asked a variety of questions designed to clarify the blurred lines of race. She describes this practice as "border patrolling."

As Dalmage (2000:40–41) sees it, border patrolling is a "unique form of discrimination faced by those who cross the color line, do not stick with their own, or attempt to claim membership (or are placed by others) in more than one racial group. Like racism, borderism is central to American society. It is a product of a racist system yet comes from both sides." People are likely to experience border patrolling from a variety of sources and also for a number of reasons (see Dalmage 2000). Border patrolling happens because most people feel the borders of race should be kept intact.

By implication, the term "both sides" reinforces the racial binary that prevailed in the U.S. decades ago and still exists among members of the nation's population. This racial binary (expressed through the language of "both sides") promotes a racial logic based on "two-and-only-two" racial categories. Most commonly, the racial binary attempts to categorize people as "white" or "black," but also as "white" or "nonwhite," and "black" or "nonblack" (see Hacker 1992; Yancey 2003). These variations in the racial binary hint at the impossibility of characterizing an entire national population into "two-and-only-two" racial categories, despite historical and contemporary efforts to do so.

In her book, Dalmage describes the differential treatment that white-black couples experience in this way (from "both sides") to highlight how this racial divide persists. Dalmage describes the opposition that white people in interracial families face as "white border patrolling" and that which black people in interracial families face as "black border patrolling." While useful for addressing this discriminatory action, the terms solidify a black/white binary. This dichotomous way of viewing race fails to accommodate racial "Others," as Maria Root (1992, 1996) suggests.

In this work, I tackle the challenge of building on Dalmage's discussion of border patrolling, and that of Khanna (2011), who speaks of the "multidimensionality of racial identity." When taken together, a need emerges for a concept that captures the way border patrollers police multiracial people ostensibly from "all sides" because of the many dimensions of their racial identities. I introduce the term, "multiracial border patrolling," to add to the existing concepts—"white border patrolling" and "black border patrolling"—to acknowledge and argue that multiracial people may uniquely experience racial border patrolling because of their racial mixture. As multiracial people attempt to assert their preferred racial identities, they may experience support and/or opposition or resistance to these preferences in the form of multiracial border patrolling.

Living "on the border," as Homi Bhabha (1991) puts it, parallels life in what Gloria Anzaldua described as the "borderlands." Both terms capture the in-between-ness that many multiracial people call home. While many multiracial people find this liminal racial location quite enjoyable, others describe the difficulties of living this shifting mixture. These difficulties often surface when other people patrol the borders of race, demanding clarification to the question, "What are you?" As implied above, questions of identity can be complicated for some multiracial people to contemplate; when posed by complete strangers, or issued as challenges by friends and family, these questions become fraught, mired in a weight of history. These questions prove tricky to answer. These questions are a form of border patrolling, or a way of policing the borders of race. When posed in particular ways, these questions can suggest that only certain answers or responses are the right ones.

Many people border patrol as if a "two-and-only-two" system of racial categorization still exists and, for many of them, this way of seeing race likely does. For people whose racial lenses sort others into "two-and-only-two" racial categories, or who fail to read between the lines by seeing shades of gray (or beige or brown), multiracial people muddy their dualistic vision. Failure to read between the color lines means that some border patrollers place multiracial individuals into single racial categories, and/or squarely into a racial group that departs from the multiracial person's known ancestry.

As a general rule, border patrollers fail to recognize the very porosity of racial categories. Instead, they hold onto their dichotomous way of thinking about race, despite the millions of people who reported two or more races on the two most recent Census surveys. Given the statistics, the limitations of the racial logic of "two-and-only-two" options appear more obvious. Thus, the practice of borderism does not always match the many ways multiracial people assert their racial identities or prefer to identify. This is especially the case with shifting, situational (protean) identities (Campbell 2007; Korgen 1998; Maxwell 1998; Rockquemore and Brunsma 2002); incipient identities[2]; and honorary memberships (see Twine 2006). It reflects a persistent misrecognition of multiracial people.

Border patrollers maintain myths of racial purity and contamination, often regarding whiteness as "pure" and blackness as "contaminated" and "contaminating" (see Myers 2005; Douglas 2002). Border patrollers often expect others' ways of seeing (or not seeing) race to align with their own, which privileges their own vision and understanding over any alternatives. As I show throughout this book, multiracial people encounter various kinds or levels of border patrolling partially because individuals do not know where best to locate them. In addition, others might sincerely be curious about them and ask questions that are guided more by a genuine curiosity and benevolence than by ignorance or the malevolence of racism and borderism.

People located interstitially present a potential problem to those who border patrol others. This may be particularly the case when a multiracial person's interstitial position is not constant, nor is constantly legible to others. Furthermore, people may border patrol when racial markers fail to situate a multiracial person into a single racial category, or when they lack intimate knowledge of the racially and ethnically ambiguous person's racial identity, family heritage or parentage, and racial/ethnic affiliations. Generally, in these types of interactions, strangers will try to gather behavioral cues; decipher and decode racial markers; and otherwise filter information during social interactions with multiracial people to determine a multiracial person's racial location. This information then allows them to border patrol, or not, as they see fit. This location, in the border patroller's mind, is almost always singular and static, seldom plural and fluid. Border patrollers may attempt to dictate the specificity of the multiracial person's racial identity, and/or insist on a singularity to this identity. Even well-intentioned and less imposing people may engage in border patrolling. Their inability to accommodate racial mixture may stem from ignorance about the multiple-race population, or (as noted above) more malevolence, expressed as resistance to embracing this racial mixture as a reality.

Additional factors influence the social dynamics of border patrolling. Borderism reflects a societal impatience with, or inability to handle, multiplicity, ambiguity and liminality or fluidity. It is easy to see, then, how easily conflicts can arise when border patrollers put multiracial people in the *wrong* racial category. This often happens because a border patroller misreads a racially ambiguous person and makes an incorrect determination about that individual's racial location. At other times, multiracial people prefer only one racial location, but that one may differ from the racial location in which the border patroller wants them to reside. This can create tensions that inform the social interactions multiracial people have with strangers and even family members and close friends.

People who border patrol may crave a fixed racial location for a multiracial person, particularly a racially ambiguous one, because they are troubled by shifting mixture. Shifting mixture is not a problem, even though border patrollers regard it as such, because shifting mixture creates a "now you see it, now you don't" effect. Shifting mixture may make racial mixture only situationally visible, by masking it at times and unveiling it at others. Shifting mixture makes multiracial identity and heritage appear and disappear. When shifting mixture is met with invisible mixture, such that a person's racial mixture is only visible to those who can read racial ambiguity, it complicates the process of correctly categorizing the multiracial person into the most appropriate racial group.

Border patrollers might be just as perturbed by invisible mixture, except that as the term implies, this racial mixture remains invisible, or at least largely undetectable. Border patrollers without a sophisticated way of looking may miss indicators that a person is "clearly mixed." If a person who a border patroller thinks is located in a particular racial group claims a different racial identity, a border patroller may get frustrated with the knowledge of the multiracial person's racial identity and heritage. Often, a border patroller expects her/his perception of a multiracial person to neatly align with that person's racial identity. This is not always the case.

Where Do Multiracial People Fit?

Dualistic sorting of multiracial people occurs as this society attempts to maintain a racial hierarchy that values whiteness and devalues blackness. This racial hierarchy generally ensures that people perceived as white receive better treatment and enjoy a higher quality of life, while simultaneously denying these opportunities and experiences to people perceived as black. Viewing white and black racial categories as seemingly "opposite," works to maintain a racial dichotomy that never truly existed yet persists in many places to this day.

These days, however, some scholars argue that this racial binary or this "two-and-only-two-races" way of thinking, is outmoded and no longer sufficiently describes the national population. Sociologists including Eduardo Bonilla Silva (2003a,b) and Herbert Gans (1999) suggest that the racial binary has given way to three categories more closely reflective of Latin American countries. This "Latinization of America" translates race by sorting people into the following: "white," "honorary white," and "collective black" racial categories (Bonilla Silva 2003a,b). That is, as the current racial hierarchy loosens its binary stance, it seems to be attempting to cleave the population into the aforementioned three categories.

Does the "two-and-only-two-races" effect turn into "three-and-only-three-races"? Where do people who are multiracial, or two or more races, fit in this system of racial categorization? According to Herbert Gans (1999), multiracial people are "residuals" or people who sort of fall into and out of racial categories. Eduardo Bonilla Silva goes a step further to suggest that, in what Telles (2014) calls a "pigmentocracy," multiracial people reside in racial categories reflective of their skin color, such that multiracial people with lighter skin color will likely take up and enjoy residence in the white or honorary white racial groups, while multiracial people with darker skin will reside among collective blacks. The idea of a pigmentocracy engages the concept of a racial hierarchy but specifically draws attention to the way society draws racial boundaries around people primarily based on skin color. In general, society distributes privileges unevenly, with people of whiter and lighter skin color receiving preferential or better treatment than people with darker skin color.

Whether it is within the context of a pigmentocracy or some other limiting artificial demarcation, racial border patrolling shows up in many ways; sometimes, this border patrolling reflects people's desire to regulate racial categories or retain the rigidity of racial boundaries. At other times, this border patrolling illustrates how race remains fluid and its borders permeable. Consider a point sociologists Lee and Bean (2007) make in their work. They posit that Americans appear much more comfortable with Asian and Latino multiracial ambiguity than with black multiracial ambiguity; they are much better equipped (socialized) to detect African ancestry than other racial/ethnic ancestry. This means that members of the general population may not see a white and Asian multiracial person as multiracial, but may misread them as only white;

they might see a white and Latino person as white instead of Latino. However, they are more likely to see a white and black person as just black. Nikki Khanna (2010) makes this point in her article, "If You're Half Black, You're Just Black." Seeing multiracial (white and Asian, or white and Latino) people as white but other multiracial (white and black) people as black reflects a kind of racial border patrolling borne out of a racial classification system designed to differentiate and devalue blackness.

That people can detect and make space for racial mixture in white-looking white-Asian and/or white and Latino multiracial people but contest the same in multiracial black people reinforces, rather than reinvents, a color line that demarcates blackness from all other racial groups. This occurs in part because racial mixture in black people, if detected, is often ignored, negated, or refused. Everyday racial discourses and contemporary ways of seeing race reflect a historical residue and legacy of race that restricts racial identity choices for black multiracial people, while opening up or expanding racial boundaries for white, Asian, and Latino multiracial people. As a society, we can simultaneously see blackness as always already racially mixed while denying this very mixture when any black multiracial people want to claim it and/or whiteness.

Whiteness can expand to encapsulate Asian and Latino parentage, but not black parentage. In many ways, blackness disappears racial mixture. This partially explains why, when compared to black multiracial people, white and Asian or Latino multiracial people can assert racial identities without any or much contestation. They are often not viewed as having a singular race (Asian) or racialized ethnicity (Latino). Rather, they can generally and more easily assert multiracial identities that are affirmed by others, which contrasts with the experiences of black multiracial people who find less public support for and validation of their multiracial identities. Moreover, unlike black-white multiracials, Latino-white and Asian-white multiracials are often identified as white, which in turn, affects the way they see themselves" (Lee and Bean 2007:23).

Other people's disbelief at the racially mixed parentage of Asian-white and Latino-white multiracials suggests that members of these groups "look" white or have a white phenotype. But what happens when this is not the case and nonwhite racial markers compromise the multiracial person's seemingly white appearance? Drawing on literature that discusses racial ambiguity, I would further complicate the existing conversation about the reinvented color line by arguing that border patrolling may be inversely related to the legibility or visibility of whiteness. The whiter a multiracial person is, the less likely they may be to border patrolled, unless they are seen as "compromising" that ostensible whiteness with the racially diverse social networks they form.

Making the face of mixture synonymous with whiteness suggests that an erasure of racial mixture is taking place in certain parts of the country; it also suggests that racial mixture remains synonymous with a racially and ethnically ambiguous appearance or face (LaFerla 2003; Buchanan and Acevedo 2004; Lee and Bean 2004; Morning 2003; Winters and DeBose 2003; Wu 2002, 2003; Wynter 2002; Zhou 2003). Where one's features "do not necessarily fit into any easily definable category" (Rockquemore 1998:208), multiracial people, as "residuals," fit uneasily into the black/nonblack divide or the triracial hierarchy, while also easily fitting into categories that they may or may not want to claim. For the white and Asian multiracial person who looks white and gets read as white, but wants to be seen as multiracial, easily fitting into the white category will likely produce privileges and benefits, at the expense of an invalidated racial identity. If multiracial people who "look white" are shifted into that category, and multiracial people who "look black" are shifted into that category, the white/black or "two-and-only-two" racial categorization system might reemerge to explain multiracial people's racial realities. This would occur because people often misperceive multiracial people's appearances as monoracial, otherwise interpreting racial ambiguity and multiplicity as singularity. However, at times, this ambiguity can intensify border patrolling for "clearly ambiguous" multiracial individuals who do not easily fit into any particular racial categories. This failure to fit can intensify border patrollers' need to know where the clearly ambiguous belong. To their frustration, border patrollers must realize that multiracial people may belong everywhere and nowhere at once.

If people rely on racial markers to border patrol, and these markers float on a racially mixed person, then people in different racial groups may patrol this ambiguity. That is, shifting mixture may make race an even greater floating signifier (Hall 1999, 1997). Multiracial people have changing faces or appearances that shift to make them look like different races (not necessarily the combination of their racial mixture, but also approximations of other racial groups). That multiracial individuals interpellate (Althusser 1971), or hail, members of "similarly different" racial groups illustrates the social construction of race, its fluidity, and the illusion of racial purity and fixity. This paradoxical term, "similarly different," updates Naomi Zack's (1997) discussion of the "same difference." The term calls attention to the ways multiracial people approximate groups that are different from them, even as they are perceived to be similar. It is this perceived similarity that ushers them into these different groups, allowing them to fit in easily to some groups, and per the above discussion, barring them from other group membership. This begins to explain why multiracial people often describe their experiences with racial multiplicity and fluidity as locating them everywhere and nowhere.

Belonging Everywhere and Nowhere: Notes on Being "Clearly Mixed"

Here I want to return to my earlier example of Bobbi. When Bobbi faced increased inquiries about her racial ambiguity and multiplicity, this increased attention suggested to her that other people were not sure what to make of her racial mixture. They wanted to know or had some "need to know" her racial mixture (see Rockquemore 1998). They wanted her to clarify her racial location, to decipher or decode the dimensions of her racial multiplicity, ostensibly complicated by her black white parentage but also by her desire to claim connections to her stepmom's heritage. Ironically, living on the borders of race meant that, for the most part, Bobbi and her siblings could enjoy their honorary membership among Filipinos, blending and blurring the borders of race even more than their membership in two racial categories already did.

While Bobbi found it relatively effortless to blend into her stepmother's Asian racial group, she had to actively assert her multiracial identity in order to clarify this racial mixture to others. That is, while she unintentionally slipped into the Asian category at times, she had to more purposefully and intentionally claim the specificities of her preferred racial identity; otherwise, they remained hidden in plain sight, where strangers could not see that she was clearly mixed (black and white). Instead, they see her as Hawaiian, Hispanic, almost anything but black and white.

What Bobbi's example illustrates is that many multiracial people can be questioned for their ambiguous appearance and policed for not phenotypically fitting neatly into any one racial category. Sometimes these questions are guided by people who are confused by multiracial individuals who looked "clearly mixed," as opposed to "clearly white" or "clearly black" or some other race. These people may want to know exactly where a multiracial person resides racially in order to know how to interact with and/or understand them.

Border patrollers attempt to reproduce racial borders for multiracial individuals. They fail to recognize the multiplicity of selves (Rosenberg 1979) that people possess or the multiplicity within categories constructed as singular. Consider a variation of this point, as Lee and Bean (2007) make a note that racial categories are "socially constructed and a great deal of ethnic heterogeneity exists within them." Arguably, the same can be said about *racial* heterogeneity within racial categories socially constructed as singular.

This failure to racially accommodate "the sum of our parts" (Williams-Leon and Nakashima 2001) prevents an understanding of the composite and sometimes competing parts of multiracial people's racial selves. This multiplicity ideally merges together to create a cohesive and coherent whole that is synthesized rather than fragmented or fractional (see Chang 2015; Stryker 1989, 1991). Arguably, when strangers border patrol others' racial multiple selves, they ignore or deny the reality of racial multiplicity. Alternately, some border patrollers do recognize this multiplicity but refuse to make space for it. They believe in the singularity of racial groups or categories and apply the same logic to social selves. This contrasts with people who question a multiracial person, out of ignorance more than malice, or benevolence more so than malevolence. Of course, the line between benevolence and malevolence is another potentially blurred line, given the prevailing racial rhetoric of colorblindness and colormuteness. As Bonilla-Silva (2002) contends, the style of contemporary racism remains polite and smiling.

When strangers border patrol people's racial multiplicity, they do not want to admit to a multiracial reality or consider Stryker and Serpe's (1994:17) footnoted assertion that, "The possibility that two or more identities may exist at the same location in a hierarchical order should be recognized explicitly." Instead, borderists prefer collapsing racial differences into similarity and singularity. In doing so, they make individuals with multiracial heritage or parentage ostensibly easier to deal with, conceptually and interactionally. Collapsing differences into coherence and the multiple into the singular, allows border patrollers to reify racial divides.

What confounds border patrollers may be that multiracial people claim any of the aforementioned racial identities in ways that depart or differ from the border patrollers' perceptions of the multiracial people and the racial identities they *should* claim. That an increasing number of people claim two or more races, *and* these increasing number of identity options, may also stir up border patrollers' racial imagination about where multiracial "best" belong. Border patrollers may also find that their curiosity about the racial locations of multiracial people contradicts any of their claims of colorblindness. While the question of how border patrollers' resolve any frustrations and cognitive dissonance created by members of the "two or more races" population, I am more interested in how multiracial people make sense of the contradictions and claims of colorblindness.

Managing Border Patrolling Amidst Colorblindness and Colormuteness

Some multiracial people confront the contradictory presence of colorblindness and border patrolling, or the regulation of race along color lines. At times, they may hear comments such as "I don't see you as (fill in race/s here)," while being asked to disclose details about their racial identities, parentage, and/or heritage. This contradiction exposes people's perceptions of the "same/difference" (Zack 1997). In the racially colorblind mind, people all look the same, while simultaneously remaining different, particularly to border patrollers who see racial divisions as fixed and static. These two contrasting positions create cognitive dissonance, for the simultaneous seeing and not seeing race at once, produces a contradiction. It makes visible what colorblind racism refuses to see: racial "difference" as embodied by the multiracial "Other."

Because of historical and contemporary patterned evidence of racial inequality and racial discrimination, people learn that access to resources and a better quality of life is primarily contingent on color. As a result, people engage in border patrolling in part to keep this racial hierarchy intact. In many cases, they do so without drawing attention to race. As Eduardo Bonilla-Silva (2003a) and Mica Pollock (2005) demonstrate, people develop discursive practices, or ways of speaking, particularly about race that appear to have nothing to do with race, except that they do. Bonilla-Silva calls this practice "colorblindness." Pollock calls it colormuteness. Upon closer inspection of these twin discourses, colorblindness and colormuteness, we can see how people talk about race even as they deny it. People leave traces of race in the racial code words they use to conceal any racist ideologies or thoughts they have. These ideas and racist ideologies reinforce the racial hierarchy by reinforcing who deserves a better life and who does not.

Colorblindness and colormuteness are curious discursive practices in the U.S. given the racist foundation of this country and the very persistence of racism. As discursive practices, colorblindness and colormuteness become suspect when people who make claims to this racial reticence and irrelevance ask a multiracial person that quintessential question, "What are you?" Racially ambiguous people often become the typical targets of this question, and all of its variations, even if those people do not identify as multiracial. People who ask these kinds of clarifying questions of multiracial people explicitly engage in behavior that characterizes border patrolling.

Here I want to introduce the irony of this reality, that many of the same people who espouse statements such as "We are all human," or "We are all the same," are also often the same people who make racialized statements about people's behaviors or hastily draw attention to problematic behavior by suggesting that such unsavory action is reflective of race. Other ways in which colorblindness and colormuteness shape the way people talk about race emerge in their curiosity about others. Consider the cumulative narrative of the multiracial people I interviewed. Most of them had stories to tell about the many questions people had regarding their racial identity, parentage, and heritage. Very few of them recognized the disjuncture between the discourse of "not seeing race" and that which accommodates such questions as "What are you?" and "Where are you from?" As I show in the first substantive chapter, these questions operate as a double-edged sword. Kerry Ann Rockquemore (1998) dubbed these interactions, "the 'What are you?' experience." Growing up in a colorblind, and colormute, society, most of my respondents themselves could not see how being asked questions about their racial locations or position across the color line betrayed these (colorblind) claims.

Because colorblind narratives continue to grip this nation but do little to satisfy people's curiosity, people present themselves as having sufficient racial etiquette, which allows them to publicly explore their racial curiosity through thinly veiled questions that skirt around race using the guise of excessive politeness (Bonilla Silva 2002; Houts Picca and Feagin 2007). In addition, they may rely on other strategies designed to acquire information and curb anxiety about ambiguity and multiraciality. Discursively, race talk enables people to navigate racial conversations while appearing interested in other issues that are not necessarily race. The ability to slip into race talk also allows people to address their anxiety about ambiguity and curiosity about multiraciality, all the while appearing polite and not policing. Relying on race talk then supports colorblindness. In some situations, people also deploy colormuteness, avoiding any direct reference to race (Pollock 2005). Both colorblindness and colormuteness facilitate the reproduction of racial categories, which endorses racial borders and supports the racial hierarchy.

These twin rhetorical strategies or practices of colorblindness and colormuteness make living in a racially divisive society interesting, to say the least. In a country with an increasingly diversifying population, claiming and choosing to not see race seems like a lofty project. The very bold admission seems foolhardy, at best, given the richness in experience and the wealth of knowledge that could be shared among people, particularly pertaining to their everyday experiences with race. People who cling to colorblind claims do not want to do the difficult work of discussing race, including their own. However, many of them do not seem to hesitate asking others about their racial identity. This seems particularly so for people who are, as I previously described, "clearly mixed," or racially ambiguous, or in/visibly mixed.

That people who deploy the aforementioned twin discourses can also ask questions that directly deal with race (in terms of racial identity) while maintaining that race does not matter captures the contradictions of race in this country. To Bonilla-Silva's research, colorblindness accommodates these and other contradictions. Border patrollers often rely on colorblindness to navigate their way through conversations about race, even at the expense of contradicting themselves. They concurrently claim not to see race and deny that racism is real, yet want to figure out what multiracial people "really" are in terms of race. This practice of border patrollers, and this attendant need to definitively decipher the racial coordinates of a multiracial person, begs several questions that I concentrate on throughout this book: How does one determine the "correct" racial category for a multiracial person? Who decides? Do multiracial people make such decisions on their own terms or do the views and perceptions of others matter more in these instances? What happens in those moments when other people cannot figure out the racial location(s) of the multiracial person in question?

To more specifically explore this matter of who is multiracial, I designed and conducted research on the multiracial population living in the Southeast United States in the mid-2000s. I set the challenge of interviewing 60 individuals of any racial combinations for this research. I created flyers to advertise my study, assuming that through "snowball sampling" I would likely attract and recruit people in particular social networks or friends of friends. The only trouble was figuring out how to ask the "What are you?" question with more grace than I found the inquiry offered. What if people—my potential respondents—were hiding in plain sight; their invisible mixture impeding my ability to ask them to consider participating in my study? I worried that soon people would take pity on me, seeing my desire to talk to strangers, and volunteer to participate despite having any known racial mixture in their heritage. These were silly concerns, in many ways, but ones that helped me identify themes that linked my experiences to that of my respondents; I reflected on my worries and recognized the traces of the authenticity tests I had been put through by others. I started to ask myself, "What if the respondents do not *look* mixed? What do I expect them to look like? (How) will their appearance impact our interactions during the interactions?"

While I believed it did not matter who showed up and how, I realized that reflecting on these questions strengthened my ability to understand much of what I focus on in this book. Even as someone who finds herself living "across the color line" (see Dalmage 2000), or in the "borderlands" (see Anzaldua 1987), I was a little bit guilty of wanting my respondents to be "clearly mixed." In actuality, I wanted what anthropologist Clifford Geertz (1977) calls "thick description," so I critically considered who indicated an interest in my research. In retrospect, these faulty initial concerns and considerations informed much of what respondents detailed in their interviews: a negotiation of racial borders. As they figured out how to answer the "What are you?" question, many of them discovered racial borders and their locations in relation to them. This book is about how they make sense of and situate themselves across these color lines and how they manage interactions with strangers, families, and friends, to feel validated and arrive at racial identities that they prefer. I also discuss instances where these preferences in racial identities are invalidated or negated and I asked respondents to share how they handled these variations in reactions to their racial identities. I turn next to a discussion of the ways studying shifting mixture creates methodological challenges.

Notes

[1] The term describes a person who has one parent of one socially defined race and another parent of a different socially defined race, regardless of their own racial mixture. This term, and the increasing literature dedicated to exploring the experiences of "first-generation" multiracial people enabled the reinvention of mixture. It also facilitated the historical amnesia and revisionism about race mixing and exposes the extent of our societal investment in socially constructed racial categories as singular and static.

[2] Incipient identities reflect the process of "becoming" in the manner that some multiracial individuals increasingly acquire information about their familial biographies, in an effort to solve "mysteries of histories." This information, and a growing desire to recover mixture or "choosing to select a varied multiracial identification that acknowledges a great diversity of racial mixing" (Campbell 2007: 926) partially explain this process of becoming. We can turn to Hansen's (1952) discussion of the third generation's attempts at cultural maintenance and preservation (of family diversity), achieved through efforts to recover the forgotten past. An example of this incipience came from Miki, who described how the convergence of experiences (border patrolling

from others, the impact of her Japanese grandmother's death, and her own maturation) motivated her to claim being both white and Asian (Japanese), and "really feel like I need to embrace it and learn about it." Other respondents expressed this desire for reclamation and recuperation of the composite parts of their heritage, such as Sophie, who was adopted into a white family that had also adopted biracial black/white children. Contrary to an Asian becoming American, Sophie described her experience as this: "I'm an American becoming Asian."

2
What Is "Multiracial"?

The question, "Why does mixed race identity matter?," begs consideration of the increasing number of people who identify as two or more races. "Mixed race" matters because a growing number of people claim this, and related, identities, including "multiracial," "biracial," and more. "Mixed race matters" reflect the growing set of concerns that people have regarding this population, particularly given the persistence of racism and border patrolling in this country. Mixed race matters encourages people to consider why the crossing, blending, and blurring of racial borders continues to garner so much public attention.

"Mixed race" matters as a contemporary issue that is arguably changing the face of America, especially as more and more young children identify as two or more races (see Chang 2015). However, several scholars debate this "increasing" number of people in the multiracial population. They argue about whether the multiracial population should be viewed through an historical or contemporary lens. Some do not create the space to accommodate both ways of viewing the multiracial population. Others see historical and contemporary mixture as not mutually exclusive. Still others contend that notions of "contemporary mixture" construct multiracial people as new and emergent rather than an existing and persistent part of the population.

For example, Rainier Spencer (2004, 2006, and 2010) takes up the charge of interrogating or "challenging multiracial identity." He questions who belongs in this ostensibly emergent "multiracial" population, noting an always already multiracial national population. Spencer is arguably a proponent of situating or understanding the current multiracial population in the context of historical mixture.

Conversely, Jessie Turner (2013) introduces and advances the idea of contemporary mixture in her work. She considers the construction of this contemporary mixture, comparing and contrasting it with historical mixture. While some might argue that contemporary mixture appears more obvious now than ever before, others disagree. Those who support the idea of contemporary mixture may see multiracial people as more "clearly mixed;" they likely recognize multiracial people in interracial families through birth and adoption, and as introduced into the population via immigration. Proponents of historical mixture would contend that multiracial people have existed in the national population since its inception.

My own research engages both of these views, respecting how both historical and contemporary mixture guide and shape multiracial identity. As I focus my attention on the present, I recognize the past. I consider how the social construction of race throughout various historical moments continues to inform people's understanding of contemporary mixture, their own and others. I open up an exploration of the central research questions, "How do people with racially mixed parentage and heritage choose to self-identify? What are their experiences with others around their preferred racial identity choices?" These questions of multiracial identity link to historical and contemporary mixture, in part because these shifting notions of mixture make it appear and/or disappear, depending on how it is being defined in a particular historical moment.

That so many multiracial people can hide in plain sight speaks to the contours of contemporary *and* historical mixture. This hiding in plain sight hints at some of the methodological challenges I faced in trying to locate participants for my study. This research allowed me to investigate some of these "mixed race matters." In this chapter, I discuss these investigations, focusing on a few of the key challenges I encountered in this research: invisible mixture, shifting mixture, and the geographies of race. Invisible mixture is any racial multiplicity that hides in plain sight. Shifting mixture is the fluid movement of multiracial identities, which includes multiracial people asserting any number of preferred racial identities or expressing protean identities. The geographies of race speak to the different meanings attached to race, depending on the geographic location. Notions of historical and contemporary mixture inform these phenomena.

First, I turn to the problem of invisible mixture to reveal the extent to which racial mixture hides in plain sight, residing in most people, whether claimed, ignored, or denied. I discuss the difficulty of studying a population that may be hiding in plain sight, or blending racial borders, by appearing to be members of single race categories. Within this discussion, I mention how my own myopia and initially essentialist thinking about racial mixture impeded, rather than facilitated, my interviewing process. Second, I discuss how shifting mixture, or the fluidity and flexibility of racial identity, makes studying racial identity messy. Next, I discuss the geographies of race, offering a brief sketch of my own racial border crossings for purposes of illustration. After presenting these methodological challenges, I discuss the sample characteristics, research methods involving in conducting interview conversations, and the process of data analysis. I conclude the chapter by foreshadowing the ways that the interview replicates or mirrors much of the social dynamic of interactions between multiracial people and other individuals.

Understanding the racial identity choices that multiracial people make and the experiences with racial border patrollers that they may have entails understanding what choices have historically been available to racially mixed people, and what choices are now open to them as well. Understanding how racial borders have shifted to accommodate mixture differently at different historical moments is relevant to this work. As others have illustrated in their own work, these choices hinge on the particular known racial heritage of multiracial people (see Chang 2015; Dalmage 2000; Davis 1991; Rockquemore and Brunsma 2002). These choices expand and contract, contingent on the appearance and ambiguity of the individuals in question, as well as the social and geographical sites in which multiracial people live. This begins to explain why the concepts of visibility, fluidity, flexibility, and geography remain central to the question of who is multiracial; these concepts are also germane to this discussion of racial identity, and the experiences of people living on the borders of race. As these topics emerged in the process of conducting these interviews, I wrestled quite a bit with them. As a result, I want to share my thoughts about them to convey the complexity of studying mixed race matters.

The Problem of Invisible Mixture, or How Do You Recruit People Hiding in Plain Sight?

The search for research participants commenced upon institutional approval of my proposed study. In order to get the qualitative interviews underway, I first needed to find ways to identify potential participants who would then need to be screened to see if they qualified for participation in my research. Before I could schedule any interviews, I had to ask people, as potential research participants, a few quick questions to see if they qualified for my study on "multiracial" identities and "interracial" relationships.

To explore the other central topic of my research—interracial relationships among multiracial people—I asked people to indicate if they were or had been in a romantic relationship for a certain length of time. If given affirmative responses to this set of questions, and an indication that the potential participant had racially mixed parentage or heritage, we then agreed on a reasonably quiet and mutually convenient time and place in which to meet for the interview conversation. As a point of clarification, these two topics, of interracial relationships and multiracial identities, were central to the broader study. However, in this book, I primarily focus on the multiracial identity choices and experiences of racially mixed people.

I momentarily put the term, "multiracial," in quotes to acknowledge that not all racially mixed people claim a "multiracial" identity. Instead, this use of quotes designates a target population, not my own contestation of this population. It acknowledges the fluidity and contingency of multiraciality. Not all people with known racially mixed parentage or heritage claim a multiracial identity, but instead may choose from a number of racial identity options. The quotes theoretically allow me to be the most inclusive and expansive in my recruitment of respondents who choose from this range of possibilities, from multiracial to what I call, "more than multiracial." This term speaks to the kinds of incipient identities, like "honorary memberships," that multiracial people develop in families that blend racially and structurally. Future research should explore these identity assertions, as space and time inhibits elaborate discussion here.

In addition to the above reasons, I deploy the quotes temporarily to underscore the contestations and negotiations around the concept, in the context of historical and contemporary mixture. The quotes draw attention to the visibility and invisibility of "multiracial" identities, or the legibility of racial mixture across time and space (the geography of race); they remind readers of the stability and fluidity or flexibility of multiracial identity, while recognize that a multiracial person does not always claim a multiracial identity; the quotes announce the ongoing debate about who is multiracial or can claim the term by crossing the borders of race without much provocation or any accusations of inauthenticity. They speak to and hint at the way border patrollers question the authenticity of multiracial people. The substantive chapters of this book address this issue of the policing of racial borders.

Even though I had a set of screening questions and my imagined target population in mind, I discovered that the very population I was searching for might be hard to find. This was not because they did or do not exist but because they were inadvertently hiding in plain sight. When I initially designed my research project, I naïvely assumed that I would *see* multiracial people in various social settings. Then I would bravely approach them, and enthusiastically invite them to consider participation in my study. It failed to occur to me that I might not *see* them so clearly after all. I had neglected to fully consider the limitations of my own "mixed like me" racial logic at the time; this logic motivated me to look for racial reflections of myself in the local population from which I would draw my sample (see Wise 2004). What if other multiracial people did not look "clearly mixed"? How would I know who to approach?" The myopic view impeded my initial search for and identification of people with racially mixed parentage. This is the inherent flaw of myopia, that too narrow a vision impedes said vision (see Collins 1993). Juanita Johnson-Bailey (1999) explores a variation of this theme in her work, where she considers how much the perception of similarities and differences between researchers and respondents impact and shape the social dynamic of such qualitative studies.

While I searched for "clearly mixed" people to participate in my research, I likely bypassed as possibilities what Marcia Dawkins (2012) calls "clearly invisible" multiracial people. Dawkins (2012) introduced readers to this term in her book of the same name, *Clearly Invisible.* I introduce the term "clearly mixed" as a complementary term that connotes a racially and ethnically ambiguous appearance as exemplified in celebrities such Rashida Jones, Maya Rudolph, Vin Diesel, Mariah Carey, and Derek Jeter. Celebrities such as Ne-Yo and Naomi Campbell may also be considered to have "invisible mixture," or racial mixture that is "clearly invisible" since many people do not recognize them as having racially mixed parentage or heritage.

About a fraction of the way through my interviews, I made this realization that I was prioritizing "obvious" racial mixture over the ostensible absence of it; I quickly proceeded to revise my recruitment strategy, ceasing to look for "clearly mixed" respondents rather than any "clearly invisible" multiracial people. I knew that not everyone with racially mixed heritage looks "clearly mixed," nor does everyone who looks mixed identify as such. Despite also knowing that people who claim singular races could almost always claim racial mixture in their family histories, I mistakenly defaulted to the typical signifiers of racial mixture at first. The revisions I made to my recruitment strategy decidedly expanded my sample, and enriched my understanding of who is multiracial.

In partial defense of my choices, I do recall having a particular interest in recruiting people who might fall easily into what *New York Times* reporter Ruth LaFerla (2003) dubbed, "Generation E.A." (Ethnically Ambiguous). I was curious to see if anyone I might interview identified as a member of this generation, or with the terms of ambiguity, ethnically and/or racially. Once I stopped privileging people I believed had more "visible mixture," I started searching for people with "invisible mixture." In the end, my efforts at a more expansive search enriched the sample of participants and the range of data I collected about their experiences. Having a combination of participants who were "clearly mixed" and others whose mixture was "clearly invisible" diversified the experiences that they narrated, which allowed me to consider convergences and divergences in their daily lives.

Before I could congratulate myself for sorting out a way to see this invisible mixture, or what author Mat Johnson (2015) calls an "optical illusion," I discovered another dilemma: shifting mixture. In addition to this "Now You See Us, Now You Don't" effect, shifting mixture presents another methodological snafu to this research. Shifting mixture means that, for some multiracial people, they may not name their racial identity as "multiracial" at the most ideal time: during the interview screening process, at the moment when I would ask them how they racially identify. If a multiracial person names one, but not all, of the racial groups that constitute their heritage, or they assert a singular racial identity (which thereby potentially masks their multiracial heritage), they may risk going undetected or unrecognized as multiracial. The challenge here is in creating enough space and comfort for potential respondents to reveal their multiracial heritage during this recruitment stage of the research. Researchers must carefully manage this interaction, as it sets the tone for any subsequent interactions (during the formal interview, if the individual qualifies and willingly participates). Researchers have to avoid creating pressurized conditions, working instead to produce the kind of dynamic that enables potential respondents to acknowledge their racially mixed ancestry and their preferred racial identities. Pressurized conditions may prompt potential respondents to conceal, rather than reveal, their multiracial heritage. This explains why, at the intersections of in/visible and shifting mixture, multiracial people can appear and/or disappear. I discuss this dynamic next.

Notes on Shifting Mixture, or How Do You Study A Moving Target (Population)?

In addition to figuring out how to recognize otherwise largely illegible racial mixture, I also found out that the borders of race not only appear and disappear, but they also move. As I traced the social and geographical migrations of racially mixed people, I was able to explore any "shifting mixture" respondents experience as the result of moving from one national context to another, and one social setting to another.

Studying shifting mixture, or fluid racial identities, is akin to studying a moving target, or race in motion. This methodological dilemma in investigating mixed race matters conveys the plethora of choices now available to racially mixed people. To be clear, increased identity options are now open to everyone, as evidenced by the honorary memberships people enjoy, as well as creative new terms that describe individuals in interracial relationships and families; terms such as "outsiders within" capture the crossing of racial lines and the significance of these relationships (see Collins 1986). France Winddance Twine (2011) speaks to this in terms of "honorary identities" within interracial relationships. As white women in interracial families with black men cultivate racial knowledge about blackness through their familial connections to these men and their multiracial children, many of the white women become "honorary black" members of their households.

While anyone can experience flexibility and fluidity in their racial identity, multiracial people must negotiate the mellifluous nature of their racial combinations in unique ways. Scholars have evidenced the different social worlds in which people live based on their membership in single racial groups. Building on this discussion, I argue here that multiracial people live in the borderlands best described by feminist Gloria Anzaldua (1987/1999) in her work, *Borderlands/La Frontera.* The borderlands are a liminal space where those worlds collide or coexist, or a bit of both. In this interstitial space (see Sandoval 2000), multiracial people may experience push and pull factors that feel like gravitational forces but are simply social ones (see Khanna 2011; Rockquemore and Brunsma 2002). These factors encourage multiracial movement, or racial migrations, such that multiracial people may be encouraged, or affirmed, in their assertion of a protean identity that claims all of the races in their parentage.

Borrowing from my own experiences in the "borderlands" helped me to understand how other people experience living on the border (see Harding 2003; Hartsock 1983). In a racially divisive society where multiracial people have so often been forced to choose "one-and-only-one" race, life on the borders of race, or in the borderlands, can be a site of conflict as well. In these interstices, many multiracial people find themselves located between socially-constructed-as-singular racial categories.[1]

In these interstices, racial multiplicity converges with ambiguity to intensify any feelings of or experiences with liminality or fluidity; this racial multiplicity often creates curiosity and provokes anxiety in others about this racial group of "Others," as multiracial people were once understood to be. Residents of the borderlands are often temporary. Their "multifacial" multiracial appearances "change face" so easily that they often confuse border patrollers and the process of racial sorting and categorization. This "changing faces" mostly happens passively or accidentally, not intentionally, although some multiracial people may manipulate their appearance to enhance a particular feature, so to speak, of their racial composition. Generally, however, many multiracial people, including those who are what actor Vin Diesel might call "multifacial," simply go about their everyday lives, but any ambiguity generates attention and curiosity in racial border patrollers.

While celebrated and applauded perhaps because it is characterized as allowing the multiracial person the "best of both worlds" (or all worlds, as the case may be), this protean identity also produces an interesting methodological dilemma or hiccup for social science researchers. Consider this: I approach an individual who asserts a protean identity, who claims white, black, and Native American ancestry and parentage. This individual satisfies the criteria for the study and indicates a willingness to participate in the project. At some points during the interview, the respondent refers to her respective racial groups, sometimes making her preferred racial identity clear, but not at other times. Throughout the interview, as I pose various questions from the interview guide, I am trying to get the fullest sense of her preferred protean identity. The respondent expresses loyalty and affinity to these three particular racial groups; that, to me, conveys her protean identity. However, at some points in the interview, she may more definitively position herself as black, and illustrates how others see her as such. She may work to claim her white and indigenous heritage as well. The dilemma is not so much in listening to this complexity and affirming this multiplicity. Rather, it is often in knowing how to affirm where a multiracial person is locating themselves in a particular memory, given a particular social setting, demographic, or other details. The richness in the thick description offered by my respondents allowed me to see that many of them were managing this very dynamic, this shifting mixture.

Given the numerous possibilities of racial identity options now available to racially mixed people to claim, I speculated that shifting mixture might combine with invisible mixture to create a logistical consideration. I wondered, "How best will I ask questions about a participant's racial identity if it shifts from moment to moment, or from one memory to another? If respondents assert protean identities, vacillating between one single race or another (or others), as well as a biracial or multiracial identity, what would be the best way to refer to their racial identities during the interview?" The fluidity and flexibility of racial identity, as expressed in protean identities, reflects this shifting mixture. Confronting and resolving these methodological problems or challenges allowed me to study this shifting and in/visible mixture in order to understand how racially mixed people make meaning of their identities and choices.

Studying the Geographies of Race and Racial Migrations

While I conducted interviews with individuals living in the South, I would be remiss not to acknowledge another kind of shifting mixture: the numerous migrations that research participants made, most often as young children who moved with their families of origin, between countries and within the U.S. These migrations informed how many of the respondents understood themselves racially, but also how they synthesized potentially competing racial paradigms and classification systems. Several respondents noted the ways that their racial locations changed along with the geographical context in which they lived; these changes occurred both for them and others, since race often takes on new meaning across and within nations (based on local and global geographies of race). To strangers, the geographical context provided a frame through which to understand respondents' racial locations. As respondents moved from one location to another, and/or one nation to another, they found that sometimes others' perceptions of their racial group membership shifted accordingly. At times, these perceptions aligned with the self-perceptions of participants, while at other times, they completed differed and thus confused the participants in the study. I summarize some of these experiences in the chapters that follow, noting the work that respondents have to engage in, in order to manage their own racial sense of self or negotiate their preferred racial identities with others.

The meanings of race can take new shape as people move from one setting to another. The specificities of a particular place inform how people understand themselves and others racially. I noticed that, even though I had lived in the U.S. for several years before beginning this research, I was holding onto at least two different ways of seeing race because of my own migrations between nations and racial locations. Gloria Anzaldua (2002:549) puts it this way:

> Living between cultures results in "seeing" double, first from the perspective of one culture, then from the perspective of another.

Seeing from two or more simultaneously renders those cultures transparent. Removed from that culture's center, you glimpse the sea in which you've been immersed but to which you were oblivious, no longer seeing the world the way you were enculturated to see it.... As you struggle to form a new identity, a demythologization of race occurs. You begin to see race as an experience of reality from a particular perspective and a specific time and place (history), not as a fixed feature of personality or identity.

What Anzaldua offers here is some acknowledgment of the way many people hold onto multiple, and sometimes competing, racial paradigms. This may occur within a nation, but certainly these ways of seeing can be multiplied the more people migrate or move around the world. These spatial migrations hint at the racial transformations that are possible, a topic I turn to towards in Chapter Six. Here, I will say that "seeing double," or having multiple ways of seeing and knowing race, is a double-edged sword. As a researcher, it means knowing that racial mixture exists in the vast majority of us, yet ignoring that reality in order to respect people's preferred singular racial identities, when chosen. It means respecting the racial rules, rather than breaking them, so as not to violate the boundaries that distinguish between racial categories.

I make these points to highlight the challenges of getting people that I interviewed to discuss these ways of "seeing double." It is difficult work to ask people to reveal their racial frameworks, and racial consciousness. Nevertheless, I made an effort to explore any evidence of the multiple ways of seeing that many of the multiracial respondents offered in their interviews. This is only the beginning step, as more work needs to be done on this. Rockquemore, Brunsma, and Delgado (2009) make a variation of this point in their article, "Racing to Theory or Retheorizing Race? Understanding the Struggle to Build a Multiracial Identity Theory." As social scientists, we learn the dominant ways of seeing race, while studying people's lived experiences. Neat and tidy alignment between the two does not always exist or emerge in sociological analyses. This suggests the need to continue researching and retheorizing race and multiracial identities specifically.

One thing that researching race and thinking about mixed race matters conveyed to me is that everyone does not subscribe to the dominant racial hierarchy. My hope is that this book reveals the complexities of racial multiplicity, as well as the complexities of race. To arrive at this appreciation, I had to begin with my own misreading of race in order to more fully see other people and their readings of race. My own search for understanding of multiracial people who were "mixed like me" enabled this "multiracial epiphany" (see Noble Maillard and Villazor 2012; Noble Maillard 2008).

Appreciating the racial migrations that multiracial people might experience involves acknowledging different ways of seeing race. Ironically, however, people who reject or resist knowing these different ways of seeing race may likely become border patrollers, believing there is one-and-only-one best way to see race. They also see the borders of race as fixed, not fluid. This stands in contrast to the lived experiences of race, not the theoretical or institutional constructions of race.

Perhaps especially because race is a social construction, there is much variation in people's perceptions of race, and much similarity. The spaces between races vary, such that no definitive "line" exists between racial groups or categories. Without such a line, there is no exact point of trespassing, yet people police racial borders as if such a definitive tipping point exists. To complicate matters, as people of any racial backgrounds move around the world, they bring their ways of seeing race to new places. As people travel, so too does race. When people move from one (social or geographical) setting to another, they carry racial frameworks with which they are already familiar. These frameworks reflect local, regional, and national differences, despite the U.S. Census and other institutional forces encouraging a hegemonic, or dominant, way of seeing race. Ideally, people learn new ways of seeing during their travels or daily migrations around the world. They recognize multiple racial paradigms, some of them complementary, some competing. To some degree, the space of the interview conversation enables the exchange of information about these racial paradigms, primarily with respondents sharing their racialized views of and experiences in the world, and the researcher sorting out these perspectives.

In part, studying shifting mixture entails studying these shifting paradigms, as people move from one (geographic) location to another, only to discover that they may have also moved from one (racial) location to another. This movement is seldom singular or unidirectional; it is more than occasional. It is often perpetual, without an endpoint or a definite destination. It speaks to what I call "the multidimensionality of multiraciality," and what Vin Diesel dubbed "multifacial," the many faces of multiracial people. Studying shifting mixture encourages recognition of any of the different racial perceptions of multiracial people made possible by these multiple ways of seeing. By seeing these possibilities in any racially mixed individual, people acknowledge that the particular racial mixture of said individual can be read in a number of ways. My research facilitates an understanding of these perceptions, as it produced opportunities for racially mixed people to describe how often they were misidentified as "some other race" rather than a product of their own racial parentage or particular mixture.

The many faces of multiraciality also speaks to the way the same multiracial person might look like a member of any single racial group, or any combinations of racial groups. This is a kind of shifting mixture, as the racial location of said multiracial person hinges on others' perceptions of them. With each reading or misreading, a shift in racial location can happen. These perceptions are partially shaped by the aforementioned competing racial paradigms, or the racial categories into which people imagine are possible to sort themselves and others. For example, let's say an individual holds a binary view of race, a "two-and-only-two" racial framework that accommodates whiteness and blackness; whiteness and nonwhiteness; or blackness and nonblackness. If this individual meets a multiracial person, the former individual cognitively holds space for that multiracial person to fit into "one-and-only-one" of the two categories, not both. Based on binary racial logic, the multiracial person is either one race or another; s/he cannot be both.[2] Otherwise, there is a perceived "failure to fit." This result may produce any number of reactions, many of which I discussed with respondents, and offer in more detail in Chapters 3 through 6.

If the multiracial person gets located in one of the two options, both of which differ from her preferred racial location, she involuntarily experiences shifting mixture. This happens as a result of slipping into a single racial category rather than being recognized as belonging in the "two or more races" population. She may wish to claim the "opposite" racial category than the one to which the border patroller perceives her as belonging, much to the dismay of the border patroller. Alternately, she may claim both of the two-and-only-two categories, opting to shift between them. Some multiracial people may discover that they are "some other race(s)" than the ones they prefer identifying as, based on others' (mis)perceptions of them, and because of competing racial frameworks. The latter is often a reflection of people's racial socialization and literacy (or lack there of), and their familiarity with the range of possibility regarding racial paradigms (or ways of seeing race). In the research study, I explored these competing racial paradigms as a way of understanding the meanings people attach to particular physical appearances and racial group categories.

I conducted the interviews for this research in the Southeast United States. I believe that the meanings that people attach to race are both specific to this region of the country, and simultaneously reflective of global geographies of race. I turn next to a discussion of my own location in an interstitial place and describe how conducting this research within a particular community created community as well.

Situating Myself within the Research, Building Bridges and Community

My decision to study shifting mixture stems from my own experiences navigating the borders of race. My own interstitial racial and spatial locations across countries inform my views and perspectives on race. Having grown up outside of the U.S. (in the U.S. Virgin Islands), I was accustomed to a slightly different racial hierarchy based on the demography, geography, and history of the Virgin Islands. The racial framework with which I was familiar shifted when I moved to the U.S., such that I learned to see race differently. The ways people perceived me also shifted with the change in national or spatial locations. In other words, my migration seemed to facilitate a racial relocation of sorts.

As a black white biracial woman who asserts a protean racial identity, I locate myself in what Gloria Anzaldua (1987) calls the borderlands; I lived there before learning its name. As Anzaldua (1987) describes in her book, *Borderlands/La Frontera*, the borderlands is that liminal or interstitial space between two cultures, typically a dominant culture and a marginalized one; it captures the "between and betwixt" of racial categories.

In more recent work, Anzaldua (2002) continued to describe the productive and generative space of the borderlands, or nepantla, where people wrestle with their self-identity. She suggests that this wrestle involves opposing forces, and that if people do not take sides "a new identity emerges. As you make your way through life, nepantla itself becomes the place you live in most of the time—home. Nepantla is the site of transformation, the place where different perspectives come into conflict and where you question the basic ideas, tenets, and identities inherited from your family, your education, and your different cultures." Nepantla is the zone between changes where you struggle to find equilibrium between the outer expression of change and your inner relationship to it.

Anzaldua's ideas registered with me, as it reflected my reality of crossing racial borders. When I read Anzaldua's work, and that of other racially and ethnically mixed women writers, I found a language that fit my experiences. In the borderlands of my own racially mixed family, people crossed cultural, racial and spatial borders, blending boundaries between them. This blending and mixing became home for me, but for others, outsiders, it was a provocation, an invitation to ask unsolicited questions.

I felt a little tinge of irony when I found myself asking my research participants similar iterations of the questions I once fielded from strangers. Studying the borders of race involves asking troublesome questions about how people manage these very borders of race. Some of the questions that I asked participants were variations of those that follow: Do multiracial people feel like they fully belong to all of the racial groups that constitute their heritage, or not entirely a part of any of the racial groups of their parentage and heritage? What are the best ways to explore the experiences of multiracial people, to fully understand their racial identity choices?

My own experiences navigating the borders of race allowed me to question those questions from others, which helped as I prepared to pose similar questions to participants. As I had wondered why people wanted answers to variations of the "What are you?" question when, at once, they claimed not to see race or its relevance in this racially stratified society, I tried my best not to perpetuate the border-patrolling behavior so often reflected in such questioning. Throughout the entire research endeavor, I aimed to study the borders of race, including the problem of border patrolling, without participating in, or intensifying the problem. Given that some multiracial people assert their preferred racial identities in the face of strong support and/or opposition from others, I worked to minimize my participation in any injuries around their racial identities.

The feminist researcher in me wanted to appear more centrally or clearly in the supportive category, though I constantly feared that I might inadvertently invalidate, and thus border patrol, some of my respondents. I did not want to border patrol or perpetuate the very problem (of racial borer patrolling) I had so often experienced as a racially ambiguous multiracial person. Thus, I always attempted to appear neutral, though not indifferent, to their preferred racial identities. I asked respondents clarifying questions, to ensure that I captured as much of the details as I possibly could, so as to successfully secure their stories and give voice to their experiences.

Conducting this research enabled me see those questions as guided by curiosity and some other motivations. It also prompted me to reflect on and attend to my own intentions and motivations for putting myself in the position to ask such questions. Drawing from my own experiences as a multiracial person living "across the color line," as Heather Dalmage (2000) puts it, sensitized me to the subject, though I had a lot to learn from my respondents' experiences. Formally following my own interests allowed me to chase my intellectual curiosities as a way to more deeply understand what Maria P. P. Root (1996) calls "the multiracial experience." While I did not set out searching for a multiracial community specifically through the research process, I found that to be an unintended yet rewarding consequence. With each interview, I felt an enhanced sense of belonging; in many ways, I was engaging in the practice of bridge-building, a process feminists describe as community-building. My interview conversations served as a vehicle that enabled these connections.

Perhaps I was also accessing existing communities, since many of the respondents referred me to their friends and family. This snowball sampling technique facilitated my ability to interview 2 sets of siblings, and small friendship networks, as well as people with little to no known social connection to each other. My ability to access these various groups allowed me to draw comparisons across individuals. I could see how siblings growing up in the same family influenced each other, but often asserted very different preferred racial identities. The same could be said about the broader communities that include multiracial people and help connect them to each other.

My own participation in the academic communities that connected me to all of the multiracial individuals I spoke to for this project also shaped my thinking about racial mixture. In some ways, in graduate school and beyond, I built a bridge between feminism and sociology, marrying the two sometimes intersecting and overlapping disciplines. Particularly within the feminist and sociological academic communities in which I participated, I came to appreciate the ways in which the scholarship and the conversations about the scholarship informed my ways of seeing, thinking, and knowing. Together, the two disciplines, Women's Studies and Sociology, informed my research design and methodology. From the kinds of questions I posed to participants, to my choice to invite participants to cocreate and help guide the process best described as "interview conversations" by sociologist Linda Blum (1999), I let feminist and sociological thought shape this investigation. You will see evidence of both disciplinary perspectives knitted throughout the book, in terms of the scholarship I use to frame my analysis, as well as in the interpretations I offer about the narratives multiracial people crafted during our interview conversations.

Just as this book brings two disciplines together in conversation, I attempted to do the same with each respondent. I successfully invited 60 individuals into such conversation by conducting face-to-face, in-depth, open-ended, confidential qualitative interview conversations (see Blum 1999) for about one to two hours. Respondents were between the ages of 18 and 57, at the time of their respective interview. It was during their interview that I solicited their consent and then they indicated their willingness to participate in my research study. All 60 individuals provided verbal and written consent, the latter of which I secured in a safe and private place.

Sample Characteristics and Technique

In terms of racial parentage, 16 participants noted having black and white parentage, 13 noted having white and Asian parentage, 3 reported having black and Asian parentage, while 2 noted having Black and Hawaiian parentage (which they distinguished the latter category from "Asian"). Five respondents reported black and Native American heritage, while two participants reported white and Native American heritage.[3] Three people mentioned having white and Latino/a parentage, while four respondents reported black and Latino/a parentage. One reported white, black, and Latino/a heritage, another white, black, Asian, and Native American heritage, and 2 others noted having white, black, Native American, and Latino/a heritage. Five respondents reported black, white, and Native American heritage. One reported having white and Other heritage; another reported black and Other heritage; and yet another reported having racial ancestry from all groups (white, Asian, black, Native American, Latino/a).

In the end, I included individuals who claimed a multiracial identity, or acknowledged known racially mixed parentage. This includes people whose parents belong to racial groups that are socially constructed as different; this even includes parents who claim a multiracial identity or had parents who belong(ed) to racial groups that are socially constructed as different.[4] The latter could theoretically include parents of the same multiple races who my respondents considered to identify differently enough from one another to constitute an "interracial" relationship. I use quotes here in case of any contestation of this description.

Rather than reinforce the idea of mixture as "something new," I also included individuals who described their heritage as racially mixed. This accounted for the possibility of multiracial parents claiming only one race, while their children (the respondents) attempted to reclaim two or more races. Including individuals with racially mixed heritage also acknowledged that those families often consist of members who compromise their "monoracial" integrity. Accommodating both parentage and heritage also recognizes that many individuals may or may not have grown up in families its members (or even others) considered "interracial" or "multiracial." I explored these nuances and contingencies in the interviews, to see the foregrounding and backgrounding of racial diversity and mixture in identity, family, and partner choice.

Focusing on individuals allowed me to ask about relational and familial experiences, while gaining a solid understanding of those experiences from the perspective of the "multiracial" person. This is important particularly at a time when multiracial identities are shape-shifting in new and different ways, and staying the same for many people. Understanding how individuals produce racial discourses about their experiences helps illuminate how they make meaning of their racial multiplicity. Do individuals learn to provide palatable explanations for the patterns that emerge in their identity options? Investigating the choices, behaviors, and attendant racial discursive practices of members of the multiracial population also draws attention to the ways such discourses connect and reconnect them to (or locate/relocate them in) racial categories of their racial combination and beyond.

Research Questions and Interview Guide

Guided by my own intellectual ambitions and curiosities in this ostensibly incipient multiracial population, I set out to interview people of *any* racial combination. In hindsight, I cannot help but wonder why I took such a broad and expansive approach, eager as I was to potentially include everyone rather than risk excluding anyone. One explanation for this decision was my then youthful ambition, coupled with a healthy dose of "I-can-do-anything-I-set-my-mind-to" tenacity. The other is that, by interviewing multiracial people of any racial combination, I could examine the liminal or interstitial quality to the lives of multiracial people, as described in the literature at the time. For example, feminist authors including the aforementioned Gloria Anzaldua and Chela Sandoval (2000) described this in-between place where multiracial people reside. Anzaldua's discussion of the borderlands and of building bridges suggested that multiracial people exist on the margins of racial categories, but also at the center from where they build bridges or connections. Anzaldua and others suggest that this bridge-building is characteristic of marginalized group members, and it reminds us of the empowered action people in which we can engage one another to build connection and community. In many ways, designing and conducting this research was an act of building connection and community.

In the end, this decision to be broadly inclusive worked in my favor, to some degree, as I could consider the similarities and differences between multiracial people of different racial combinations. If I had only interviewed people who identified as two particular races, I would not have been able to compare and contrast multiracial people of different racial combinations. For example, by not setting definitive racial parameters for participation, I could see how some white and Asian multiracial people experience border patrolling similarly to, and/or differently from, white and black multiracial people. By interviewing a wide variety of multiracial people, I could consider their lived experiences and compare them to the existing literature, as well as to one another.

In conceptualizing these interview conversations as a space for consciousness raising and honest exchanges, I employed feminist methodologies throughout, in order to encourage respondents to critically reflect on their lives and feel empowered by the interaction (Babbie 1998; Harding 2003; Hartsock 1983; Phoenix 2001; Reinharz 1992; Sandoval 2000; Smith 1999; Twine 2000). I asked people with racially mixed parentage and heritage a set of questions as outlined in an interview guide, and encouraged them to cocreate the interview conversation, to make the dynamic more reciprocal. Having an awareness of real or perceived power differentials between researcher and respondent (Acker, Berry, Esseveld 1983; Fine, Weis, Powell, and Wong 1997; Reinharz 1992; Sandoval 2000; Smith 1999; Twine 2000) allowed me to remain sensitive to and supportive of respondents in their efforts to extricate or communicate some of their experiences for my consideration and analysis.

Both the respondents and an interview guide allowed me to address specific topics of interest and informed the interview conversations. Attending to and incorporating topical areas of interest generated by the respondents attempted to democratize and decolonize the process (Reinharz 2000; Smith 1999). In creating an iterative and interactive environment, I invited respondents to identify omissions and oversights in the interview guide. Using a guide provided some structure and consistency, but flexibly accommodated emergent and relevant themes I initially neglected, but eventually noticed. Thus, the guide provided a starting point from which to ask questions and establish rapport, as well as an opportunity to introduce and explore previously unexamined issues.

In addition to advertising my research project through the distribution of flyers, I also relied on snowball sampling to acquire additional respondents. That is, as I interviewed multiracial people, they referred me to people they knew who identified similarly or had racially mixed parentage. This snowball sampling revealed some of the existing connections people had to each other, which then allowed me connections to them. In the moment of interviewing, and then more clearly in retrospect, I could see how many of the respondents who participated in my study were already in community with one another, beyond those respondents who are related to each other.

In my study, I interviewed two sets of three siblings. I included respondents who identified specifically as biracial or multiracial, and others who identified as a single race. A few alternated between a biracial or multiracial identity and a transcendent or raceless one, while others alternated between racial categories, to express more of a protean identity. While I provided the respondents with a written copy of the questions I planned to pose, I did not provide this information prior to each interview conversation. Several respondents did note, typically before the start of the interview or immediately afterwards, that they had spoken to their parents about their upcoming interview. Together, they speculated about the questions I might ask, and then talked about how the respondent would answer those hypothetical questions. I found this interesting, given some of my findings that deal with the family environment, parent socialization, and the existing models of multiracial identity formation. Because multiracial people occupy a liminal position in the current racial hierarchy, and multiracial children occupy an ostensible position of deference to the elders in their respective families, they are constructed as in a position to listen to and learn from others. Their own racial consciousness and embodied knowledge seldom get recognized as viable forces influencing individuals in their families of origin. If people experience social life differently depending on their relative group position, then members of interracial families experience social life similarly, on the basis of their shared membership in such families, yet differently, based on their respective racial locations.

As I will illustrate in later chapters, multiracial people, particularly as they enter late adolescence and young adulthood, may find that they are better informed about their racial realities than their parents. This is particularly the case, I would argue, among parents described as belonging to a single racial group. For multiracial people managing the borders of race, their experiences across these borders of race are informed by, but often differ from, the interracial families their parents (or partnered caregivers) form. I expressly wanted to acknowledge and consider these differences where they existed, and to explore the racial realities of multiracial people in interracial families. Doing so allowed me to see similarities and differences between individuals in interracial families.

In the broader scope of the project, I also focused on the dating histories and romantic relationships of multiracial people. While I do not focus on that in this book, I will note that much of the racial socialization from and racial identity of the parents of my respondents informed their own partner choices *and* their racial identity (see Joyner and Kao 2005; Roberts-Clarke, Roberts, and Morokoff 2004). How parents identify themselves racially plays a huge role in the way their multiracial children identify. The quality of the relationships and strength of connections that family members have to each other also greatly impact how they understand themselves racially, on both individual and familial levels. The process of parental racial socialization, or the way parents talk about race with their multiracial children, also shapes the racial identity formation process for these children (see Dalmage 2004b,c; Thompson 1994; Thornton 1997; Thornton, Chatters, Taylor, and Allen 1990). Since socialization is an ongoing process that last a lifetime, these early parental messages shape the family's social environment, and may continue to be of significant influence on the multiracial child's choices, in terms of racial identity and romantic partners. Because these parental influences shape so much of the day-to-day messages that multiracial people receive throughout their lives, it is important to consider and study them. In Chapter Four, I discuss some of the surprising patterns that I observed about multiracial families, including the social pressures and messaging to multiracial adult children to make particular choices in terms of racial identities and romantic partners. Next, I discuss the ways in which I analyzed the data I gathered during this research study.

Data Collection and Analysis

With the permission or consent of each respondent, I took handwritten notes during each interview conversation to ensure that I had some written record of the narrative were the other recording device to have failed. I conducted the interviews until the point of saturation, the juncture where respondents thematically and categorically begin to sound like or echo each another. Once this happened, the interviewing culminated.

At the end of each interview, I transcribed them verbatim, or word for word, analyzing them using Grounded Theory Method (Strauss and Corbin 1998, 1997; LaRossa 2005). I began with open coding, conducting a paragraph-by-paragraph analysis of the interview transcriptions. In fracturing the data during this microscopic analysis, I identified concepts related to the respondents' identities and everyday experiences navigating race as multiracial people. I analyzed the data for indicators of these concepts, discovering the relationship between concepts, and ultimately seeing the concepts take on dimension from the data. I moved through the stages of axial coding onto selective coding, where I was able to identify "multiracial border patrolling" as the central organizing theme. I developed the dimensions of border patrolling as applicable to identity and partner choice through my analysis and examination of racial discourses. I considered whether respondents experienced others' reactions as affirming or an expression of curiosity, with indifference, or resentment. I asked myself questions to help clarify the connections between concepts: Did other people interact in ways that validated the multiracial person's identity and romantic relationship? Both? Neither? How did the respondent's racial identity influence others' perceptions of race, such that the respondent evaded or faced intensified scrutiny publicly?

Taking a microscopic look at the transcripts also allowed me to see that a variety of people had reactions to the multiracial respondents' identities and partner choices. Adding this dimension facilitated my arrival at the theory that the patrolling of racial borders is neither solely negative nor singular in its source or origination. Instead, I discovered many types of border patrolling, and that many different groups engage in this behavior discursively. Weaving these connections allowed me to arrive at the core category of "multiracial interracial border patrolling," with the conditions including the actors involved: strangers (border patrolling "from the outside in"); family and friends (border patrolling "from outsiders within," "insider others," or "insiders without"); and the self/the respondents (border patrolling "from the inside out"). Delineating and dimensionalizing the various types of border patrolling allowed me to see that exploring racial borders served different purposes. This exploration then translated into the types of border patrolling for which I found evidence: benevolent, beneficiary, protective, and malevolent. In the following chapters, I discuss and illustrate these terms in more detail.

Before concluding this chapter, I turn to one of the primary shortcomings or limitations of this study: gender asymmetry in the sample. As I explain, despite my best efforts, I was unable to recruit similar numbers of women and men for the study, as was then suggested. I was encouraged to reflect on the lack of men participants and disproportionate number of women participants in the sample, to provide possible explanations for this pattern. At the time, I was operating within the parameters, if not constraints, of the "two-and-only-two" gender binary, using only two gender categories to guide my recruitment. Given the changes in my own thinking about the limitations of the "two-and-only-two" gender binary, I do not necessarily maintain that the gender composition of my sample compromises the quality of my research. Instead, I would argue, it amplifies the voices and experiences of individuals willing to participate, and draws attention to the gender continuum. In many ways, this conundrum of a persistent "two-and-only-two" gender category, now opening up into a continuum, reflects and intersects with similar shifts in individual and collective understandings of race.

Limitations to the Sample

In the end, of the 60 individuals[5] I interviewed only 8 identified as men and 52 identified as women. While I made efforts to encourage men's involvement in the research project, I was less successful at securing their participation than that of women. An admitted shortcoming of this research, the gender imbalance suggests that men may be more reluctant to participate in interviews for a number of reasons: they may view these interviews as the gendered woman space, rather than a gender neutral space; they may be socialized not to "tell stories" or see the act of storytelling as another gendered woman act; they may not have much of an awareness of their racial identities, if hegemonic or dominant masculinity and male privilege protect them from having many of the experiences described by the disproportionate number of women in the sample.

Despite these potential reasons, no men explicitly provided reasons for declining to participate in this qualitative research. Instead, many of them expressed an interest in participating in an interview, but never scheduled one. This may have a bit to do with maturity and responsibility, or reflect that many of the young men might not have taken me or my research study seriously; additionally, they might not take themselves seriously enough to imagine all of the important contributions their narrative would make to the collective whole.

I might also speculate that some people, but perhaps men in particular, might have imagined the interview as a space for (further or any) contestation and invalidation of their racial authenticity and/or their masculinity. By possibly viewing interview questions as extensions or replications of any interrogations they face in their everyday lives, these men would feel reasonably tentative about putting themselves in harm's way. The consent forms and formal review of these forms by the Institutional Review Board served to minimize this harm for and protect all participants, but some men may have averted participation in order to avoid having to "save face" or perform masculinity and race. This performance partially departs from that discussed in Khanna's (2011) book, *Biracial in America*, as related to forming and performing race.

Some scholars point to the intersections of race and gender as possible explanations for the disproportionate sample distribution by gender. As Kenney and Kenney (2012), Kivel (1996), Bradshaw (1992) and others have argued, multiracial women are often sexualized and exoticized; such sexual objectification and the surrounding myths might convince men that they have little to contribute to or discuss in the interviews. Men with racial heritage might feel gender-specific pressures related to their racial identities, with these very pressures dissuading them from participation. Unfortunately, their lack of participation impedes my understanding of any significant differences in the ways that they assert racial identities and make partner choices, but points in the direction of future research (for this lack of participation warrants its own investigation). The limited number of men in my sample precluded me from comparing the identity and partner choices of men and women with multiracial parentage or heritage.

The gender asymmetry possibly suggests that women may feel more socially motivated than men to "be nice" by participating in such research. Accounting for this "social desirability" effect still leaves some questions unanswered: Why do women tend to participate more in social research on multiracial people? Is what they share gender specific, or gender neutral? Are there experiences that multiracial women have that are specific to their social locations, or generalizable to multiracial men, or even the general population?

Researchers offer speculation and insight from their own investigations. The gender imbalance implicitly supports existing research that suggests women uniquely experience racial mixture, at the intersections of gender and race as they experience these social locations); in part, this occurs because so much attention, in social institutions and social interactions, focuses on women and their bodies (Rockquemore 2002). Finally, the gender asymmetry serves as motivation for continued this research, with different or newly devised strategies for more effectively recruiting men.

As additional and related demographic information, all but two of the respondents had at least some college education, with the majority of them having attended a large urban research institution in the Southeast. The majority identified as heterosexual, while one reported being bisexual and another reported questioning their sexual identity at the time of the interview. As noted earlier, many generations of multiracial were represented in the age range of respondents.

While I certainly would have liked to diversify the sample in terms of gender, as well as the other aforementioned variables, I am satisfied with the existing composition of the sample. The respondents who did participate centered their voices and shared experiences that enrich the way people "think mixture." They echoed and departed from existing narratives, complicating and expanding ways of seeing, knowing, and talking about mixed race matters.

Limits to a "Mixed Like Me" Logic

In the initial conceptualization of this project, I naïvely believed that I would have an easier time talking to other multiracial people, presuming them to be "mixed like me." A play on Tim Wise's (2004) book, *White Like Me*, the concept, "mixed like me, " speaks to the perceptions of racial similarities and any limitations stemming from those perceptions (see also Gallagher 2000). Upon preparing for the interview process, I speculated that my shyness might prove more of an impediment than other variables affecting my ability to acquire information from respondents. However, once I successfully identified and recruited participants, I failed to fully consider how my own appearance, identities, and understandings of race would impact how others saw me, and how we talked about race.

During the interviews, I recognized that larger issues created in a "pigmentocracy," like colorism, were likely at play (see Telles 2014; Hunter 2005; Herring, Keith, and Horton 2004). Even though I did not reveal my racial identity to respondents, I still felt that I, too, was managing my multiracial identity with them. In my estimation, respondents likely revealed and concealed parts of their personal histories partially on the basis of their perception of me, racially. That is, I sensed that respondents with whiter skin color generally shared experiences that completely contrasted with my own. Conversely, I observed similarities between my experiences and that of respondents whose skin color approximated mine. These points highlight the variation in who is multiracial, and in "the multiracial experience" (see Root 1996). The different racial combinations of parentage, and different skin colors of respondents created differing racial realities. Discovering and exploring these differences speak to the importance of qualitative interviews with multiracial people of various racial combinations. It broadens the collective understanding of how multiracial people manage the borders of race.

Throughout the interview process, I employed the feminist praxis of listening to and affirming the lived experiences of multiracial people who took the time and expend energy to share their lives and stories so that others can hear their truths (see R.N. Brown 2013, 2008). Nevertheless, I wondered, if not worried, about how completely respondents might share their stories, particularly if they did not see any similarities in our appearances, and by extension, a real or imagined lack of shared experiences. I realized that the very topic—multiracial identity—could become both an obstacle *and* a vehicle to the interview conversations. I had to devise ways to manage my own multiracial identity with respondents. I had to open up and hold space for them to clearly, to the best of their abilities, explain to me how they understood race, racial identity, racial categories, and racial hierarchy. Each interview conversation created an opportunity to explore as much of the nuances that the respondents attached to particular terms regarding race.

Throughout the research process, I kept in mind issues that Carla Goar (2008) addresses in her work, including debates about researcher objectivity, the impact of colorblind racism on social science research, and race neutrality. Goar (2008:159) argues, "The idea of race neutrality serves to restrict our knowledge of racial groups." She challenges colorblind notions that the race of the researcher remains irrelevant to the research. Instead, Goar (2008:159–160) contends, "[R]ace is an important status characteristic that affects the way individuals perceive social phenomena. To suggest that individuals who possess different ascribed statuses may observe things differently is certainly in line with the literature, but violates the basic premise or objectivity: that trained empiricists be capable of removing all personal and subjective understanding as they proceed with research endeavors." As I illustrate throughout this chapter and book, people with racially mixed parentage or heritage may possess ascribed statuses such as race that are debatably "the same difference" (see Zack 1997). It is this very same/difference that complicates yet enriches the interview process, ensuring that it is dynamic and facilitates discovery.

Similar to other social interactions, the interview process has the potential to create the space for negotiation. These negotiations simulate that which occurs in the social world, but differ to the degree that the research setting influences these interactions (see Stryker 1980). This largely explains why feminist researchers work to neutralize power asymmetries, to minimize some of the ways power differences shape these interactions (see also Lamphere, Ragone, and Zavella 1997). Interestingly, the dynamic of the interview allowed respondents to offer their definitions of various terms. It was, for instance, during the interview conversation, that I was able to ask respondents to elaborate upon their understandings of terms, and clarify connotations of particular concepts.

Suggestions for Future Research

The exploratory nature of this qualitative research accommodates the aforementioned gendered asymmetry and other demographic similarities, but suggests the need for triangulation in future research. Had I acquired additional (sufficient) funding, I would have hired additional interviewers, in an effort to offer potential respondents more variety in whom they could connect to (in terms of race, gender, and sexuality) during the interview conversations. I want to discuss one of the ways that I noticed this impacting and shaping the interviews as it relates to the interactional dynamic during the research (see Stanley and Slattery 2003).

In my observation, and because of the research design, my decision to conduct interview conversations with respondents meant that much of the social dynamic of those interview conversations simulates or mimics that which would occur naturally in other social settings. Any recognizable power asymmetries aside, the participants asserted their agency in ways that are not characteristic of more traditional interviews or other settings outside of the research context. For example, the research setting was purposefully designed to allow respondents to elaborate on their views, on their racial identity choices, their family life, their relationship histories, and other topics they found relevant to the research. In other settings, they might not be given similar amounts of time to detail these topics.

In seeing the research setting as a simulacrum of society, I eventually understood some of the social dynamics I was dealing with in the interview conversations were simply reflections of the broader social world. Just as respondents managed the borders of race as a multiracial person in society, they might have done so during the study.

Concluding Thoughts

In thinking about some of the interviews I had with research participants, I am inclined to attribute the success of some of those interview conversations to some combination of compatibility or similar personalities, as well as to a shared knowledge about being "global mixed race" (see King-O'Riain, Small, Mahtani, Song, and Spickard 2014). That is, a number of the respondents who had been born outside of the U.S., lived outside of the U.S., or were first-generation Americans, shared this experience of managing the borders of race in more than one national context. These respondents conveyed how much discovering and navigating racial borders were often difficult and painful lessons; they demonstrated how their lived experiences with crossing racial borders confused them initially, particularly in places like the U.S. where "race doesn't matter," rhetorically speaking. They described the authenticity tests they endured from family members and friends, and how the same people also validated and affirmed them at times. Again, to see the research setting as an unintended yet potential site of these authenticity tests is to see it as a reflection of society.

Even though I anticipated most of my respondents would share some of the same social locations or characteristics with me, not many of them did. As a result of this, I am convinced I learned more about the nuances of mixed race matters than I fully expected at the inception of this investigation. The research process reminded me of the difficulty of finding similarity in multiraciality, within or among a diverse group of multiracial people of various racial combinations. I also appreciated finding some similarity in surprising places, particularly at the intersections of social differences (in terms of race and gender). Because of the dynamics of race, these similarities and differences can shift from one moment to the next. Perhaps this is why Suki Ali (2003) described studies on the multiracial populations as endeavors of "researching the unresearchable."

Here I would argue that both of the stability and fluidity of multiraciality makes this research so dynamic and difficult. Studying shifting mixture and the ways multiracial people manage their identities in public and private proved to be as rewarding as it was challenging. It proved interesting to witness that management of identities, or the blurring, blending, and brightening of racial borders.

Notes

[1] These categories include White, Asian, American Indian or Alaska Native (or Native American), Black or African American, Native Hawaiian or Other Pacific Islander and Some Other Race. While the category Hispanic/Latino/a can include individuals of any race, it is also a racialized category as well.

[2] Here, I borrow from and adapt the terminology of "two-and-only-two" from Betsy Lucal (1999), and adapt it to also include the limitations of these options allowing for only one choice or racial group.

[3] Here I use "heritage" instead of "parentage" to highlight that these respondents spoke about their family heritage more generally, and differentiated between having relatives (versus parents specifically) of certain combinations.

[4] I rely partially on the work of Rockquemore and Brunsma (2002) to describe this population, and the possible racial identity options they choose.

[5] I largely centered my recruitment efforts on "first-generation" mixed people, those with self-identified monoracial (white, black, Asian, Native American, Latina/o) parents; but also included those who self-identified as mixed who had parents who asserted a singular identity with acknowledged multiracial heritage (a singular mixed identity)[5]. This allowed the latter group to reclaim and recover mixture that may have been masked, denied, or unclaimed by the parents, or disallowed by society at the time (for example, given the persistence of the one drop rule).

3
Managing Racial Identities in Public Spaces

In the introduction of this book, I noted that many multiracial people face borderism from "all sides." This acknowledges what I consider the "multidimensionality of multiraciality," or the many dimensions and expressions of multiracial identity, and the varying appearances of multiracial people. The multidimensionality of multiraciality speaks to the many ways that multiracial people may encounter questions from others because of the plethora of perceptions that others have about their racial identities and locations. Rather than simply crossing over one color line, multiracial people may appear to perpetually cross many color lines or racial borders. Any racial ambiguity in their appearances and any fluidity in their preferred racial identities may accelerate or amplify the frequency of crossings. These crossings typically provoke racial policing or patrolling.

With racial border crossing comes racial border patrolling. As discussed in the existing literature, racial border patrolling has focused on people perceived as belonging to one racial group and trespassing into others (see Dalmage 2000). For multiracial people, this trespassing arguably happens by default, presumably intensifying as they move out of their interracial families of origin and into their own chosen families. This trespassing also happens because multiracial people inhabit multiple racial locations—that liminal space known as the "borderlands" (see Anzaldua 1987). Typically, border patrolling becomes a process of sorting the multiracial person into the right racial category, rather than recognizing the various racial groups to which they lay claim. Border patrolling tends to ignore "multiracial" as a racial reality for people of two or more races; it works instead to reify the racial order, by privileging singular racial categories through the assumption that most people fall into them.

Sometimes, the border patrolling of multiracial people happens when borderists presume that "multiracial" connotes a particular kind of mixture. For some, the term "multiracial" solely means "black and white." This was even true for some of the respondents in my study who admitted that they initially imagined the term "multiracial" meant "mixed with black and white." For others, the term "multiracial" recognizes more variation in racial combinations, on a continuum of the Census categories. This continuum means that people can claim anywhere from two to six races, or no race to some other race(s). Still others employ some combination of creativity and resistance to avoid being boxed into the available options; these individuals often generate descriptors of their own, as evidenced by clever terms such as "Cubarican," which recognizes the Cuban and Puerto Rican ancestry of a person. Others create these terms specific to their racial mixtures, as evidenced by the term, "Caubliasian."

In order to figure out where multiracial people locate themselves along this continuum and within the dominant racial classification system, people often pose the quintessential question, "What are you?" What could be seen as a clarifying question is also, as Heather Dalmage suggests, a loaded one. Dalmage (2000:1) asserts, "More than five hundred years' worth of socially, politically, economically, and culturally created racial categories rest in the phrase 'what are you.'" The "What are you?" question may prove as troublesome as any responses multiracial people provide. These responses may be contested in one setting and affirmed in others, or by some individuals and not others. Some groups of people may likely express this contestation, while others express affirmation. For multiracial people, or individuals arguably living on or across the fault lines of race, navigating the borders of race involve handling this question and its twin, "Where are you from?"

These and other questions about multiracial people and their racial identities are often about race, even as they appear not to be. These relatively direct inquiries betray the dominant racial discursive practices of colorblindness and colormuteness. While authors Eduardo Bonilla-Silva (2003a,b) and Mica Pollock (2005) respectively provide an excellent treatment of these topics in their work, I mention these dominant discourses to provide a context for much of the social interactions that people have in this society. For multiracial people, the questions strangers ask can pierce directly through colormuteness or the generalized silence and reticence around racial matters. Strangers making claims of colorblindness, or this way of not seeing race or its relevance, falsify these claims when they pose questions about the racial identity or location of a multiracial person. How does a stranger pose questions about race without noticing race? How might someone contend that race is irrelevant yet question the racial identity and location of others?

According to Bonilla-Silva (2002), the contours of colorblindness accommodate these contradictions. Charles Gallagher contributes to this conversation by noting that it is not race that people evade but discussions of racism. I argue here that colorblindness and colormuteness operate in such ways that people can remain reticent about race *and* racism. Asking people questions about their racial identities and locations departs from and proves disloyal to these two dominant discourses. Instead, these inquiries reveal the relevance of race and the continuing significance of race and racism in this society (see Feagin 1991; see also Doane and Bonilla-Silva 2003). These inquiries also reveal the level of (or lack thereof) sophistication in talking about race. Twine and Steinbugler (2006) refer to this as "racial literacy." Racial literacy is the extent to which people can effectively discuss race with sensitivity, knowledge, and awareness. The more effective and skilled a person is in discussing race, or the more fluent they are, the greater their racial literacy.

The dominant discourses of colorblindness and colormuteness work to compromise people's racial literacy, potentially limiting their ability to effectively discuss race in a variety of settings with any number of diverse actors. As a result, a large number of people likely possess limited knowledge of race or lack any substantial racial literacy. They might reveal and/or conceal what they know about race in particular settings, including social interactions in public with multiracial people. Sociologists Leslie Houts Picca and Joe Feagin (2007) call this two-faced racism. Two-faced racism allows people to present a polished-up version of their racial ideologies in public, while reserving the more problematic or questionable comments and views for private conversations, typically sharing them with "like company" or people presumed to be racially similar or perceived as sharing the same racial group membership and racial ideologies. It is in public spaces, then, that people who practice this two-faced racism ask questions to multiracial people to figure out where the latter belong. Strangers will likely pose these questions politely and inquisitively, if they follow the rules of racial etiquette and two-faced racism. If they break these rules, then they are likely to express something more malevolent, something akin to antagonism or the like. Asking questions in this way or expressing malevolence signal their break from the conventional rhetorical styles of race and racism. In other words, they are also breaking with the contemporary practices of colorblindness and colormuteness. This break actually aligns with explicitly hostile historical expressions of interpersonal interactional violence or vandalism (see Duneier and Molotch 1999, among others). Contemporary society is increasingly accommodating of both styles of interactions, effectively maintaining two-faced racism, in light of recent examples of interactional social conflict and institutional inequities.

In this chapter, I describe some of the patterns I observed in how multiracial individuals interpret and respond to strangers' questions and inquiries. This is the first of three chapters to focus on the policing of racial borders. Here, I consider the public interactions that multiracial people have with strangers. In Chapter 4, I focus on similar interactions but with family and friends, and Chapter 5, focuses on how multiracial people internalize these interactions to understand their racial sense of selves. Focusing on these three different social groups complicates the concept of borderism by demonstrating how everyone in a racially divided world can participate in racial border patrolling.

What Prompts People to Border Patrol: On Racial Ambiguity, Fluidity, Incongruity, and Multiplicity

In the interstitial space between the borders of race, many multiracial people metaphorically reside. This in-between space, or the borderlands, symbolically represents a racially, spatially and culturally interstitial place where two or more races, spaces, and/or cultures converge, coexist, or overlap. Many multiracial people call this liminal space home and can be seen and unseen as floating signifiers of race and of racial mixture. Some multiracial people look "clearly mixed," where the specificities of their racial composition may remain unclear or in question to others, and at times, even to themselves. In order to understand more precisely the exact coordinates of their multiple racial locations, strangers often ask questions to access any specificities that multiracial people are willing, or able, to provide.

Multiracial people are often seen as a specific racial group, somehow distinct from all other racial groups and members of the population. This is a fallacious notion, as F. James Davis (1991), Rainier Spencer (2010), and others contend, since the majority of the population could claim some racial mixture. Nevertheless, the idea of singular racial categories remains more appealing than multiple ones for its simplicity, as racial singularity suggests simplicity while racial multiplicity suggests complexity. Singularity easily accommodates individuals who do not want to name or claim their complete heritage, or do not know the full details to be able to claim such complexity. Arguably, singularity does not as easily seem to accommodate people with known racially mixed ancestry who opt for this singularity, or chose singular racial identities.

Like most other people, racially mixed people want to enjoy the same freedom to choose their preferred racial identities. They choose from the various multiracial identity options available, including but not limited to one or more races. Nevertheless, many racially mixed people are not always granted this choice, at least not without contestation or question. For visibly mixed or recognizably multiracial people, racial singularity, and any attendant simplicity achieved, often proves elusive. Multiracial people with racially ambiguous appearances are often denied the luxury of asserting their preferred racial identities. What happens to multiracial people whose appearances are racially ambiguous or are incongruous with their preferred identity or are mellifluous, fluid, shifting? How do strangers handle the ambiguous, incongruous, and mellifluous parts of multiracial identities? Border patrolling can rely on the in/visibility of multiraciality, where the legibility of multiracial people's racial mixtures frequently prompt this patrolling behavior while any "invisible mixture" allows multiracial people to elide questions or even recognition as a racially mixed person. Throughout this work, I will show how multiracial people manage any tensions between being "clearly mixed" (when their racial mixture is visible to others) versus having any "invisible mixture."

The racial ambiguity of multiracial people creates an interesting effect, allowing them to quietly blend into racial categories (their own or others) without question or contestation, or provoking or attracting attention that generates questions about their racial identity. This is a double-edged sword for multiracial people who are racially ambiguous. They may slip into racial categories and blend so convincingly so as not to be border patrolled, yet slip out of (or be forced out of) the racial groups constitutive of their parentage and heritage by border patrollers. That means that some multiracial may look more like members of other (single) race groups and be afforded entry into them. When they claim their preferred racial identities, however, they may encounter resistance from border patrollers who note how little the multiracial looks like their (fill in the blank) preferred racial identity. In this way, border patrolling proves to be a form of racial authenticity testing for multiracial people. That strangers expect multiracial people to authenticate their racial identity is a central component of border patrolling. Border patrollers wrestle with any tensions that exist between multiracial people's perceived identity and their preferred identity.

In part this border patrolling happens because many multiracial people in this population are "multifacial," meaning they have physical appearances that approximate more than one race. They are perceived as belonging in groups that they may or may not claim. As a result, many multiracial individuals often cross more racial borders than their own; they accidentally cross these racial borders, moving into racial groups that they appear to belong to, but do not. They confound border patrollers who see them as members of certain racial groups, even as those racial groups remain outside of the multiracial person's known ancestry. Put simply, being "multifacial" means having an ambiguous appearance or one that others consider "clearly mixed." Being clearly mixed makes it difficult for others to determine to which racial groups said "multifacial" multiracials belong. As a result, some multifacial multiracial people may be "passing" as members of racial groups apart from their own racial combination[1] (see Khanna 2014).

Being "multifacial" can compound the border patrolling that multiracial people experience in their everyday lives. Because of the "curious racial equations"[2] produced by "multifacial" multiraciality or racially and ethnically ambiguous people, many respondents reported encountering borderism. Border patrollers attempt to answer their questions or resolve Other status by trying to "solve a problem like racial mixture." When they experienced this questioning as curiosity, most multiracial respondents interpreted these social interactions as benign mechanisms to understand "the multiracial experience" (Root 1996). I call these interactions, "benevolent border patrolling."

The Benevolence of Border Patrolling

While some of the respondents in my research loathed the "What are you?" question, others welcomed it. They proved quite gracious and generous in curbing the curiosities of strangers by providing responses to their various clarifying questions. The experience of benevolent border patrolling involves curiosity without the usual antagonism of malevolent border patrolling. As the term implies, benevolent border patrolling is experienced as something benign. The respondents generally characterize social interactions with strangers as such when they get the sense that the strangers are exploring the racial realities of the multiracial people of whom they ask questions. This "sense" that some multiracial people may rely on is what Phillip Brian Harper (2005) calls "felt intuition." Felt intuition is a way in which people sense the intangible or imperceptible or rely on the "evidence of things unseen," as James Baldwin (1995) said. It is an important skill to have and is likely honed during times when strangers insist on imposing their own perceptions of multiracial people's racial locations onto them. This imposition is less characteristic of benevolent border patrolling and more so of malevolent border patrolling. For multiracial people, any felt intuition may operate as an additional navigational tool to public interactions that can begin as benign or benevolent but then turn hostile and harassing, sometimes without a moment's notice.

Without access to the particular border patrollers who my respondents encountered, I cannot specify their intentions. However, I do want to point out the possibility of people masking their individual racism by employing benevolent border patrolling as a mechanism for relocating racial mixture to its "rightful" place. However, the accounts of many respondents suggested that they interpreted and experienced benevolent border patrolling most often as a sincerely innocent interaction. These conversational exchanges allowed others to discuss racial mixture as it continues to take on new meanings.

Many respondents reported enjoying any reciprocity that resulted from the initial inquiry and welcomed opportunities to share some of their rich and interesting racial biographies. The reciprocity in these social interactions speaks to the expression of agency because when multiracial people ask strangers similar questions and reciprocate the "interest," they disrupt this idea that only some people have a race and/or interesting stories to tell about their racial identities and backgrounds. Typically, people socially constructed as "different" or seen as "exotic" are often expected to engage in this public education, particularly with members of dominant groups or positions. Black lesbian feminist Audre Lorde (1984) made this point in her work, noting the ways marginalized and oppressed people are expected to educate their oppressors about their humanity. Here, I would like to extend or complicate Lorde's point, noting that this educating and informing ideally involves everyone.

Given this society's tendency towards colorblindness and colormuteness, any impromptu interactions that involve opportunities for education, learning, and sharing should be welcomed. This is particularly so when such interactions are mutual or reciprocal and any power asymmetries are acknowledged and managed accordingly. These opportunities have the potential to enhance people's racial literacy. With varying skill levels of racial literacy, people enter into conversations arguably made easier by higher levels of racial literacy or more difficult if such literacy is low. In general, this literacy reflects people's ability and willingness to engage in conversations about race, and conveys their racial competence, racial consciousness and racial sensitivity.

The interactional dynamics of these conversations are facilitated or impeded by people's varying levels of racial literacy; they can also be exacerbated or accommodated, informed in part by people's different ways of seeing race. These differing ways of seeing speak to different racial paradigms that prevail, which shape discussions of race. People can discuss these different paradigms, including their merits and flaws, given their racial literacy supports these conversations in respectful and effective ways. In part, border patrolling captures both a gap in racial literacy among actors in an interaction and any gaps between individual ways of seeing race and the dominant one encouraged by and centered in this society. Understanding how race operates on these individual *and* societal levels supports shared learning and more reciprocal interactions.

Through this framework, one might see multiracials in an instructive role, when the reality is that even multiracial people can lack racial literacy or be ill-equipped to navigate conversations about race and the specificities of inquiries around racial identity. While some of the multiracial people in my study found questions from strangers to be more of an interrogation or imposition, others found them to be an interactional invitation. Individuals in the former group include respondents like Juanita, a black-identified woman who claimed her African American, Native American, Creole, Puerto Rican and white heritage. During our interview, she noted, "I'm always entertaining people because I already know it's coming and it's always, there are always questions." Individuals in the latter group noted how much they wanted to share their stories with strangers, with dignity and pride. They did not lament the situation for what it partially appeared to be: "the responsibility of the oppressed to teach the oppressor their mistakes." (Lorde 1984:114). Instead, they viewed such social interactions with strangers as opportunities to share knowledge of their lived experiences.

Not all multiracial people are always already in possession of racial knowledge about themselves, their families, and their individual and collective histories. Some may not be equipped with this information. Still, for others, this racial knowledge of self and family remains elusive, in cases of adoption for example, or the erasure or loss of important documents including birth and death records, or the collective absence of historical records of African slave families. Through the refusal to keep any such records on African slave families, this information was effectively eradicated or disappeared by the white ruling class. In addition to the specificities of people's individual and collective racial heritage remaining veiled, silenced, or never spoken, some multiracial people may not wish to unveil or reveal these histories when speaking to strangers. Sometimes, the specificities of histories remain mysteries, such that multiracial people never hear or learn about them, because no one tells these stories privately either. When pressed for details during border patrolling, multiracial people may not have much information for public disclosure whether or not they even inclined to disclose that information.

Some multiracial people, however, can strengthen their experiential knowledge, cultivated through the habitual crossing of racial borders publically and privately, in their racially mixed families that blend, blur, and/or brighten racial boundaries, contingent upon the mix. This experiential knowledge and felt intuition are strengthened by the very precarity some multiracial people feel living on these racial fault lines (Almaguer 2008; Harper 2005). In fact, one could argue that limited racial categories, or options that fail to fit people's lived experiences, partially produce this precarity (see Butler 2004). Butler describes this precarity and feelings of vulnerability as everyone increasingly has these experiences. Multiracial people navigate this precarity and any attendant uncertainty, unpredictability or incivility from strangers in a number of ways. Precarity can stem from learning about historical and contemporary forms of racism and antagonisms so often directed at people of color, including many multiracial people and their interracial families. Given these antagonisms, historical hostilities, and racial ideologies about group differences, social interactions maintain some level of unpredictability and have the potential to be conflictive. When social interactions go smoothly, people can engage in sharing information that facilitates racial understanding.

Consider the experience of Gloria, a black white biracial woman in her 20s. Gloria was one of the few black white biracial participants to describe experiences of benevolent border patrolling. She reported that she sometimes opts for "Other" and often gets misread as black and Puerto Rican. Gloria noted that people ask questions about her appearance because they "look at you and can't figure out what you are, so they just ask. So I tell them so they know." She also mentioned that people often tell her, "'You have a nice complexion,' and usually think I'm from Florida or California or the islands...I usually don't get 'black and white.' Everybody gets that mixed up." Though they incorrectly access her racial identity, they often compliment her. This may mask more malevolent border patrolling, but not to Gloria. She interprets others' questions as well intended, through a lens of benevolence.

Gloria, who was born in the Midwest, explained: "I would say I'm mixed. I would say right off the bat I'm mixed. I'm white and black." She indicated that she usually says that she is African American to avoid the "hassle." This suggests that these social interactions remain sites of racial negotiation, where strangers may intend to innocently ask questions that may have an alternate impact on the multiracial people to whom such questions are posed. In addition, Gloria hints at the extent to which multiracial people iron out the specificities of their racial multiplicity for simplicity sake, a topic I turn to more fully in Chapter 5.

Gloria's comments show the shifting mixture she expresses as she claims different dimensions of her identity to different people in different settings. Social research and more literature provide evidence that and specifically illustrate how people code switch in this manner, (see Waring 2013 for further discussion). Her comments also narrate how her mixture shifts depending on how other people see her. The two inform each other, as multiracial people may internalize others' perceptions of them, or alternately choose to reject them to arrive at their own self-understanding.

Code switching or shifting more formally than casually allows Gloria the space to reclaim or recuperate her mixture during social interactions. She flattens out that mixture in her formal identification. This respondent expressed a complicated combination of feelings regarding her multiracial identity. "I like to say that I'm mixed. I like to, I like to feel different, though. I kinda like it." In the process of self-Orientalizing and exoticizing herself, Gloria communicated the multiracial cliché: "I feel like I get the best of both worlds."

Other black multiracial respondents shared similar responses. Take Jessica, a black-identified black and Asian Indian woman. She expressed awareness of the ways other multiracial people might find the inquiries strangers posed to her to be malevolent. However, she interpreted these interactions as benign, and provided an example of her experiences with benevolent borderism:

> See, I find people get offended when they're asked that question ["What are you?"], but I never did because I'm always happy to say, "Oh, well, you know, I'm half black and Indian." I'm happy about who I am so I'm always, you know, ready to tell people who I am, what I'm mixed with, and I'm happy to, um, take care of their curiosity...because I'd rather them know what I am than for them to think in their minds, "Hmm, what is she? Is she Latino? Is she Middle Eastern? She's *something*."

One part outgoing personality, another part pride in her heritage, Jessica epitomizes the gracious accommodation of questions. She immensely enjoys sharing information about her racial heritage because she sees it as an opportunity to clarify and celebrate her racial mixture. She appears to anticipate people posing these questions to her, sensing their curiosity and seeks to satisfy that curiosity. This speculative knowledge, the aforementioned felt intuition, helps position Jessica in the driver's seat. Directly answering strangers' questions allows her to assert her agency in ways that dispel the tropes about multiracial "confusion." Nevertheless, people may continue to see her as "confused" in the cliché way, if they misunderstand the ampersand. That is, Jessica asserts a protean identity: she claims a preferred black identity while acknowledging that she is racially mixed (black and Asian Indian). Because of this, she may appear to be a contradiction, or even "confused," despite her knowing *exactly* what she prefers.

When strangers fail to see "multiracial" as a viable option, they may intensify their border patrolling behavior to figure out which one category best fits the person in question. Alternately, if strangers refuse to recognize the multidimensionality of multiraciality, they may conclude that the multiracial person is the confused one, not them. In these cases where strangers fail to see the numerous possibilities of multiracial identities, they may end up contesting multiracial identity options more malevolently. However, when others simply seek to satisfy their curiosity, strengthen their racial literacy, or understand the various racial combinations that make up "multiracial," they may still be engaging in border patrolling behavior but doing so from a place of ignorance or benevolence. In the latter example, people may know that they do not know how to talk about racial multiraciality smoothly and effectively but they want to learn. They may make comments that reveal their ignorance but their questions are often issued from a place of benevolence; through an acknowledgment that they know little about "the multiracial experience," as psychologist Maria P.P. Root (1996) put it, they demonstrate a willingness to learn, at times at the expense of reinforcing racial borders.

These moments, where my respondents interacted with strangers, draw attention to the dimensions of their multiracial identities. I would argue, however, that opening up these "exchanges" provided opportunities for both parties to practice their racial literacy. This racial literacy reflects sensitivity about racism and an ability to discuss racial issues from an informed position, not one of ignorance.

Twine and Steinbugler (2006) address this in their work on the gap between whiteness and white racial literacy. I argue here that everyone, not only whites, could stand to improve their racial literacy and ability to communicate effectively about race and racism. In part, respondents who felt these interactions connoted benevolence may have been accustomed to "bridging" or building bridges between racial groups (see Keating and Gonzalez-Lopez 2012; Anzaldua 1987; Moraga and

Anzaldua 1983). Conversely, they may have welcomed opportunities during these exchanges for all involved parties to practice and grow their racial literacy.

When pressed, most of the respondents admitted that these sorts of "exchanges" were largely uneven. However, this unevenness or lopsidedness did not appear bothersome. Instead, some respondents reciprocated the questions; they practiced this as a way of being polite, of extending the idea of "racial etiquette," to include talking about race by showing interest in people showing an interest in them. Otherwise, the rules of racial etiquette discourage the sort of direct questioning and engagement that the respondents described having with strangers.

In reflecting on these interactions and the interpretations of the research participants, I imagine that the process of asking questions satisfied or curbed other people's curiosities while making multiracial people more curious about their own biographies and family histories. These questions may encourage self-reflections among multiracial people, some of whom may also be searching for their own satisfying and self-affirming answers to the "What are you?" question, or what to call themselves racially, to paraphrase Heather Dalmage (2000). In a sample of mostly young people, many of the participants seemed to be working out the specificities of their preferred identities, while others had already arrived at this knowledge, appearing firmer or more unwavering in their racial identity articulations. The impact of these questions on multiracial people in the former category may be read as benevolent if they utilize these interactions as a way to express themselves and experience validation of any of their preferred racial identities. In other words, these interactions with strangers may help younger multiracial people crystallize their identity or express the various dimensions of their racial multiplicity to others. This could mean that, contingent on who is asking (i.e., what the stranger looks like racially), multiracial people might reveal different sides of their racial identity to different people or they may claim a more consistent (but not necessarily a singular) racial identity.

Throughout the interview process, I remained aware of and sensitive about potentially replicating the very dynamics about which I was inquiring and investigating. In effect, I was asking respondents to reflect on what Kerry Ann Rockquemore (1998) calls, "the 'What are you?' experience." However, I did not want to reproduce the very power asymmetries that I have experienced during similar interactions with strangers in public. It was through my interviews that I discovered the different ways multiracial people view these interactions. Several of the respondents interpreted strangers' questions (such as "What are you?")

through a lens of innocence or benevolence. This frame pushed me to reexamine my own a priori assumptions and interpretations of these sorts of interactions. I always understood these questions to be border patrolling from a place of malevolence, filled with antagonism or entitlement; these interactions operated as a mechanism for soliciting information that otherwise might be considered impolite to request. I always felt the questions were guided by a "need to know" in what racial group (never groups) to place a multiracial person, that providing this information was imperative, and that *not* providing this information was more audacious than being asked in the first place. I wondered, "What could possibly be benevolent about these questions?" While I knew my own experiences would simply serve as a point of departure from which to understand other racially mixed people, I had no roadmap with which to comprehend these interactions as such. In fact, my personal experiences with street harassment (which would become my thesis research topic) often centered on my racially ambiguous appearance. Nevertheless, I was inspired, if also puzzled, by the possibility of multiracial people enjoying interactions with strangers in public. I tried as best as possible to tuck away my suspicions of "smiling discrimination" (Bonilla-Silva 2013a) in order to fully appreciate the abundance of information to the contrary of my own. I struggled with the contradictions created by the benevolence of border patrolling. Given that the prevailing racial rhetoric is one of colorblindness, strangers' inquiries about multiracial people seem a clear violation or betrayal of this implicit and collective agreement to *not* see race and *not* talk about it. When strangers ask subtle or pointed questions about the racial location of multiracial people, they stand in direct contrast to the claims of "not noticing race" or "not seeing" racial differences.

To me, the malevolence of border patrolling is captured in Lorde's (115) concern with managing marginality and facing oppression: "For in order to survive, those of us for whom oppression is as American as apple pie have always had to be watchers, to become familiar with the language and manners of the oppressor, even sometimes adopting them for some illusion of protection." Nevertheless, respondent after respondent shared a similar story. They did not see these interactions and social dynamics as expressions of malevolence or opposition to them or their multiracial identities and families. They *enjoyed* responding to these inquiries. They conveyed a sense of knowing people are curious, perhaps because they are familiar with the fuss around "Generation E.A.," (Ethnically Ambiguous), the ostensibly growing multiracial population, and the public's attendant fascination with this generation (see LaFerla 2003). Ultimately, they recognized that their responses curbed some of that curiosity in others and themselves.

Consider Sarah, another multiracial Asian respondent, who self-identified as an "Anglo Indian" (British and Asian) young woman. Like Jessica, Sarah proudly embraces and celebrates her racial mixture; like other white Asian multiracials, she positions herself as not "full" or "all" Asian or white, but both. For Sarah, growing up in an interracial family meant that she was familiar with others' border-patrolling behavior. Between herself (with her own racially and ethnically ambiguous appearance), her brown-skinned sister, her British white mother, and her Malaysian Asian stepdad, they all provoked a lot of racialized attention and curiosity. Nevertheless, she positively interpreted people's attention and regarded what she viewed as their attempts to racially decode her and her family with compassion. Sarah explained:

> Every day somebody says, "What are you?" (In response) I just will answer but my mom will say to them, "Just a human being." It *really* makes her mad but it doesn't make me mad. I don't mind. It's just curiosity. It really pisses my mom off because when we go out to eat, it'd be my sister and I who are half white and half Indian, my dad who's Chinese, and my mom with a British accent, so people are like, where are these people from, like "Who *is* this family?" She gets so mad. I don't mind....I don't know what they think. I really don't know. We look nothing alike. She has a British accent. My sister and my mom look alike even though my sister's darker...her features, she's like a darker version of my mom. People don't think that I look like my mom....Egh. I don't care because I know that we have a good relationship. It doesn't bother me but it irritates her.

Sarah's nonchalance about or indifference to being border patrolled contrasts with what sounds like frustration in her mother's reaction. Sarah struck me as a vivacious, intelligent, energetic young woman who likely attracted as much public attention for her racially mixed appearance (within her multiracial family) as for her perceived beauty (see also Streeter 2003). I tread lightly here, so as not to risk endorsing or advancing the trope of the beautiful-by-default multiracial person. Instead, I would argue here that her outgoing personality, combined with her kindness and compassion, drew much of this attention to her. This attention was likely amplified when she was in public with her family, given the variation that she describes in their appearances and racial identities. Strangers may ask questions as a means of learning about the particularities of a family love story. Perhaps some people might be disapproving or in opposition of interracial families and race mixing but others might be guided by an interest in learning more about the ties that bind seemingly disparate members of multiracial families together.

Without many other opportunities to directly engage these individuals, benevolent border patrollers might not even think to pursue answers to their questions elsewhere (in the memoirs, personal narratives, or scholarly articles and book publications of multiracial families). They may simply not know what other sources to consider. In some ways, the "best" source is someone like Sarah, whose willingness to answer border patrollers' questions may help them make sense of how people from different racial groups (and nations even) migrate into each other's lives to create racially mixed families. Like Sarah's family, many people cross racial borders within and across national borders, in addition, to form the families that they call home. This movement both echoes and foreshadows any future movement among multiracial people who cross racial and national borders to find love and form their own families.

Notably, Sarah's comments about her mother's irritation with border patrollers' questions (whether benevolent or otherwise) draw attention to something interesting. There appear to be some instances where members of interracial families deploy colorblind discourses to deflect some of the attention. Through the use of colorblind discourses, Sarah's mother is able to achieve what Audre Lorde (1984) outlines by humanizing her family or having them recognized as human beings, not solely "representatives" of race or regarded as racially deviant. Sarah's mother could be viewed as quite subversive in her use of a colorblind frame. However, her mother might also equally be misinterpreted as being colorblind for minimizing race in her attempts to minimize the unsolicited or unwanted attention her racially diverse family receives. Her efforts to minimize the racial spectacle that surrounds her family, however, seem self-protective and honorable, not the typical race-evasive style characteristic of colorblindness. Thus, her behavior contrasts considerably with people who simply take a colorblind stance to avoid the discomfort of dealing with race-based discussions, typically from a position of privilege. While Sarah's mother arguably occupies this position of privilege as a white woman, she also occupies a precarious position as "outsider within" (see Collins 1986). She is an interracially married white woman with adult multiracial children. By acknowledging the humanity of her multiracial or interracial family, she counters any historical and contemporary efforts to "Other" and/or "Orientalize" them (Said 1978). Her stance restores their humanity in ways that this society has systematically employed efforts to the contrary.

In this instance, the minimization of race makes other people share or take on the burden of race work. They are unable to ask questions or make casual observations without having to perform what Amy Steinbugler (2012, 2007) calls "race work." While this is work typically performed within couples, I stretch the term here to apply to the interactional work involved in the questioning of multiracial people and their interracial families. This work speaks, ironically, to some people's refusal to speak directly about race while at the same time posing explicitly racialized questions to strangers. It captures the work performed by members of interracial families, who are expected to accommodate the racial curiosities of others rather than reserve the right to respectfully decline this information. Coopting the rhetoric of colorblindness affords some members of interracial families the "luxury" of opting out of responding to these various inquiries.

Humanizing partnerships and families still seen as deviant in many ways marks a subversive strategy for addressing border patrolling (and the ugly history of animosity and intolerance for interracial unions). This possible strategic use of colorblindness stands in contrast to the aversive, avoidant kind guided by racism, not antiracism. This qualitatively marks a small but significant difference in understanding how people rely on or deploy colorblind narratives in their everyday lives.

Sarah's example shows how multiracial people and their families are impacted by borderism. They may choose to interpret it positively as she did, for the most part, or regard it more ambivalently or negatively, as did her mother. These two interpretations illustrate the difference between these two kinds of border patrolling, or borderism as an an invitation to border patrollers to explore their racial curiosities about multiracial people and alternately as an interrogation, a topic I turn more fully to later in this chapter.

Sarah further explained her experiences in fielding questions from others:

> Do you know what? That's what throws people off because people say, "Where are you from?" and then I say, "England," and then they look at me like I have seven heads because it's not what they want to know....Like people will say, "You're really pretty. Where are you from?" But they might just be saying, "Well, you're pretty" just to figure out *where* I am from. A lot of people notice that I am different, but it's not ever in a negative way, I don't think, although I've told you about some of the negative experiences I've had but most of the time it's quite positive, I think, which is probably not common for most people....I think it's mostly positive and I love it! I would not want to be all Indian, and I would not want to be all white. I love to be mixed.

Like Jessica and other multiracial respondents, Sarah feels a sense of gratitude about her racial mixture. She displays a solid racial literacy in her responses to people's inquiries, sensing they were searching for clues about her racial mixture in her answers to their questions. Sarah's comments suggest that she knows that people are trying to locate her racially, geographically, and socially.

Sarah's "face is a map of the world," given her cosmopolitanism and global consciousness; these thingss are increasingly characteristic of transnational multiracial people (see Neal 2013; see also Tunstall 2006). Sarah's responses surprise them and also defy racial logic, since Sarah could be read as a white-looking American woman, not a British multiracial one. In addition to negotiating these national and ethnic differences, Sarah felt being white and Asian troubled the existing and prevailing racial hierarchy. Her mixture falls outside of the always already "black and white" mixture so often presumed by the term "multiracial." Her racial multiplicity might have meant fitting poorly into a black/white binary; a lens through which borderists try to view her multiraciality. She suspected that people racially perceived her through this dichotomous frame and shared these impressions of how others view her: "I think as white probably, because every—you're either white or black in this country, it feels. So I think as white and it just goes back to the stereotyping (which is you know, I 'talk white,' 'dress white'), I think sometimes people may think I'm Spanish, but not Indian ever. But I think what you're asking, I really think white."

Like many of the multiracial participants in my research, Sarah recognized that her racial ambiguity facilitates her multiracial movement through racial categories and across multiple color lines, as Lee and Bean (2007) note in their work. Because of her lighter skin color, Sarah is able to cross these color lines relatively effortlessly because people perceive her as more white than Asian or multiracial. Seldom do people see the other "ties that bind," making Sarah "more than multiracial;" that is, she feels more than her own racial mixture that is white and Asian Indian. She also feels Malaysian, in a sense, given her deep and meaningful connection to her father and his country and culture. In our interview, Sarah spoke of the ways her connection to and relationship with her stepfather have informed her racial and ethnic identity.

If given the freedom to do so, Sarah conveyed how much she wished she could add that detail to claim a Malaysian dimension to her identity. She subtly suggested that society would not know how to accommodate this nuance or make sense of the interstitial races and spaces that she inhabits. Sarah acknowledged that her multiracial identity disrupts the racial binary, thereby provoking some of the curiosity people conveyed about her. She is not at all confused about her own racial identity and generously shares with others her healthy perspectives about being multiracial. In fact, she successfully manages a transnational, multiracial identity, a discussion upon which I elaborate in the final substantive chapter of the book.

Like Sarah, other multiracial respondents reported an awareness of the way their racially and ethnically ambiguous appearance provoked the attention of others. Sometimes, this ambiguity makes multiracial people's racial mixture disappear, such that they are what Marcia Dawkins (2012) refers to as "clearly invisible," while at other times, this ambiguity is apparent, signaling that the multiracial person is "clearly mixed." These terms play on historical and contemporary notions of racial mixture, as well as individual and collective notions of racial mixture. Despite evidence to suggest that racial mixture has been embedded into this society since its inception, border patrollers hold onto the myths of racial purity (for whiteness) and racial singularity.

Without "clear" indicators of race, racially ambiguous multiracial people challenge malevolent border patrollers' needs for categorical adherence. These types of borderists insist on one-and-only-one racial location for multiracial people. However, any ambiguity in multiracial people's appearances and/or incongruity between those appearances and their preferred identities can provoke these types of border patrolling behaviors. Many multiracial people do not easily fit into the existing racial categories or conceptual schema *and* multiple, competing ways of conceptualizing race exist. Both of these realities can prove a source of agitation for malevolent border patrollers, despite the difficulty of *any* racial classification adequately capturing the complexity and fluidity of multiracial identity.

Some multiracial people look "clearly mixed," in that they can approximate various racial and ethnic groups. Their racial ambiguity creating some shifting mixture, these multiracial people possibly attract others from any of the racial and ethnic groups that they happen to approximate. The social laws of attraction or patterns of people gravitating towards "like others" play out in the lives of some multiracial people, where the "like attracts like" can be any of these approximated racial groups, as well as the ones that are a part of the racially mixed person's heritage.

Theresa, a multiracial-identified woman with White and Asian Filipina parentage, was one such person. I approached Theresa about participating in my research because she appeared "clearly mixed" to me. While more curious than confused about her mixture, I asked Theresa if she would be willing to share some of her experiences about being multiracial. She agreed, offering lots of great insight and observations about her experiences. For example, she commented on the number of people she attracts socially, who mistake her for a member of their own racial and/or ethnic group. She also explained the confusion that *others* had about her racial identity:

> I know I confuse people....Just because I've had people from/of all different nationalities come up to me, and with my job, I'll have people who are Asian come up and speak Japanese to me. I've had people who are Spanish come up and speak Spanish to me. I've had Korean people come up to me and speak, you know, Korean, so I've had the whole thing. I'm just kind of used to it. A lot of people think that I'm Hawaiian, too.

Like Sarah and other White and Asian respondents, Theresa often fields a number of inquiries from Latino/as. People presume she speaks Spanish. Her lack of fluency in Spanish limits her interactions with Spanish-speaking Latinos who read her as similar to them. As she noted, "I think they get disappointed in the fact that I can't *speak* their language but I never really felt that they were disappointed that I *wasn't* Hispanic." I attribute people mistaking her as Spanish, in part, due to the particular Asian ethnic group that she claims: Filipina. To me, her Filipina heritage reveals itself in her appearance, with its mix of White European, Spanish, and African ancestry. People see her as Spanish in part because of her appearance and as it relates to this history of colonization, to historical mixture. In other words, she could claim that she is Spanish because she is Filipina (see Root 1997). Sociologist Anthony Ocampo (2016) explores this in more detail in his book, *The Latinos of Asia: How Filipinos Break the Rules of Race*. The multiraciality embedded in national histories and populations intersect with particular individuals, making mixture at national, familial, and individual levels. The narratives of Theresa and other multiracial respondents with Filipino/a heritage speak to the many layers of mixture made possible through conquest and/or consent. These complex histories inform the public interactions multiracial people have with strangers.

Because some people are unable to identify Theresa's exact Asian ethnicity, they take guesses. As a general rule, this is a typical practice of strangers, according to some of my participants. People take a look at their multiracial and often ambiguous appearance and then attempt to decode or decipher this racial multiplicity and any ambiguity offered up in their appearance. They attempt to identify their exact racial coordinates, so to speak, without seeing the impossibility of being exact.

It is impossible to know someone's exact racial location but this is the information some border patrollers futilely search for from multiracial people.

Even some multiracial people rely on these false notions of racial boundaries to describe others as more centrally and wholly belonging to their respective racial and ethnic groups while placing others (including themselves) much more marginal to these groups. For example, Theresa noted having "had Filipino people ask me if I was Filipino, and you could tell that they are 'full blooded' and when I say yes, then they kind of get excited, like, 'Oh, a long lost family member,' kind of thing.... And then we start talking about food." What Theresa refers to here is racial or ethnic kinship, the construction of imagined (and real) pan-communities organized around ethnic and racial identities, such as Filipino and Asian ones. Given the mixture that Ocampo (2016), Gambol (2016), and others argue already exists in and among Filipinos, Theresa's reference to a "full-blooded" Filipino proves interesting. It is equivalent to saying, "clearly mixed," or at least hints at its irony all the same.

To say that someone is a full-blooded Filipino is to also say that they are always already mixed; in some ways, this acknowledgment might serve as an affirmation, rather than a negation, of Theresa's Filipina and white mixture. Theresa provides an example of this possibility even though this affirmation does not become a reality. She notes that some people "who've looked full blooded, they'll say, 'Are you mestiza?' which is mixed. And I say, 'Yes,' and they go, 'Oh.' But it's not like, 'Oh!' (excitement). It's like an, 'Oh.' (disappointment)." As with other white and Asian respondents, Theresa makes references to 'full blooded' Filipinos. Her reference echoes that of Lexie, in that both women attempt a discursive differentiation between themselves as multiracial Asian women and "full" Asian (singular racial identity). As I interpret it, this is meant to be a comparison or point of contrast. It is a rhetorical or discursive way of the multiracial person affirming their identity, by contrasting it with a "full-blooded" racial group member. References are made about "fully" nonwhite ethnic/racial groups while references to "full-blooded" whites are never mentioned.

Questions of authenticity remain embedded in these distinctions and beg the question that nags many multiracial people, "Are you really (insert race here)?" "Are you 'Asian enough'?" or "Are you *really* Native American?" The experiences multiracial people share suggest that their positions within the racial categories they want to claim are not always guaranteed, but rather are precarious ones that require ongoing negotiations in order to secure membership however temporarily or permanently. As they (in/voluntarily) play versions of "Guess My Race" and its twin, "Guess My Ethnicity," multiracial people learn to manage their identity with strangers, which can strengthen the racial literacy and awareness of everyone involved. With greater experiential knowledge and felt intuition (Harper 2005), multiracial people can more easily walk through these conversations. However, there is sometimes no telling when a benevolent interaction will begin or become more malevolent. I discuss some of these instances next.

The Malevolence of Border Patrolling

During my interviewing, I discovered that many respondents, including some of the ones who spoke about benevolent border patrolling, spoke of instances of border patrolling as much more interrogative than inquisitive with border patrollers more insisting than exploring. Sometimes, multiracial people found public interactions with strangers benign and welcomed the chance to share stories from their "multiracial experience." At other times, they found these interactions to be initially inviting, but then eventually invalidating, as border patrollers expressed a number of reactions to their asserted preferred racial identities. The intrusive quality of these interactions, often coupled with a sense of entitlement, made them more malevolent than benevolent.

During these moments of malevolent border patrolling, strangers may work to dislocate a multiracial person from their preferred racial social location and/or invalidate their preferred racial identities. Thus, malevolent border patrolling much more blatantly and mercilessly polices race mixing and racially mixed people. Malevolent borderists can appear to have a profound and unwavering sense of knowing more about multiracial people's racial identity than the multiracial people themselves. Malevolent border patrolling is so for just that reason.

Imagine the experience of being a private person and being out in public where strangers repeatedly recreate "the 'What are you?' experience" for multiracial people. Imagine that generosity of the multiracial people to offer insight into their racial identities and family biographies. Now imagine those strangers explicitly challenging, refuting, or rejecting this information. Next, imagine them making unsavory or stereotypical comments about the racial groups to which they initially believed these multiracial people belonged. This is malevolent border patrolling.

So, too, are the racial microaggressions, or the daily indignities, hostilities, and slights that racial minorities face. According to psychologist Derald Sue (2010), these microaggressions can generate microinsults, microassaults, and microinvalidations. Linking the literature on microaggressions to that on border patrolling produces a more robust understanding of the everyday penalties incurred by multiracial people perceived to be engaging in racial trespassing or making transgressions for crossing, blurring, and blending the borders of race. Many of the respondents in my sample described interactions that reflect malevolent border patrollers expressing these microaggressions and invalidations, along with more explicit antagonism and opposition to their racial ambiguity, fluidity, and multiplicity *or* singularity. As many of the following examples suggest, malevolent border patrollers seemed to prioritize their view of the respective multiracial person over her/his own view. This presumptive posture appears to guide much of malevolent border patrolling in the first place. Why else might a malevolent border patroller put his/her perception of a multiracial person ahead of that person's self-perception and preferred racial identity? Why would such a border patroller prioritize her/his own views over the person from which s/he seeks information to answer any "What are you?" questions or who might clarify any confusion? For preliminary answers to these questions, let's turn to a few examples provided by some of the respondents.

One of my first respondents was quiet and thoughtful Leilani. She was one such private person who reported experiencing the more racially microaggressive dynamic of border patrolling (see Sue 2010). A white-looking black and Hawaiian woman in her early 20s, Leilani asserts a protean identity. During our interview, she noted that she contends with people's questions and authenticity tests because both her ambiguous appearance and racial combination strike some people as unique. When people find out that she is black *and* Hawaiian, some will say,

> "I've never met a Hawaiian person before" or something like that, and it also will be stereotypical sometimes. "Oh, you're from Hawaii. Do you know how to hula?" "Do you speak Hawaiian?" and I'm like, "Why?" "Do you surf?" And all this. Another thing is that I don't know how to swim so they're like, "How are you Hawaiian and don't know how to swim?" I didn't move to Hawaii until I was already 8. By then, I mean I would love to go to the beach, but I was afraid of drowning.

Leilani used her great sense of humor to deal with others' pointed inquiries and stereotypical thinking, as evidenced by the references to Hawaiian language, hulas, and surfing. This thinking suggests that Hawaii is evocative of these activities; it also links geographic locations to gendered and racialized behavior, conjuring up the commodity fetishism of Hawaiian women. When Leilani disrupts these stereotypes, she gets confronted by the border patroller for not living up to or embodying the stereotypical sun-worshiping and swimming surfer girl. The contestation reveals the extent to which the image of Hawaiian women appears more real than an actual Hawaiian woman.

In some ways, it might have been easier for a border patroller to express this doubt about Leilani (because she does not do stereotypically Hawaiian things or act very Hawaiian based on this logic), rather than to say directly, "Well, you don't *look* Hawaiian." In this instance, it seems more socially appropriate or acceptable to discredit one's identity based on her/his activity rather than appearance, although both become sources of evidence to authenticate or disqualify some multiracial people from all of the racial and ethnic groups that they claim.

It seems that people rely less on stereotypes of blackness when interacting with her, perhaps because of Leilani's invisible mixture. To some people, Leilani's light skin color, reddish hair color, and freckles explain the "invisibility" of her blackness. To others, like me, her blackness is not necessarily invisible, but rather hiding in plain sight. Leilani's appearance reminds me of distant cousins of mine, who have darker skin than she does but whose appearance blurs racial lines all the same. Arguably, people who live across the color lines are not always "tripping across the color line" (see Dalmage 2000). Malevolent border patrollers constantly trip as they discover racial borders or figure out that there are many ways of seeing (or not seeing) race. Some express borderism by thinking of race in terms of "two-and-only-two" options: black and white. As a woman who breaks this binary, Leilani contends with strangers who seem reluctant to accept her claiming two or *more* races. One stranger even refused to make space for races beyond black and white. Leilani noted that strangers tell her, "You don't look like a Hawaiian." This prompts Leilani to ask, "'Do you know what a Hawaiian really looks like?'…and I had someone actually say to me, 'Well, if it's not black, it's white.' And I'm like, 'No, it's not.' And that was a bad day. I just didn't understand how she could be so ignorant." The stranger held so firmly onto the black/white racial binary that she effectively disappeared Leilani's Hawaiian heritage by forcing her to choose "black" or "white." Leilani's honest admission about the pain she felt at this invalidation draws attention to the toll that these microaggressions and invalidations take on some multiracial people, perhaps especially those with racially and ethnically ambiguous appearances that move beyond black and white. Notably, the language of objectification surfaces here as it does in some examples that follow, when the stranger says "it" as opposed to "you." This is a small but significant linguistic difference, but one that points to the gap between multiracial people as objects ("it") versus subjects ("you").

The incongruence between Leilani's preferred (black and/or protean) racial identity, her (white) appearance, and the way others perceive her prompts much of the malevolent border patrolling she faces. Leilani also describes herself as having a "red," "yellow," or "lightly tanned" skin tone that borderists often perceive as white. "I guess because most mixed people that I know are darker than I am, so you can pretty much tell [that they are mixed] but I guess my skin tone is closer to being white." Because of this perception, white border patrollers (see Dalmage 2000) say a variety of things to Leilani, including, "'I thought you were white. We just thought that you liked to hang around a lot of black people, just trying to be black,' whatever that is." Usually, whites "are just really surprised" when they find out how she racially and ethnically identifies. As they accumulate more complete and accurate information about her racial heritage and background and explore their curiosities to make sense of Leilani's ambiguity and friendship groups, border patrollers gain a richer picture of Leilani. This information may address any cognitive dissonance that results from the incongruence between Leilani's physical (white) appearance and her asserted black and Hawaiian identity. This may mitigate their *future* borderism. To my knowledge, no studies formally investigate this. An optimistic view of borderism recognizes that with each answer a borderist acquires, s/he also acquires insight and understanding that ideally enhances that individual's racial literacies and strengthens her/his lenses (ways of seeing race) thereby minimizing, or altogether eliminating, future border patrolling.

The example above illustrates how atypical it is for people perceived as white to socialize with people perceived as black. These patterns of social segregation compound the problem for white-looking multiracials who are not "just trying to be black" but, in fact, identify that way. Research suggests that friendship networks in contemporary society are profoundly skewed racially. As Christopher Ingraham (2014) of *The Washington Post* notes, "In a 100-friend scenario, the average white person has 91 white friends; one each of black, Latino, mixed race, and other races; and three friends of unknown race. The average black person, on the other hand, has 83 black friends, eight white friends, two Latino friends, zero Asian friends, three mixed race friends, one other race friend and four friends of unknown race." Ingraham cites data from the Public Religion Research Institute, or PRRI, which indicate that the friendship networks of both whites and blacks are more racially homogenous than not. However, at least 75% of whites have exclusively white friendship networks. This national context puts the above-illustrated border patrollers' comments into broader context. It also begs the questions, "Are most people racial border patrollers?" "Do most people internalize the current contemporary racial hierarchy and classification system and police the borders of race in their own lives, and then by extension, in those of others?"

Leilani recalled an instance that illustrates how racial border patrolling reinforces the color line and serves as a mechanism that polices multiracial people's choices in identity *and* friends. A young, white woman interacted with Leilani in this way: "She just asked me one day, 'How come you hang around so many black people? Not that I'm saying there's anything wrong with black people but I was just wondering, because I always see you with black people.' I was like, 'Because I'm black.' Her eyes got so big. I was like, 'I'm mixed.' I said, 'My mother's black and my dad's Hawaiian.' And she's like, 'That's so interesting.'" Likely incredulous and embarrassed about misreading Leilani as white or presumably "not black," this white woman border patrolled her by imposing this white identity on Leilani; she further tried to draw the color line between, rather than around, Leilani and her friends which reinforces the exclusivity of the racial divide. Conversely, Leilani imagines herself as belonging to categorical blackness and seems to draw no distinctions between herself as a white-looking multiracial black woman and her friends with darker skin color. They all consider each other black. Malevolent border patrollers reject the idea that Leilani, or other white-looking multiracials, deserve to be included in the black category.

Deploying a discursive variation of the expression made popular in the sitcom *Seinfeld*, "Not that there's anything wrong with that," the white woman attempted to save face and minimize any backlash from such front-stage racism (see Houts Picca and Feagin 2007). Author Judy Scales-Trent (1995), a self-described white black woman, detailed similar experiences Leilani shared in our interview. Both women were border patrolled by whites because of the illegibility of their blackness or the invisibility of their racial mixture; both women had to determine their points of disclosure, or when to "come out" as racially mixed, to people who regulated racial borders. Buchanan and Acevedo (2004:121) describe this in their work to demonstrate some of the difficulty of managing the borders of race when identity and appearances do not align or create incongruity. They argue, "[A]s new relationships are initiated, individuals are likely to face a resurgence of questions concerning their ethnic/racial identification that may challenge their sense of self (Root 1999). Such questions reflect others' perceptions of the individual as racially ambiguous—lacking phenotypic features indicating a clear racial category to which the person belongs." Many of the racially ambiguous multiracial people had these experiences not only in interactions with strangers but also in their social relationships with friends and family, including romantic partners. I return to this topic in Chapter 4.

These examples of malevolent border patrolling offer further evidence that people are supposed to "stick to their own kind" so as not to confuse the implicitly coherent composition of existing singular racial categories. Leilani discovered this the more she was border patrolled based on social expectations of homogeneity and homophily (see Korgen 2002). These racial rules suggest that people should not blur racial borders by choosing friends and family members of different races. These social patterns of homogeneity and homophily ensure the erasure of the racial mixture that always already exists in the population. Nevertheless, people who identify as multiracial are often the ones who appear to challenge these normative expectations.

Leilani's experiences echo Kimberly DaCosta's (2004) point about the extent to which we internalize racial classification schemas in this country and reinforce racial borders through socialization. Because "like attracts like," and patterns in social behavior indicate that we (should) gravitate towards people who we perceive to be similar to us, Leilani was being border patrolled for looking like a white woman socializing with black people. Who is to say that those said black people identify as such and not in any other ways? The limitations of legibility, as is the legislation of integration, are revealed here. The desire to keep socially constructed racial categories intact by denying racially mixed people a place in the categories they would prefer only reinforces, rather than undermines, the persistence of mixture in this society. That is, were Leilani to take up residence in categorical whiteness, she would not only be "passing as white" but also allowing mixture to exist more peacefully there, because it would remain largely invisible, instead of among darker-skinned black people where she could be seen as more obviously "passing as white," if that were her intention.

If social behavioral patterns (such as racial homogeneity) ceased to exist in our racially divisive society, there would be little opportunity for border patrolling to persist. People could freely enjoy the company of one another irrespective of race or other perceived differences and similarities. However, the persistent racial hierarchy and insistence on "correct" racial categorization make social integration a liability. Even as people challenge these racial borders and the people who police them, they often fail to get their point across or be understood in shape-shifting and change-making ways.

As Leilani's experiences demonstrate, racial border patrolling can even be based on how people sound, not solely on how they look. Though her blackness was not always visible to whites, she believed in the audibility of her blackness. Her voice audibly made blackness visible: "Most people tell me that they can tell something when they hear me talk.... In one of the classes, we learned that black females have a deeper sounding voice than the softness of a white woman's voice. I don't know or more raspy or something like that, but they tell me once they hear me speak, 'Oh, I knew you had to be something. I knew you weren't just white.' I was like, 'Okay.'"

It was apparent to me throughout the interview that Leilani spent a lot of time thinking about these mixed race matters. Other respondents displayed similar levels of awareness about how their physical appearances shaped others' perceptions of them racially. Much of Leilani's experiences were echoed in the narratives of most of the respondents who looked white or had light skin color but had some known black ancestry. For the most part, these individuals lamented their invisible mixture. They feared the charge that they were trying to pass or were "acting white." Accusations of "acting white" stung the most for multiracial respondents with black *and* white parentage. The accusation confounded them since they claimed whiteness as a part of their racial sense of self. They were not attempting a convincing performance of race; they want others to embrace all of the composite parts of their racial identities.

Consider the experience of Campbell, a black and white biracial woman, who looks like a white woman to some people. Campbell frequently faced the charge of "acting white" and found these accusations hurtful. Primarily launched by black people who perceive her as white (in appearance, action, and identity), "acting white" is a charge Campbell puzzles over the irony of identifying as biracial but being accused of acting white. She explained:

> When I was in high school, they wanted me to be white because they would say that I think I'm better.... It's kind of crazy but they didn't want me to be part of the black race because I acted a certain way or I dressed a certain way or I did certain things. You see what I'm saying? It's like, "Oh, you don't belong with us." Because "you're acting this way" or "You look this way." I just thought that was kind of strange. And it hurt sometimes but I was like, "Whatever."

Campbell makes it clear that words do wound, a point that critical race scholars Richard Delgado (1993), Mari Matsuda (1993), and others explore in their work. Racial border patrolling makes little to no sense to Campbell for a number of reasons. As someone who has grown up racially mixed in a family where people have crossed racial and other borders, Campbell does not understand the importance others place on maintaining these various divides.

For a moment, let's contrast Campbell's experiences with those of Leilani. Because Leilani has such light skin color, she was presumed to be white. Campbell, on the other hand, has a slightly darker complexion but lighter hair, and was accused of acting white. Both women, among many others in the sample, reported experiences that negate their preferred racial identities. They encountered border patrolling with a frequency matched mostly by other multiracial black respondents. This stands in contrast to many of the white multiracial respondents who experienced some border patrolling but also enjoyed some of the privileges of their "honorary whiteness."

Campbell suggested that her behavior and almost-white phenotype primarily provoked this perception and accusation of her as "acting white." It appeared as if Campbell's whiteness became more visible or detectable in the predominantly black spaces she inhabited during her youth. Her approximation of whiteness—physically, behaviorally, and socially—suggested to border patrolling strangers and school-aged peers that she was both privileged and a racially treasonous person. Seeing her in this apparent "privileged position" led to their claims of her being "less black" and more "like white." While these terms are not necessarily inaccurate (since she asserts a black white biracial identity), the implication is framed as a disqualification. That is, Campbell *is* white (and black), but the redundancy did not discourage school peers and friends from calling her white; which called her racial group status and loyalty into question, rather than offer her some affirmation.

Some of Campbell's own racial ideologies complicated, rather than legitimized, the malevolent borderism that she encountered. Having self-described "good hair," for example, reinforced her privileged positions within a gendered racial hierarchy that rewards her physical approximation of whiteness and celebrates mixture as a site of beauty (Rockquemore 2002; Hunter 2005; and Herring, Keith, and Horton 2004). These ideologies often pit her against women with darker skin. Her "failure" to pass tests designed to authenticate blackness actually affirm her multiplicity. This point contrasts with that of Rockquemore (2002), who posits that multiracial women can experience this as an invalidation of their blackness. A "failure" to authenticate blackness can also be understood as an implicit validation, albeit an unintentional one, of a multiracial identity. That is, while Campbell experiences malevolent border patrolling as rejection, she could reinterpret this behavior as a validation of her racial multiplicity.

Throughout our interview, Campbell seemed less aware of how her social behavior might, in a similar fashion, have been regarded by blacks as her rejection of them. Being rejected by blacks for "acting white" begins to make the multiracial legible. It is paradoxically invalidating because it ignores, in this case, a black white biracial person's blackness, while validating her whiteness or racial mixture. For malevolent border patrollers, this racial mixture serves as a provocation of this borderism.

Her example proves counterintuitive in that sense as it exposes everyday challenges to white superiority. Interventions to privileged whiteness may come in the form of contestations to multiracial people who look white. These contestations can be understood as a malevolent borderist's critiques, on the individual level, of a multiracial person. These contestations can also be understood as a critique of institutional racism and the attendant privileges white-looking multiracial people enjoy at the expense of their darker-skinned contemporaries. Even the multiracial person can perpetuate these privileges by endorsing particular ideologies and engaging in behavior that they understand as beneficial to them or that advances their position in life. Many respondents reported other interactions that proved similarly charged and injurious. Sometimes the injuries stemmed from border patrollers questioning the possibility of a multiracial person's preferred racial identity, or more specifically, regarding said preference dismissively or as impossible. That is, some of the questions border patrollers asked my respondents implied an impossibility to their particular racial and ethnic combinations. These insinuations served as a mechanism to invalidate or deem the multiracial identity "inauthentic."

One such respondent was Sa, a self-described "British, Brazilian, Blackfoot Indian black" woman who explained, "My father is black and Blackfoot Indian and my mother is British/Brazilian so I guess you could say European and South American." She used strategies similar to Leilani (discussed earlier) in disclosing details about her racial background. Sa noted that she gets asked the "What are you?" question often, or in her words, "every *single* time I meet somebody." In response, she replies by saying, "I'm a person." On the surface, this looks like a colorblind response, but it remains her way of evading the question (not denying race). This discursive move allows her some agency and the possibility of minimizing the burden of emotional labor produced from constant racial interrogations. While the frequency with which she receives racial interrogations bothers her, Sa never resists or refuses to respond, but *does* draw the line at being called "exotic." She quipped, "I mean, I have people tell me that all the time.... I hate when people say that to me, 'Yeah, you look exotic.' I'm like, 'What am I? A bird?!'"

Sa reiterated the frequency with which she faces border patrolling from strangers in public, admitting to the injurious impact of borderism on her:

> I deal with this *so* much, and it really bothers me because a lot of (people I know), they always do this to me, like, they discredit my blackness or whatever. Anytime, I don't know, there are all these situations where they're like, "Well, you're not really black, so what are you talkin' about?" Like, anytime I speak out on any issue that relates to black people, or anything I might, like, they might bring up a little candy, or, you know, something that you used to eat when you were younger, and they were like, "You weren't eating that over there in England, so you can't identify." Like, it'll be something like that, but it'll be something really racial, like, "Oh, well, you're not all the way black, so you don't understand." You know what I'm saying. And even when I speak out on the whole, you know, issue with black people kind of like using the white man as a crutch, to not be anything in life, like, to constantly be like, "Oh, well, I'm oppressed so that's why I'm not doing anything with myself because I'm just going to be oppressed anyway." And, like I have really strong feelings about that, and I speak out against that, and people are just like, "Well, you're not black anyway, so what are you talking about? You can't identify with this situation. You're not getting oppressed because you're, you know what I'm saying, you're multiracial." And I'm like, "Oh, really." They (others) definitely don't see me as "multiracial." They definitely identify me as a black female. So if anything, I'm going to get it just as bad as any other black female would. So I don't know, it's just situations like that—I, I always have people, like, make certain comments sometimes that kind of discredit, you know, or anytime I do anything that's outside of the box, anytime I listen to a type of music that's not black, anytime that I put on anything that's not black, you know, anytime I *use big words*, I'm not black (emphasis hers). You know what I'm saying? It's crazy.

Sa's reflection on her experiences serves as a critique of both the logic of colorblind racism and the motivations of malevolent border patrollers. She draws attention to the fictitious notion that black people do not use sophisticated language, have expansive music tastes, or cultivate cosmopolitanism as an identity formation (see Neal 2013).

Even as she locates herself in multiple racial and ethnic categories, Sa is expanding the meaning attached to categorical blackness by challenging the very connotations or associations that people make with being black. She complicates this through her shifting mixture, which likely undermines her critique in the eyes of malevolent border patrollers. Ironically, the very people policing her racial identity and performance may partially benefit from her behavior for, as she notes, she is often simply seen as a black female. In this regard, if Sa deploys her racial privilege, she may do so at her own expense. She is penalized for thinking or doing "anything that's outside the box," even as her individual action supports a collective gain by countering myths that limit what black people can (or cannot) do.

Like Sa, many multiracial people who claimed racial identities composed of black and "some other race" encountered a lot of malevolent border patrolling. Sometimes the border patrolling was negating but not so nefarious. Some respondents reported confronting not their own confusion, but that of others, or being confused by the border patrolling behavior of strangers. Theresa, who I mentioned earlier in this chapter, related her experiences with malevolent border patrollers who ask, "What are you?" and, "Where are you from?":

> "Um, where I'm from?.... I'm from Long Beach." And, "What are you?"—I usually say female, if I get, "What are you?" Just to give them a hard time, because I think that question is just hideous. *What are you?!* (Emphasis hers) [When I'm in the mood] I usually say I'm part Filipina, and then people usually dig a little more and that's...when I'll say, "Well, my mother is American but she does have some Native American."

While mildly irritated and frustrated with the intrusiveness of others and the way they pose the question, Theresa still volunteers information about herself, in part perhaps to move away from the objectifying "*What are you?*" to a humanizing, "*Who are you?*". Articulating her mixed race heritage allows her some agency while making her multiracial identity visible and legitimate. By sharing some of her heritage and biography, she addresses people's curiosity in a challenging but self-satisfying way. Asserting her agency in this way reminds border patrollers of her humanity, implicitly communicating to them more tactful ways to ask questions.

Interestingly, Theresa subtly speaks the language of borderism herself here. Notice how she describes her mother as American but also Native American. Throughout our interview, this reference to any indigeneity remained in the background of her narrative about her personal and familial ancestry. One might see this as internalized border patrolling, a topic I turn to in Chapter 5.

Jessica, a black-identified woman of black and Asian Indian parentage, and Flora, a biracial-identified woman with black and white parentage, echoed Theresa's thoughts about the inconvenience and imposition of the clunky questions that border patrollers ask. Jessica's comments also show how her being from the U.S. might dissatisfy the malevolent border patroller by disrupting the idea of the always already "exotic other" multiracial person:

> That [Those indirect questions] kind of frustrates me, not necessarily—well, it doesn't necessarily frustrate me.... I don't know if they're trying to ask me what my background is, or where was I born, so sometimes I'll be like, "Well, I was born in Kentucky." And they'll be like, "Oh, okay, ...so um, where's your mother from? Where's your dad from?" So sometimes *that* can be a little weird. I prefer if people kind of get straight to the point. Just ask me, "So what are you? What's your background?" or ask it in a clear manner so that I know what it is they're trying to ask. Sometimes I really don't know. Are they trying to ask me what my background is? Or are they trying to ask really where I'm from?

Flora reacted similarly to some of the ways strangers choose to interact with her. Citing their circuitous approach as off-putting, Flora frowned upon the obtuse and race-evasive style of borderists' discourses. Despite seeing right through the veneer of racial etiquette, she graciously entertains their thinly veiled and questionably colorblind inquiries:

> The only time I find it offensive is when people try to dance around the question. Just—you can ask me just as easily as anything else. I was working once and this gentleman came in and I always get the words ethnicity and race, not race, or something else, ethnicity and [nationality]. That's exactly it! Ethnicity and nationality. Well, this time I didn't get it mixed up and I told him that I was American because he asked me my nationality. He goes, "No, no, no. I didn't mean that. I mean, 'Where are you from? Where are you from?'" [So I told him] "I'm from New Jersey. Like, what are you trying to ask me?" Finally, he said, "No, what are you mixed with?" "Oh! You're asking my race? I am Caucasian and African American." That's the only time it's offensive.

Flora's example highlights much of the work that multiracial people have to do to figure out these interactions or what information inquirers really want; they do this as these inquirers attempt to figure them out racially. In my interpretation, the inquirers become malevolent border patrollers when they refute or reject the responses multiracial people provide.

Sometimes, border patrollers have to confront the geographies of race to fully understand where to situate some multiracial people. At the intersections of the questions, "What are you?" and "Where are you from?", respondents like Maritza appear. A black Panamanian woman, Maritza shared her experience of managing border patrollers' understanding (or lack thereof) of race and nation and what I call the "global geographies of race"; she also experiences what Elizabeth Spelman (2001) calls "the problem of the ampersand." The ampersand makes space for multiplicity in identity. For Maritza, the ampersand accommodates and celebrates the simultaneity of her being *both* black *and* Latina. The problem lies in some people not knowing or accepting that people can and are both black *and* Latina.

In contrast to some of the other Latina multiracial respondents who reported facing contestation of their preferred racial identities from other Latinas, Maritza felt that strangers who are Latinas are more likely to validate her identity and experiences. It is the people unfamiliar with the racial variation among Latinas who are more likely to invalidate her identity or engage in malevolent racial border patrolling. As she hints, their ignorance about her birthplace and the existing variations within and across race and ethnicity (or their intersections) requires her to offer information and clarification to others. She generously provides ample explanations about her identity so that they might better understand her experience crossing racial, cultural, and geographical borders. Claiming both parts of her parentage also enables others to reconcile any tensions between "black" and "Latino," such that they could see the two terms as coconstitutive, not mutually exclusive, categories. She shared what this possible resolution sounds like in her life:

Well, like if I go to a...party...and I would talk to some of the girls. "Well, so where are you from?" And I always say I'm from Panama. And they were like, "So you speak Spanish?" and I'm like, "Yeah!" So they say, "Well, (stumbling) where, so you're not black then." And I'm like, "Yeah, I'm black. I'm a black Hispanic." "Oh, okay. Well, how can you be?" "Well, because Panama is, you know, a Spanish country." So, in that context, then, I have to explain that, but if I was to talk to someone that was from either Puerto Rico, Colombia, whatever, and they asked, "What are you?" I'm like, "Panamanian." "Oh, you're

Hispanic." And that's it. They don't ask, "*How* are you Hispanic when you're black?" They automatically know.[3]

It is interesting to compare and contrast Maritza's narrative with that of Flora, in part because Maritza is black and Hispanic but finds her Latina heritage denied or contested, while Flora appears always already Latina to strangers. Flora shared some of the ways these perceptions and interactions play out, and the way being brown gets regarded in the South:

Despite the fact that I'm black and white, most people think I'm Hispanic. So that makes me even more mad when they say, "Can I get someone who can speak English?" I'm like, "I can speak English just fine, sir." Yeah. "What can I do for you?" But then I forget that my age is something, too. Most people don't think that, you know, when they walk into a floral shop, that I'm the person running it. Like in any form or fashion, so they're usually like, "Can I speak to a designer?" or "Can I speak to someone who knows more?" "You know, I'm actually it."

…Sometimes I get shy and I just completely shut down….Yeah, someone thought I couldn't speak English and that's why I was so quiet. "Oh, she just can't speak English" and I remember I looked up and died of laughter. I just said, "Oh, no? I can't speak English? I just didn't really know you." And she goes, "Oh, I thought you were Hispanic and you just couldn't understand me." I was like, "No, I can."

Author Richard Rodriguez (2002) might argue that Flora typifies the type of "brown" (woman) who muddies color lines; sociologist Ann Morning (2000) makes a variation of this point in exploring how Latinas help us understand "who is multiracial." She also considers the blurring that occurs between and within these false racial categories ("multiracial" and "Latinas").   Clara Rodriguez's (2000) book, *Changing Race*, also draws attention to the demographic shifts created by a growing Latino population, and the resulting browning of America.

Based on Flora's accounts, these strangers did not see her as she saw herself: an English-speaking biracial woman. Instead, they saw her appearance (caramel-colored skin tone, curly hair, and curvy body) as an approximation, if not indication, of her being "Latina" or "Hispanic," *and* being fluent in Spanish. They went a step further by presuming that she was not in the position of authority that she held at her place of employment. Thus, strangers lacked the racial literacy to read her as biracial, as well as the racial and cultural sensitivity to recognize her as the "person in charge." Strangers' false and unsavory readings of her reinforce racial and ethnic stereotypes and result in their failing to see her in alignment with her self-perception: a biracial woman in a position of authority, with a college degree, and an ability to speak English fluently. This misreading of her is not only inaccurate but also offensive in the attendant stereotypes that swim around strangers' perceptions of Flora. It is offensive in its implications that she lacks the requisite literacy and credibility, perhaps even citizenship status, to be legally employed in this country, particularly in a position of authority. The malevolence of border patrolling masks or muddles many of the important details of multiracial people's identities and lives, which get lost in translation, so to speak.

Flora articulates the antagonism that she feels as a result of others' misperceptions of her as a Latina. To be clear, Flora was not angered or insulted by this misrecognition but rather by the presumptions people made based on their (mis)perceptions of her. Unlike some respondents who got annoyed at others' misrecognition, Flora felt frustrated by the false frames in which strangers viewed her. Flora felt this malevolent border patrolling compelled her to clarify herself to complete strangers, to legitimate her position of authority, and clarify both her English language fluency and her multiracial (black and white) identity.

In contrast to Flora being presumed to be Hispanic, Maritza struggles to make that part of her heritage visible. As a darker-skinned woman, Maritza is ostensibly "too dark to be Hispanic" in the eyes of strangers ignorant of such human variation in the U.S., Panama, and elsewhere. Based on prevailing and persistent racial rules, most strangers see Maritza as "just black." Few are able to move "beyond black" to see that she *knows* Spanish because she *is* Spanish, or Panamanian in particular.

Maritza described to me how regularly she dealt with strangers and their questions about her racial and ethnic ambiguity and multiplicity (see Chapter 6 for further detail). For Maritza, her Panamanian identity is hers to claim but other people's ignorance impedes and complicates that process. Instead, Maritza must contend with perpetual questions from strangers frustrated by her invisible mixture or those who cannot see that she can be both black and Panamanian.

It is this invisibility and the ostensible impossibility of racial mixture, coupled with the crossing of racial, ethnic, and national borders, which agitates malevolent border patrollers.To be black and Hispanic or Latino (and/or some other race/s) at once presents a paradox to border patrollers, a perplexity intensified by the Spanish language ability of people presumed to be "just black." Writer Roberto Santiago

(1995:93–4) argues that not claiming both would be a denial of self and challenges the idea of proving and performing race when he writes: "This debate among us is almost a parody. The fact is that I am black, so why do I need to prove it?" Many respondents, including Maritza, spoke to this point about bearing the burden of proof.

Among black multiracials, racial complexity has often been canceled out by hypodescent or the rule that a person with "one drop of black blood" is "just black" or only black. Based on this racial logic, when black cancels out all other racial mixture through hypodescent, to be both black and Hispanic is beyond contradiction. It gets registered as an anomaly and impossibility. Impossibilities do not exist. This is the illogic of race in the rule of hypodescent. Despite much of the public fascination with racial mixture, some racially mixed people are still often denied such assertions because they do not fit within race logic. This is particularly the case among darker-skinned multiracial people who are most consistently denied membership in multiple racial groups; moving "beyond black" is not seen as an attempt to claim the "sum of one's parts" but rather is misconstrued as an ostensible exit strategy from blackness. Countering racial hegemonies entails engaging people who openly express disbelief in racial multiplicity, particularly in regards to certain combinations. These efforts reveal the racial knowledge that many people living on the borders of race cultivate when they are confronted with challenging questions from strangers.

Several respondents described ways that they had to explain their own identities, as well as their family ties, to strangers. One respondent, Sanchez, a black and Puerto Rican young man, described being asked to explain the connection between his immediate family members. Since his Puerto Rican mother "looks Korean to people," he experienced borderism because strangers have trouble making sense of him being with his black father and "Asian-looking" Puerto Rican mother. An alternate explanation is that malevolent border patrollers may be as equally perplexed by or disapproving of a partnership between a black man and Puerto Rican woman as they seem to be in their misreading of them as black and Asian.

Other respondents addressed sensing or facing this opposition directly. For further illustration, I will return to Leilani, who became familiar with racial border patrollers by being in public with her immediate and extended families of orientation (and sometimes their families of procreation and choice) (Dalmage 2000; Katz Rothman 2001). She also navigates what feminist sociologist Amy Steinbugler (2005) called "visual dislocation." According to these authors, interracial families and multiracial children are often seen as not belonging together. Steinbugler in particular posits that members of these families are dislocated from one another because strangers do not see them as an organized whole. Visual dislocation works to fragment these families by drawing lines that racially divide rather than fully encircle them.

When strangers fail to recognize or accommodate multiracial identities, they also have a hard time doing the same with racially mixed families. Leilani suggested that strangers fail to see her as mixed and as a part of her interracial family. To borderists, Leilani neither sufficiently resembles nor race-matches her parents. Her racial ambiguity then visually dislocates her from her family, leaving her to appear an inexplicable outlier, rather than an understandably central component in the familial order of things.

Along with other scholars, Steinbugler (2009:92) argues that "interracial couples and families can feel unrecognized or unseen" in public spaces and interactions. Leilani described the cognitive dissonance that she and her mother create for malevolent borderists who divided "black" from "white."[4] "Like if I'm just with my mother, we do get looks like, '*What* is she doing with her?'" To resolve this dissonance, Leilani believes that borderists decipher the mother-daughter duo in this way:

> Well now that I'm older, they usually assume that we are friends first but when I was younger, they would assume she was someone—my caregiver or somebody—a babysitter or something like that, but the first thought in their mind usually was not, "Oh, that's her daughter," or "Oh, that's her mother." Sometimes people, they think they are whispering but they are really not. And I can hear them, you know, what they are saying. Like I can remember a particular incident from when I was younger. They were like, "Oh, that must be her babysitter because she got good hair so that couldn't be her daughter," and she was supposedly whispering this to her friend. And I didn't feel the need to tell my mom that I heard it because she really would've got upset.

Leilani uses humor to deflect some of the nonverbal signs of border patrolling: knitted brows, quizzical looks, and the sideways stares of others (Rosenblatt, Karis, and Powell, 1995). Leilani has learned, through experience and advice from her mother in particular, that border patrollers are "just not worth your time. They're not doing anything for you." She felt no differently about multiracial-identified people asking her questions; in fact, the racial locations of border patrollers make little difference when it comes to who asks her intimate questions about her race, friends, and family. She was equally annoyed by the imposition from anyone, and wondered, "Why does it matter? I guess that's how I feel." While her experiences and narratives suggest that race *really* matters to border patrollers, they also illustrate the conundrum: she wishes that race did not matter so much to others that they felt entitled to ask her these questions.

Because Leilani views questions about race as personal and indicative of others' ignorance, she usually reciprocates the inquiry, primarily to purposefully expose its intrusiveness and abruptness. Her distaste for borderism results in her refusal to share details with people who ask what she calls "the roundabout questions" ("Where are you from?") to figure her out racially. She disdains the questions that produce the "'What are you?' experience" that Rockquemore (1998) describes. Leilani asserts her social agency and reclaims her humanity by choosing to say, "I'm a human being." She should not be misread as producing what seems like a colorblind and colormute transcendent racial identity. In reality, she has the racial literacy to discuss race but opts out of doing so most of the time. She employs this as a strategy to challenge the imposition of malevolent border patrolling and the expressed entitlement of border patrollers.

She reciprocates the questioning, reserving the right to access information about others as they do with her. She reports that when she reciprocates or reflects this borderism, she confounds others who react with impatient incredulity. They will rhetorically ask, "Well, isn't it obvious what I am?" to which she responds, "No, because it's not obvious what I am to you so why is it obvious to me what you are?" This exchange provokes curious, dissatisfied looks from border patrollers who normalize their inquiries and express surprise when the targets of their questions ask them questions in return. In other words, border patrollers expect that multiracial people will answer their questions without returning the questions for them to answer. Leilani's experiences parallel those of several other respondents, exposing the patterns that unfold in interactions in/visibly mixed people have with strangers in public.

For racially mixed people with skin color that does not "match" their preferred racial identities, they may find interactions with strangers to be tense places of negotiation. Many of the examples the respondents provided hint at the kinds of mental and emotional labor multiracial border crossers engage in during public interactions with strangers. Border patrollers may expect them to clarify who they are yet convey malevolence when they dispute or contest the preferred identities of multiracial people, advance racial stereotypes about groups to which the multiracial people do not even belong, or otherwise convey unsavory ideas about the multiracial people and any of the racial groups into which multiracial people move as a result of being malevolently border patrolled. For some respondents, these moments of misrecognition and misidentification meant that they became targets of the "wrong" racial epithets or stereotypes. I put "wrong" in quotes here to highlight that all racial epithets and stereotypes are wrong, and almost always injurious or adverse upon impact, despite anyone's best intentions; I also do so to suggest that these injuries might be doubly so for multiracial people who are called the wrong offensive term or are characterized stereotypically in groups outside of their own heritage or parentage. This is one of the liabilities of shifting mixture in a society that remains racially divisive and generally insensitive to racial differences. And, as Maritza and others will attest, this happens on a regular basis.

Conclusions

The irony of much of the multiracial experience involves the incongruence between multiracial people's preferred identities, their appearances, and the ways others perceive them. Malevolent border patrolling highlights this irony. Several of my respondents addressed the way that they prefer to claim their particular heritage and the specificities of their familial histories. Yet, malevolent border patrolling impedes this process and sometimes moves them into altogether different racial categories. It must be an unsettling? kind of dislocation to be denied membership in the multiracial racial groups of one's family heritage while also being casually relocated to other racial groups, primarily based on the appearance of the multiracial person and strangers' perceptions of them. The narratives above and the additional ones that I listened to reveal these and many other challenges of the invisibility of racial mixture.

Malevolent border patrolling also exposes how people (over)rely on the notion of race as biological and read too closely into appearance to determine someone's racial identity. This offers partial explanation as to why people who fall outside of particular categories can be placed in them anyway, most simply because they "look" like a member of said group(s). The difficulty, as participants described it, is in belonging to but being denied membership in, many racial and ethnic groups. If one does not look sufficiently (insert race here), or behave accordingly, one risks racial disqualification, identity invalidation and possible racial relocation (a topic I revisit in Chapter 6).

I would argue here that the narratives of my respondents suggest, through their experiences with borderism, that race is as much, if not more, an achieved status rather than an ascribed one. Throughout this work, I detail the efforts that many multiracial respondents have made in order to "prove" or authenticate their identities and to accomplish the real or imagined goal of having strangers affirm their preferred racial identities, rather than have them invalidate identities typically understood as determined by birth. The ongoing negotiations of identities suggest that race is both inheritance and achievement and is just as much a social characteristic to be accepted and celebrated, as it is to be contested and updated. These contestations make space for new understandings of race and potentially shift how we categorize race here in the United States.

Notes

[1] The respondents in my sample asserted a variety of racial identities and referred to themselves with a variety of racial labels (often in addition to the existing racial categories). Some referenced themselves as "white," "black," "Asian," "mixed," "brown," "Flip" (Filipino), "Black Hispanic," "Black Panamanian," "Blackerican" (Black and Puerto Rican), "Blasian" (Black and Asian), "Anglo Indian," and more. In choosing these labels, the respondents were able to acknowledge and communicate how they understood their racial sense of selves at that moment in time. They also discussed how they negotiated this racial sense of self during interactions with others who had little intimate information about their racial inheritance. These negotiations proved particularly interesting, given the changing contemporary racial landscape of and specific to the South.

With much of the experiences the respondents shared having taken place in the South, one must keep in mind that the local racialization process often diverges from other parts of the country. The geography of race in the South contrasts, for example, with that of the West, in that a white/black racial polarization persists in the former, with new waves of immigration agitating this tendency towards white and black (Jones and Smith 2001). These flows of new immigrants not only erroneously make "Mexican" synonymous with "Latino" but also suggest that in places in the South, a tri-racial system exists that positions Latinos as "not white" and "not black." Not only then does this support the idea of three racial groups, it erases the existence of overlapping categories and the possibility of Latinos being of any race(s). Furthermore, this social construction of race largely masks multiraciality. This contrasts with the geography of race in the West, where immigration flows have increased the number of Asians and Latinos there, as well as interracial marriages, but also made more visible the multiracial populations that are recognized as such much more easily there than in the South (Farley 2001; Lee and Bean 2007; Rockquemore 2002). Thus, the ongoing debate about which racial hierarchy best applies continues, and impacts how others racially see (or refuse/are unable to see) others.

[2] Examples of these equations follow: Black + Asian + Native American = Hispanic; White + Asian = Hispanic; and White + Black = Hispanic.

[3] Other Hispanics, particularly from the Caribbean and Latin America, have more likely been exposed to racial variations within and between categories so this predisposition to these differences creates a racially and ethnically mixed habitus. This also equips them to recognize these differences, rather than disqualify them. The idea of "automatically" knowing illustrates how different racial paradigms are operating that allow some people to see black and Hispanic as compatible and sensible, versus irreconcilable, a point made by Rodriguez and Cordero-Guzman (1992).

[4] By splitting them into color-coded groups, borderists missed the relationship between mother and daughter, rather than recognizing this relationship and lumping them together as "family." This lumping and splitting (Zerubavel 1991, 1997) reflects the cognitive decisions that borderists make and how those decisions impact their perceptions of and interactions with multiracial individuals in interracial families of orientation and/or procreation.

4

Managing Racial Identities with Family and Friends

> With racial ideologies and practices so reliant on family for meaning, family writ large becomes race. Within racial discourse, just as families can be seen as naturally occurring, biologically linked entities who share common interests, whites, Blacks, Native Americans, and other "races" of any given historical period can also be seen this way. The actual racial categories of any given period matter less than the persistent belief in race itself as an enduring principle of social organization that connotes family ties (Collins 1998a:65–66)[1]

As I discussed in Chapter 3, strangers explore their curiosity about the racial mixture of many of my respondents by asking questions such as "What are you?" and "Where are you from?" People with multiracial heritage and parentage can choose to interpret and respond to these questions in a number of ways. Many of my respondents reported enjoying the process of sharing information with strangers, and happily answering questions about their specific (multi)racial identities. Other respondents expressed less accommodation of these inquiries; citing power asymmetries as one source of discomfort and the intimate quality of what they considered personal questions as another.

What happens when individuals close to multiracial people start to have similar sets of inquiries? What if these inquiries begin to take the shape of borderism, such that the multiracial people involved feel policed or interrogated (versus questioned) about their identities? How do multiracial people make sense of family and friends engaging in potentially borderist behavior? How do multiracial people interpret borderism from family members who themselves likely face(d) borderism? What does it say about our society that even people with lived experiences of borderism in their own interracial families or within multiracial friendships or social networks participate in and perpetuate border patrolling? Do these individuals register the irony of these moments, in border patrolling, when they themselves may have been border patrolled because of their own racial identities and involvement in interracial relationships or communities? Do targets of borderism in one generation become border patrollers in the next?

To appreciate the different ways people participate in and respond to borderism, I consider the aforementioned contradictions. These contradictions often emerge under oppressive conditions that prompt people to internalize behavioral patterns of the oppressor (see Collins 2005). Understanding that primary and secondary group members include family, friends, neighbors, coworkers, and others with whom people have more meaningful and sustained social interactions with and connections to, I consider their influence on multiracial individuals' experiences.

In this chapter, I explore the paradox of family and friends engaging in borderism directed at members of their own families via many of the multiracial participants in my research. This borderism has different shades than that in which strangers engage, primarily because of the greater familiarity among family members. This intimacy creates a different level of knowledge from which family members might question their multiracial relatives; this backdrop gives them greater access to biographical information from which to pose these questions. Rather than protect multiracial people, the individuals who engage in this borderism often neglect to respect the racial identities of multiracial individuals. Instead, they police multiracial people's preferred racial identity options. This policing may reflect attempts, on their part, to resolve any cognitive dissonance created by multiracial people fitting into or falling out of racial categories. This "fitting in" can result from multiracial people actively making moves to blend into certain racial categories. "Falling out" of racial categories tends to occur when multiracial people's physical appearance is incongruous with their identities. Having an appearance that departs from others' expectations might mean that border patrollers locate multiracial people in racial categories different from those that the multiracial person would choose for herself or himself. Any inconsistency or incongruity between a multiracial person's preferred identity and appearance could result in a racial relocation; that multiracial person could be socially moved into another racial category or any number of racial categories. In this way, multiracial people sometimes fall out of the racial groups of their heritage or parentage and into new and different ones primarily, but not exclusively, defined by border patrollers. What I consider in this chapter is the curiosity that this shifting of mixture occurs *within* interracial families, when such borderism might make more sense when initiated by strangers.

By blending racial categories, claiming two or more races (or only one), and/or by having an incongruent identity and appearance, multiracial people can defy expectations and perceptions. Whether or not they look "clearly mixed," multiracial people may appear to belong to a racial group or groups that are not part of their racial heritage. In trying to figure out where, or wrestling with how, to make a multiracial person fit into their racial schemas, border patrollers attempt to keep racial categories seemingly neat and cohesive. Border patrollers seldom achieve their goal because race is a social construction and the property of cohesion is as illusive as race. Through their actions, border patrollers reveal their coercive power as well as the power of race as an illusion (Bonilla Silva 2003a,b; Oliver 2003). They often refuse to recognize that the meanings people attach to race may differ. These differences reflect any variations in racial socialization across time, space, and place throughout the life course. These differences also reflect any alternate interpretations to systems of racial categorization. As Omi and Winant (2014) suggest, racial formation projects present this system as a fully crystallized form, rather than a free-flowing model.

As systems of racial categorization differ from nation to nation, people learn a variety of racial meanings. These meanings are sometimes, but not always, shared. In general conversations, people may agree and/or disagree about the meanings of race and the prevailing racial categories. When the subject is a particular person, these agreements and/or disagreements may become tenser, seemingly because there is more at stake.

Border patrollers may hesitate to acknowledge how meanings of race can change or shift, even as social interactions create the space for this negotiation to occur. They may fail to recognize that race changes for a variety of reasons and reflects potential variability and fluidity in terms of people's preferred identities, others' perceptions, and formal racial identity options. Individuals who experience their racial identity as flexible and fluid experience changing race. Many of these individuals may face "changing race" when other people misperceive them as "some other race(s)" than the ones they claim for themselves. Even multiracial people who consistently choose a specific and singular racial identity may face changing race as others perceive that individual in any number of ways. Finally, as racial categories change, people may choose their racial identities differently than before (or not). They may depart from existing categories if they feel the introduction or formal recognition of another category better reflects how they see themselves.

Border patrollers prioritize their perception of reality, or of these racial illusions, because they may be discomforted by the idea of racial multiplicity and fluidity. They may be equally discomforted when multiracial people choose singular racial identities or articulate a racial specificity that betrays a "clearly mixed" appearance.

Multiracial individuals arguably complicate the property of cohesion in racial categories. They are seen as disrupting the presumed cohesion in these categories. Despite any individual and collective denials or opposition to race mixing, racial mixture is both a contemporary and historical process, one that Turner (2013) elaborates upon in her work. This ongoing mixture means that many multiracial people are also unseen—hiding in plain sight—because of the generations of people passing, blending into one category or another (or others), or racial border crossing—the blurring of racial lines. Sometimes, these actions—this passing, blending, and blurring happen actively and, sometimes, they happen accidentally. This slippage reflects the act of blurring lines or blending racial categories in the borderlands. It reflects the interstitial spatial and racial locations in which multiracial people reside (see Sandoval 2000).

In these interstices, some people pass into categories that may not even be their own, a thought that might haunt border patrollers who are hung up on ideas of racial purity and racial contamination. The notion of racial purity is a fiction that persists despite evidence to the contrary. Often, border patrollers neglect the historical and contemporary reality of racial mixture throughout the national population in this society. This mixture does not solely exist in people who claim or assert a multiracial identity but, rather, in a large percentage of the national population (see Davis 1991). Nevertheless, many individuals encounter forms of border patrolling that contest this very mixture exists on individual and collective levels; the dominant discourses about race erase much of this racial mixture on a collective level, even as more and more people personally attempt to claim racial mixture, acknowledging their racially mixed parentage or heritage.

The racial classification system, constructed by the Office of Management and Budget and administered as the U.S. Census, reinforces the idea of racial singularity by creating categories that speak to and encourage the population to claim racial singularity or specificity, even as the choice for racial multiplicity continues. The construction of this classification system limits information, even as it ostensibly opens up the range of choices that people can make regarding their racial identities. The specificity both narrowly defines and clarifies any blurred lines, through the suggestion that claiming a single race is clearer than claiming multiple race. As I argue elsewhere in this book, the social construction of race ensures that this exacting racial knowledge, this specificity, technically eludes people. A person who claims a single race is biologically no closer to the center of said racial group than a person who claims two or more races. However, ideas of racial purity and authenticity breathe life into this perception.

As the Census works to enumerate the population, it reflects how racial formation works in the U.S. with racial categories further solidifying the socially constructed nature of race. It also reflects the way society supports the notion that people who claim a multiracial identity are the only ones who embody racial mixture or have experiential knowledge of living in the borderlands or in the blurred spaces of racial borders and boundaries. To the contrary, many people negotiate these blurred lines as they develop interracial friendships and relationships or navigate life in racially mixed families, through birth, adoption, cohabitation, and/or marriage.

Yet, even from within these families, individuals experience a racial socialization that endures the lifetime. They learn the dominant ways of seeing race in this country and, more specifically, within their families. Just as strangers attempt to figure out where to locate people with racially mixed parentage, so too do members of multiracial or interracial families, friends, and others in the primary and secondary social group networks. That is, individuals in interracial families may not fully understand intergenerational racial differences or they may simply hold differing racial perspectives and perceptions reflective of different racial realities.

From their own described positions as "outsiders-within" (Collins 2000, 1991, 1986), "insider-others" (Twine 2006, 2003), or "insiders-without" (Reddy 1997), some members of racially mixed families lack the racial literacy and consciousness to fully support and understand the range of identity options available to all family members. In particular, knowledge and understanding of the plethora of identity options for family members with multiracial parentage may not match those individuals' lived experiences. People "raising biracial children" (Rockquemore and Laszloffy 2005) or "raising mixed race" children (Chang 2015) may not understand that their children might identify in a multitude of ways: as any singular race, with multiple races or racial combinations, as "some other race(s)", as "raceless," as primarily one race with a deemphasis on others or, as I found, "more than multiracial." Being "more than multiracial" speaks to the ways that multiracial people claim both biologically and socially inherited racial heritage, as informed both by biological parents, family storytelling, and the blending of families which may introduce more racial variations into the mix. I return to this topic in more depth in Chapter 5 but mention it here, as many people with multiracial heritage experience their identities by moving "beyond the binary" and the boundaries of their racial heritage. They consider the composition of their families and want to incorporate that complexity into the way they express their preferred racial identities. This can complicate race and our collective notions of racial heritage within families as well as the reactions to those racial articulations among its members.

As the research shows, multiracial individuals may opt for singular, border, blended, protean, and/or transcendent identities (see Rockquemore and Brunsma 2002). My research revealed, as well, that some multiracial people form honorary memberships that emerge in the process of their membership in families that blend structurally and racially as a result of some social-structural reconfiguration or the merging of multiple families into one (see Twine 2011). Just as individuals in interracial relationships and families may cultivate these honorary memberships or experience their own kinds of shifting mixture, so too might multiracial members of families (see Keating 2013; Twine 2011). These honorary memberships further blur the borders of race since the significance of these social ties and the richness of their meanings are not always immediately obvious or transparent to others. These kinds of ties might confuse members of interracial families who have only ever claimed a static singular race or have not had to consider how the daily navigation among the borders of race shape and reshape their racial identities. Borderism becomes part of the process for members of families to share information about their racial realities, particularly as each person's identity influences others, albeit to differing degrees. The racial group membership of each family member potentially gets reconfigured as a result. This influence potentially shifts the racial identities and social locations of family members. This may result in a dislocation from and relocation within and between racial categories. Alternately, it may create or reflect fluidity and liminality in these identities and experiences.

All too often, however, some family members falsely see themselves as emboldened and empowered to define the racial realities and identities of others. This situation can be complicated if the latter operate with a different set of race rules or cognitive racial schema than that of the multiracial members of the family. Because of their everyday exposure to and relationship-building experiences with multiracial individuals in their families, the discourses produced by these family members and friends who border patrol multiracial members of their families can differ from that of strangers. Because they usually have more personal knowledge about the specificities of the respondents' racial backgrounds, family members may feel that their interactions with the respondents entitle them to make determinations about the "best" racial locations for multiracial family members; they racially border patrol as a result. These border-patrolling family members may ignore how their positions as outsiders-within do not always align with that of the multiracial members they attempt to racially police. This awareness, or lack thereof, results from social interactions between the two parties drawing attention to any real and imagined differences in the perceptions and realities of all involved.

Throughout this chapter, I provide ample examples to illustrate this tension of borderism. I pay close attention to the irony that emerges when individuals in interracial relationships and families engage in borderist behavior directing it at multiracial members of these interracial families. It may appear counterintuitive that some of the people socially closer to the respondents engage in borderist behavior; however, the intimate knowledge and greater familiarity that stems from this proximity may mean that family members and friends have more detail with which to police and reinforce racial borders. It might also be a reflection of the different ways in which families individually and collectively identify themselves racially; the racial socialization within these families; and, the varying levels of racial literacy and consciousness possessed by family members. These factors draw attention to differences in how families understand themselves. That is, just as multiracial people choose and manage the various racial locations or labels attached to them, so too do families. Consequently, not all members of a family would always agree that theirs is an "interracial" one or has "multiracial" members in it. It is in these situations of contestation, when and where families disagree, that multiracial people may more likely encounter borderism from family members. This point is an important one intended to disrupt the idea that everyone within interracial families sees their family unit as such, and/or sees the multiracial members of their family as such. In some ways, the shifting mixture of multiracial people can be seen as potentially strengthening or diluting the racial mixture of families and any changes in racial consciousness (as described by Twine 2011 and others) can compromise the integrity of family units believed to be always already interracial ones.

Borderism, then, becomes a way for family members to interrogate the racial composition of their family unit and make sense of their racial reality, given what they know of one another's racial identities, consciousness, and preferred social locations. This borderism can be experienced any number of ways, some of which reflect people's desires to buffer their multiracial family members from racial microaggressions, hostility and adversity, and some of which reflects people's motivations to maintain any racial privilege they might be privy to or already enjoy. Next, I discuss the dimensions of borderism that emerged among the family and friends of my multiracial respondents.

Types of Border Patrolling

Based on my interpretation of respondents' reported experiences, family members and friends participated in any variety of four different types of border patrolling: benevolent, beneficiary, protective, and malevolent. These patterns of behavior emerged from the data analysis—the variations of borderism becoming clearer with each new interview I conducted. This analysis revealed differences between and within social groups, such that not all borderism is alike. That is, strangers border patrol multiracial people based on limited and available information (primarily physical appearance) or upon accessible information (gained through social interactions where multiracial people share this knowledge with strangers). While some family members and friends racially border on this basis, they moreso racially border patrol on the basis of more intimate information about the multiracial person's (real versus imagined) racial background and heritage.

In my analysis, I found that respondents shared narratives demonstrating these four types of border patrolling. While not mutually exclusive categories, these types of borderism capture different discursive practices, motivations, and behaviors. First, I summarize the qualitative nuances differentiating the types. Then, I provide examples from respondents' narratives demonstrating each type of border patrolling behavior. I attempt to capture some of the slippage between types, as they overlap and entangle each other.

Benevolent border patrolling involves family members and friends politely and perhaps unintentionally policing the identities and partner choices of respondents. This type of border patrolling reflects more of an innocence or ignorance about race generally, rather than the injurious quality of malevolent border patrolling. When they inquire about the (multi)racial locations of multiracial people, benevolent border patrollers do not tend to refute the knowledge they acquire or express hostility or angry incredulity at multiracial people, like malevolent border patrollers tend to do. Rather, they simply may not understand the plethora of racial options from which multiracial people can currently choose, including but not limited to "multiracial." In other words, they may not know that it is possible to claim two or more races, or that millions of people did so in the most recent enumeration of the national population (see Census 2010). Benevolent border patrollers are often curious about the racial locations of multiracial people but they may lack the racial literacy to effectively ask questions that might better clarify these racial locations. Like other types of border patrollers, benevolent border patrollers sometimes have different racial frameworks from the multiracial people with whom they interact. Unlike other types of border patrollers, they do not purposefully guide a multiracial person into a particular racial category. On the basis of their own views, they may refuse multiracial people their racial multiplicity or whatever their preferred identity. They may believe, out of innocence or ignorance, that multiracial people must choose "one-and-only-one" race because benevolent border patrollers do not know that multiracial people can claim the sum of their parts in ways that are affirmed by others. They puzzle over multiracial people in part because they know very little about how much the racial landscape has changed to increase people's freedom to choose their preferred racial identity. Ironically, however, benevolent border patrollers can inhibit that very freedom, as they learn these racial lessons for themselves.

Beneficiary border patrolling involves interpreting mixture through the lens of higher social status, with beneficiary border patrollers working to see respondents in a "better" light. By encouraging multiracial people to align with whatever racial group gives them the most privileges and benefits, beneficiary border patrollers often invalidate respondents' *preferred* racial identities and encourage them to racially identify in socially "desirable" ways. This would entail choosing racial group membership in the more or most elevated category. This speaks to the racial hierarchy and the differential value associated with racial groups and their members.

This strategy or practice of beneficiary border patrolling can be seen in the example of an Asian white multiracial person "opting for white" to purposefully elevate her/his racial position in society (Rockquemore and Arend 2002). This is often done intentionally to access, or otherwise benefit from, white racial privilege (see also Rothenberg 2005). By extension, beneficiary border patrollers may also encourage multiracial people to partner with people who will improve or enhance access to social and material privileges, i.e., individuals in racial groups with high(er) social status, especially whites.

Protective border patrolling involves trying to prepare multiracial people for potential and actual encounters with racial discrimination, particularly if they have been "passing" as some other race(s) and buffered by any racial privilege that they are able to enjoy. This type of borderism builds on the essentialist assumption that discrimination and disadvantage will be inevitable for racially mixed people, despite evidence to the contrary. The term captures the desire to shield multiracial people away from the injuries of racism, microaggressions, and everyday injustices and violations embedded in social interactions and the broader society.

People might observe some slippage between beneficiary and protective border patrolling. The former, beneficiary border patrolling, can involve encouraging respondents to choose singular racial identities, and/or form homophilous and racially homogamous relationships, just as the protective border patrollers might do. Rather than trying to benefit from positioning multiracial people in privileged racial categories, however, protective border patrollers try to minimize any inevitable injuries these individuals will likely incur in this racially divisive society. Protective border patrollers may intend to deflect some of the racialized gaze that reads multiracial people as "spectacular," "special," and "exotic." Their attempts to minimize the attention that multiracial people often face are designed to buffer the respondents from the racial surveillance that prevails in this society (Browne 2015).

A particular variation of protective border patrolling involves parental border patrolling (but could also include extended relatives in some cases). Parental border patrolling often operates under the guise of "cultural maintenance" with parents communicating to their multiracial and multicultural children the importance of being "culture keepers" (Kibria 2002, 1995). As I illustrate in examples provided later in the chapter, some parents conflate "culture" with "race," using "culture" as a code word for "race." This false interchange of terms does little to camouflage questionable (often hostile) feelings, yet many parents use the terms interchangeably because it is considered safer and easier to discuss culture than race.

Because some interracial families are also international or immigrant families, they may experience culture and race differently here versus abroad. For these families, messages about cultural maintenance are at odds with the families' level of assimilation and the multiple meanings attached to race that shift with time, space, and place. That is, many interracial families may want to preserve their cultural heritage and traditions, supporting more of a pluralistic perspective. Conversely, other families have sometimes undergone some cultural dilution by way of assimilation; some may attempt to recover their culture(s) of origin by encouraging their racially mixed children to identify with the minority culture(s) and race(s) in order to preserve that "difference." As race, culture, and nation remain difficult to disentangle, so too is the deciphering of the practice of parental border patrolling as benevolent, beneficiary, protective and/or malevolent. Perhaps it is up to the reader to decide.

Finally, malevolent border patrolling involves more blatant and explicit invalidation of identities. Friends and family members, including significant others, who border patrol in this way use harsher and more explicit or abrasive language, including racial epithets and other racially charged words to do the following: 1) disqualify the respondents; 2) reject their preferred racial identities or view them as "inappropriate" or "inauthentic" identities (including making racially disloyal partner choices, as discussed in a later chapter); 3) impose their assessments of the "right" choices on respondents, which negates their agency and infantilizes them; and 4) seem more racially divisive and invested in the racial divide.

Borderists' locations within and connections to interracial families often do little to dissuade them from border patrolling the multiracial people in their lives. Their own firsthand encounters with borderism, as immediate and extended members of interracial families, do not always disrupt the border-patrolling behavior directed at the multiracial respondents. Perhaps the policing that significant others experience explains why they participate in this process but for differing reasons. What appears as borderism may be race-evasive strategies linked to a lack of racial literacy or the inability to effectively communicate with multiracial people about race and racism throughout the lifelong socialization process.

The borderism that stems from family members and friends often involves resolving potentially competing perspectives of their perceptions of the multiracial person's identity. A part of this process involves identity negotiation, such that individuals with multiracial ancestry and fluid identities must resolve any incongruence or dissonance within their families. If differences are seldom (or never) discussed in families, for instance, the very identities that these individuals choose to assert both reflect and sometimes depart from the racial socialization they receive from parents and others and the social identities imposed by others.

Racial socialization in a racially divisive society takes on many dimensions and reflects the process in which parents were likely socialized; the process also opens up the possibility that multiracial individuals, in childhood and/or adulthood, have the agency to shape socialization, just as socialization shapes them. Much of this socialization remains cloaked in colorblindness and colormuteness, with multiracial people learning lessons about their racial identity from their family as well as friends, the media, and other agents of socialization. Sometimes these lessons do not make enough space for multiracial people to privately claim their preferred racial identities, so they may resist the racial messages they receive during this socialization process that lasts a lifetime.

Multiracial individuals who challenge this racial socialization and familial expectation often arrive at different identities than the ones they are taught to embrace (i.e., choosing a racial identity that contrasts with the one imposed by one's immediate and/or extended family). For example, this can involve reclaiming identities previously denied some family members in a recovery of mixture such that "multiracial" will survive until the next generation (Bratter 2007), even after its death in the previous one. That is, it is important to recognize how family members and friends themselves may have been socialized to assert a singular and static racial identity, even when they themselves are racially mixed or have shifting subjectivities. Because of these social pressures to choose "one-and-only-one" race, these family members and friends may replicate this lack of choice onto others. For some multiracial people growing up in interracial families, this may entail having the family appear to be racially homogeneous. An example of this appears in the form of black white multiracial parents who have only opted for black and raise their child as black, not multiracial, like them. However, as that child learns more about his racial identity options, he may claim a multiracial identity that the parents do not affirm, because they fail to see multiracial as a viable option for him or anyone else with similar racial parentage. In this way, family members in interracial families are not unlike more racially homogeneous families in that they see themselves in certain ways racially. In addition, they also interact with each other and others outside of the family in part on the basis of these shared racial subject positions.

The broader social environment interacts with the family unit and its individual members to reinforce messages about the familial and individual identities of those involved (whether the family appears interracial to outsiders, or is understood as such to its *own* members).

Growing Up "Multiracial," Learning to Be Mixed?

What lessons do multiracial children learn as they grow up in interracial families? How do multiracial children learn about the racial identity options possible and available to them? What messages do they receive from family members, friends, and others? As Rockquemore and Lazloffy (2005) suggest in their book, *Raising Biracial Children*, this practice of raising biracial children involves consideration of the children's preferred racial identities. Sharon Chang (2015) addresses much of the same themes in her book, *Raising Mixed Race*. Many people presume the preferred racial identity of children who grow up with racially mixed parentage is always already a multiracial one. This is not always the case. As other scholars have substantiated elsewhere, and as I summarized earlier, multiracial people can assert a variety of racial identities. In my research, I posed similar questions to people with racially mixed parentage or heritage. My analysis uncovered a few surprising findings. While I expected that not everyone in this category would consider themselves mixed or assert a multiracial identity, I did not expect people to reject the "multiracial" label, such that it did not resonate with them at all. That is, not all of them shared the same experiences of growing up "multiracial" in families with members who possess different levels of racial literacy. As a result, the multiracial respondents had varying levels of "multiracial" racial consciousness. Their experiences begged several questions, "What languages, or racial discourses, and what literacy do immediate and extended families speak when discussing race (or remaining silent or colormute)? Are these shared racial literacies or do multiracial people develop new modes of communication—a differential consciousness—or the hybrid language of the facultad that Anzaldua (1987) describes in her work on conocimiento (see also Sandoval 2000).

Often the experience of growing up in an "interracial" or multiracial family means that its members learn how to navigate race and the racial surveillance that stems from others' reactions to racial mixture. As I discovered during my interviews with individuals of various racial combinations, not all multiracial children grow up in interracial families or in ones that are consistently so. Family dissolutions and reconfigurations (related to marriage, divorce, separation, birth, and death) alter the composition of these units. Just as families blend in terms of membership, they blend racially as well at times. Like the shifting of racial identities, families sometimes shift in their understandings of race, individually and collectively.

While I had previously recognized the fluidity of racial identities, I neglected to do the same for families. As a result, I acknowledge here how a family might think of itself as interracial at one time and not at another. How a family racializes itself reflects and impacts how its members understand their racial identities, individually and collectively. Families that blend may do so racially and in composition. In families with multiracial members that identify with a single race are border patrolling their own. Not all families that are "interracial" have members who look mixed or appear physically different from one another (have visibly different skin color). Families whose members blend their own racial borders will likely not be border patrolled (on the basis of appearance). Instead, they may be privy to the borderism directed at more visibly mixed interracial families or families whose members do not racially resemble one another.

As I mentioned earlier, people negotiate race at the level of identity, individually, but also relationally, within their families, communities, and the broader society. Individuals growing up in households that adopt colorblindness and colormuteness might find asserting their preferred racial identities more difficult than in households that encourage more open and honest discussions about race. Learning about race in color-conscious households arguably facilitates racial sensitivity and literacy.

For multiracial people growing up in colorblind and colormute "interracial" families, they face a set of challenges around their assertion of racial identity. If they assert a preferred racial identity that compromises how the family unit sees itself, then this produces a tension to be negotiated and, ideally, resolved. The potentially shifting, "situationally interracial" family also impacts how its multiracial members are border patrolled (do they blend in more or less?). Even within families that do not appear interracial, it is important to acknowledge how members might claim similar racial identities or divergent ones.

For many of my respondents, learning about race did not necessarily involve learning to be mixed. In wanting to maintain the illusion of racial purity and singularity, some respondents were reportedly told, as children, to identify as everyone else did in the family. Racial lacunas existed in many of the respondents' families and households, creating both silences and curiosities about any untold stories. The silence surrounding family heritage inspired many respondents to ask questions and discuss the "mysteries of histories" in their racial backgrounds. Some of this silence stemmed from extended family members' opposition to interracial unions within families. At other times, the silence numbed painful pasts, embarrassing family details, or other specificities that families wanted to conceal. The silence was a way to manage negative emotions and associations within their families. Those family secrets generated more, not less, interest for some respondents who wanted to hear those truths. As Nash and Viray (2014), Brown (2013), and Brown (2012) and others illustrate, truth-telling practices and telling stories can heal. To this point, families might benefit from more openly discussing racial traumas within their families, as a way of processing these injuries and acknowledging (where applicable) the multiracial reality of their family composition.

A multiracial person whose family members do not validate a multiracial identity may grow up as the only person in their family to see their family unit as "interracial" or interracial in a particular way. This process becomes especially messy in the context of the honorary memberships I describe elsewhere. As family members in monoracial groups establish enough racial literacy to gain these honorary memberships, their own potential shifting mixture calls their racial "authenticity" into question. Understanding these processes for the multiracial people I interviewed would require interviews with family members and in-depth ethnographic research in their families. As I did not conduct those studies during my research, I am limited to discussion and speculation about the dynamics of shifting mixture on many levels: individual, familial, and societal. Stated simply, multiracial people shift the racial mixture in families and society.

Since many individuals are uncomfortable with shifting mixture, even those who are a part of multiracial or interracial families, they tend to manage this mixture with varying degrees of success. For many families, colormuteness and colorblindness were the literacies strengthened through silence and a refusal to recognize race and racism. I turn next to discuss how *not* talking about race becomes a form of border patrolling.

Benevolent Border Patrolling: Who Said Anything About Race?

In this society, one could presume that interracial families have more racial literacy than members of the general population; however, this is not always the case. Anyone can internalize racism and adopt the dominant discourses of colorblindness (Bonilla-Silva 2003a,b) and colormuteness (Pollock 2005). Often, benevolent border patrolling produces innocent but important ruptures in a family's colorblindness and colormuteness, allowing for multiracials to discuss their identities alongside other family members. These ruptures may invite other members to engage in racial discourses and heighten their racial consciousness (and racial literacy).

Individual family members who lack racial literacy may benevolently border patrol their own (immediate and extended) families because they do not understand racial complexity and the range of options available. As more and more people cling to colorblindness and colormuteness as the default dominant racial discourse, they will continue to lack the racial literacy that would help them to more effectively navigate conversations about race.

Many of the respondents' families practice colorblindness and colormuteness, opting not to see or discuss race. As a result, some respondents reported a kind of "suffering in silence" as they struggled to put the puzzle pieces of their family's racial composition together or make sense of their own racial identity. Several respondents did not grow up "learning to be mixed" as they were not racially socialized as "multiracial." When a family wanted to create a racially singular and cohesive unit, they strongly encouraged, if not expected, everyone in the family to identify as part of the same racial group.

Trusting or internalizing their own parents' perceptions of their racial identities, many of the respondents generally accepted and embraced their parents' racial identification of them, at least initially. As the respondents developed a sense of self in relation to and independent of their families, some began to assert preferred (private) racial identities that ran counter to the way their parents (or siblings) saw them. This created some tensions, at times, but generally prompted conversations that revealed some of the families' rich racial complexity, a complexity cloaked by colormuteness and colorblindness. At other times, these conversations were flattened, prohibited, or altogether avoided as family members worked to assuage painful histories or truths about their heritage, individually and nationally.

These conversations addressed the racial lacuna in families and allowed for some respondents to explore the "mysteries of histories." This lacuna, or silence, stemmed from painful pasts, details of which family members considered embarrassing or shameful, or, at other times, the silence related to extended family members' opposition to interracial unions within their families. It operated as a variation of the saying: "If you can't say something nice, don't say anything at all."

These silences did not take on different valences depending on the racial composition of the families. Instead, they connected to and reflected a confluence of personal and collective racial traumas, the extensive violence that racism created and sustains in this country, and the profound impact of that violence as experienced through discrimination, sexual exploitation, limited opportunities, and so on. In "Bodies Don't Just Tell Stories, They Tell Histories," Walters, Mohammed, Evans-Campbell, Beltran, Chae, and Duran (2011) explore the relationship between everyday racism and the experiences of trauma (and that impact on wellness). As respondents in my research revealed, they offer narratives that speak to the legacy of racism and its injuries; they tell stories about how their families handle historical injuries from persistent racial inequalities. Not everyone wants to revisit the past or celebrate their histories given the way stories can trigger memories of traumas. This appeared to operate as a dynamic for some respondents.

For example, Keisha mentioned that, out of respect to her elders, she's learned to not ask her black grandmother questions about the family's racial ancestry because "she gets upset to the point of tears." Being forced to be deferential and respectful also speaks to the difficulty of dealing with racial traumas of the past and present. Maintaining silences occurs at the expense of preserving any *positive* racial memories for future generations. Other part-black respondents noted how infrequently family members discussed race with or around them. For example, Sa, a young woman with Black, Blackfoot Indian, and British/Brazilian parentage, noted that, "They don't talk about race." In learning about the racial rifts within her family resulting in part from some opposition to her parents' interracial marriage, Sa discovered that being multiracial meant sometimes living on racial fault lines. She described how colorism created conflict with and accusations from relatives resentful of her position higher up in the racial hierarchy and the beauty queue (Hunter 2005) (see also Bonilla-Silva 2003b; Russell, Wilson, and Hall 1992; Thompson and Keith 2004). In being viewed as "better than," she felt policed, but no regret, for being multiracial.

Other respondents reported a generalized silence in their family surrounding race matters. This lacuna can operate as a form of benevolent border patrolling in the sense that the "mysteries of histories" veil difficult details and painful pasts. This practiced silence ignores the important intergenerational transmission of knowledge about how to handle what Derald Sue (2010) calls "racial microaggressions," or the everyday injuries and injustices that create harm for racial minorities. This lacuna helps family members elide the discomfort of discussing race and its specificities that might be experienced as a form of trauma, as it relates to and departs from experiences with microaggressions (see Sue 2010). For example, Walters et al. (2011) discuss the link between historical collective traumas and the implications and adverse impacts on individual lives. As individuals negotiate their racial group membership, they also negotiate the historical residues of these groups. This can result in a sense of pride or shame, as related to traumatic events. People often respond to the latter through silence; a quality Vanessa (a black-identified multiracial woman with Native American, Black, and White parentage) describes in her father specifically, but also in her family generally:

> Oh, with my father...he's quiet, isolated, to himself. He never really brought that up. So when I did find out, it was through my grandmother. My grandmother started to explain things about her husband. He passed away. She started showing me pictures and things like that. When I looked, it was kind of curious the way he looked to me. He looks to me like an Indian, curly hair, high cheek bones, and he was very white-skinned. So he's—and she's dark-skinned. So my father took, I took the complexion of my father, which is brown. That is how I started to understand things more because my father has features that I wondered about. They are not typical African American features, so when my grandmother would talk about it, she would explain things. It made a lot of sense.

While no one volunteered generous amounts of information, they did indulge Vanessa's curiosity to her minimal satisfaction. With most of the family photos in black and white, Vanessa posited, "You have to ask more than you want to know." Her persistence helped to heighten her self-understanding, as she gained greater access to this familial and ancestral information.

Arguably, the silence of racial socialization, in the form of colormuteness and colorblindness, facilitated her singular black identity. She was not actively discouraged from claiming a multiracial identity, but being readily presented with information about her family's blackness encouraged that identity for her. Having additional ancestral information offered more reluctantly operates as a form of benevolent border patrolling, as it guides her towards blackness and a racial identity that seems chosen for her on a familial level. Multiracial people who push for more information, "more than you want to know," may arrive at an identity different than the one preferred by their parents, extended family members, friends, community, or even society.

Generalized silence, or the racial lacuna, becomes a form of border patrolling in its failure to acknowledge the complexities and richness of people's heritages. This familial reticence masked or distorted racial specificities and centered singularity, constructing families and respondents as "monoracial." Given the range of social problems that families must deal with in their lives, they may not prioritize the management of race in relation to any number of other concerns they have on a daily basis. Constructing or presenting the family unit as racially cohesive may strategically simplify social life. Alternately, it may reflect a denial of race and a refusal to recognize how powerful racism remains and in the way it structures and shapes the quality of our everyday lives, for better or worse. Constructing a racially cohesive unit may offer the family a way of appearing as such: socially cohesive, integrated, intact, whole. In addition, such cohesion might mitigate some of the social problems these families face (in response to racism, or other social forces).

Just as individuals have been found to choose one ethnicity, individuals and families may choose one race for similar ease and simplicity. Opting for a singular race is often done strategically to access privilege or minimize disprivilege (Harris-Perry 2011). That families conveyed to respondents these messages of racial singularity meant that the respondents were implicitly and/or explicitly discouraged from claiming their preferred racial identities—a reality that contrasts with contemporary arguments couched in neoliberal ideas about identity as free choice. Wallenstein (2002:250) argues:

> This is America. You can be anyone you want to be. At least, that is far more true after *Loving* than it was before. The notion of changeability has come to apply more to race than it long did, so racial identity is more like religion, occupation, and place of residence—more subject to individual choice. Yet it is generally far, of course, from simply a matter of individual choice. And in any case, how to identify oneself when a simple category is demanded and none seems to apply? Finding a solution to this question, many people have come to call themselves "biracial" or "multiracial."

Despite his contention, respondents with part-black parentage or ancestry felt less freedom to choose (Lee and Bean 2004; Rockquemore and Brunsma 2002; Khanna 2010, 2011). The persistence of hypodescent (Khanna 2010), coupled with many of these parents' participation in the Civil Rights Movement and racial consciousness, provided some context for the benevolent border patrolling that many respondents faced.

Hearing accounts of their parents' pride in blackness signaled a subtle disinvestment in mixture to some multiracial people with black parentage. Some respondents challenged this disinvestment and relied on their (limited) knowledge of familial racial mixture to delimit, rather than limit, the ways that they asserted and performed their racial identities. This delimiting of racial identity happened within and across racial categories.

Some respondents noted the lack of recognition of them as "multiracial" by primary and secondary group members (significant others) who benevolently policed their racially ambiguous appearances. Leilani, a Black Hawaiian woman, noted, "A lot of times during the winter, one friend in particular, she's always like, 'Girl, I can't wait until summertime so you can get your tan back, because you look pale.' And

I'm like, 'Okay, thank you. You look pale, too.' This is a black friend. She's light skinned so I told her that she was pale, too." This exchange illustrates how some friends of multiracial individuals benevolently border patrol them. As a Black Hawaiian with red hair, light skin, and freckles who has been misread as "Puerto Rican, Mexican, Colombian, and Polynesian," Leilani is often told that she looks white; she is seldom read as black or multiracial. Not only is Leilani's comment funny, but it reveals how she benevolently (playfully) border patrols her black (light-skinned) friend (as she herself comments about her friend's potential racial mixture).

> Very few people have recognized me as being black. Actually just yesterday this [black] girl told me, "I just thought you were a very light-skinned black female." But there's very few instances of that.... Sometimes I feel like people that I do consider to be my friends who are black try to discredit my blackness because I'm not fully black.... It's just that "I was raised by a black mother. You were raised by a black mother. So really, what's the difference?"

Leilani presumably appeared "too much like white" for her black friends to accept her as black. She strategically managed her multiraciality by highlighting commonalities between herself and her friends. This attempt reflected her desire to build bridges, rather than reinforce racial divides across color lines (see Moraga and Anzaldua 1983). She tried to forge connections, despite feeling the tensions of these social divisions. She felt she would have had an easier time cultivating these connections had her father been black. She believes many others would have viewed her as "more authentically black." This is notable in that it challenges the idea of women as "culture keepers." It also troubles the historical reality of black mothers birthing multiracial children, all of whom were recognized as black, even if to varying degrees. The implication that having a black father facilitates the connections to other black people generates more questions than answers. For example, "Is black masculinity and manhood a more "authentic" version of blackness than black femininity and womanhood?"

Leilani's comments speak to, and challenge, the role black mothers play in the process of racial socialization (Collins 1991). That socialization, scholars argue, differs depending on the race of their children (although black woman are socially not allowed to have "white" babies). The socialization of light- versus dark-skinned children might differ. Books such as Kerry Ann Rockquemore and Tracey

Laszloffy's (2005), *Raising Biracial Children*, suggest the process *is* different socially because of the way multiracial people are treated during social interactions and in society in general (not because they are biologically different) (see Spencer 2010).

David, a white Latino, discussed many of these experiential differences in our interview. His comments echo that of Leilani. David reportedly faced benevolent border patrolling from graduate school friends. He shared experiences of living in the South:

> When they would see me take off my shirt, you know, early in the Spring—"Oye, [David], el sol es gratis." Which means, "Listen, David, the sunlight's free." And so my whiteness as a phenotype has always been, you know, sort of on me in my home. Now, in school, especially later in life, there was always this ambiguous, "What is, what are you?" Asking my college roommate, "What is he? Is he Lebanese? Or what is he?" That kind of stuff. So obviously, there was always some external, not sure where to put me, um, and so I grew up with that biracial experience but I've changed the way I've owned that as I just became more aware of the power and privilege issues.

David offered ample examples of his own awareness of how his appearance shapes his reality, as evidenced in his observation, "My whiteness as a phenotype has always been...sort of on me." Unlike light- or white-skinned respondents who attempt to maximize the perks of being multiracial, David does not exploit his whiteness. Instead, he uses his whiteness to trouble this racial privilege, by drawing attention to the disparities that exist in a racially divisive society. Even though he does not intentionally access white racial (and male) privilege, he enjoys it nonetheless. He may take a critical stance against privilege, or attempt to reject it, but he knows that it operates in his favor because he looks white and because that is the way that privilege works.

David understands and remains knowledgeable about white racial privilege in part because he educates and involves himself in difficult conversations about race and racism; he considers himself a social justice activist, or someone who works to challenge and eradicate the racial inequities that so discomfort him. He negotiates his white privilege from his precarious position as a white Latino. Being both white and Latino creates some cognitive dissonance. It simultaneously establishes and compromises his credibility, grants him racial privilege and undermines it all at once. His antiracist activism and heightened racial consciousness contrast with many of the white-looking multiracial people I interviewed, many of whom attempt to activate or secure the privileges of whiteness. David's example provides a useful transition to discussing the contrasting behavior exhibited by many of the multiracial people that I interviewed, namely the desiring of whiteness for all that it affords (Seshadri-Crooks 2000). This desiring of whiteness, or of improving one's position in the racial hierarchy, can become another form of borderism: beneficiary border patrolling.

Beneficiary Border Patrolling

While most of the multiracial respondents spoke of the various ways that they managed their multiracial identities or a shifting mixture that reflects identity changes between different singular racial identities, a handful of respondents were not interpolated by the term "multiracial" at all. Initially puzzled by this, I probed for further detail and requested elaboration. The explanations and narratives that I heard revealed a way that some multiracial people were growing such an identity, experiencing what I call "incipient mixture," as they learned racial lessons and explored their families' biographies.

One respondent, Soraya, a White and Asian multiracial woman described her experiences growing up with her white mother. She explained to me that she asserted a white identity, like her mother, in part because of conversations the two of them had regarding family, race, and identity. At one point she questioned her mother, whose response to Soraya's question, "What race am I?" was, "You're white like me." Because of this interaction, and with an appearance that approximates whiteness, Soraya chose to assert a white identity. After her white mother and Asian father divorced in Soraya's youth, Soraya likely found it easier to assert a shared identity with her mother. That would likely deflect personal questions about her and her family, minimizing any potential pain provoked by the inquiries of peers, friends, or neighbors. Inheriting and sharing her mother's whiteness also minimizes other people's intrusive questions; much of the malevolent borderism is kept at bay when multiracial children closely approximate a parent, particularly in single-parent households. These resemblances deflect much of the malevolence otherwise directed at and documented by multiracial (adult) children who experience visual dislocation from their parents.

I also argue that asserting a white identity offered Soraya other benefits. She could enjoy all of the privileges of whiteness, without any of the penalties of being a visible racial and ethnic minority or having a multiracial and multiethnic heritage. She indicated that people primarily learn that she is "half-Indian" based on her name. She can otherwise largely conceal, and selectively reveal, that she has multiracial heritage as she desires.

Some of the racial lessons that she learned about race and racial identity may help her maintain her white identity individually, which in turn maintain the family's collective identity as white, as opposed to interracial, particularly given the predominantly white spaces that she inhabits. This appears as a significant social force. Contrary to the "best of both worlds" narrative, "opting for white" makes the most sense for some multiracial people who feel that whiteness is their preferred racial location. Arguably, choosing this location or moving towards whiteness works to secure white racial privileges that might not otherwise be easily distributed to respondents like Soraya.

Curious if she expressed her preferred white identity in ways that others validated, I inquired about this with her. Soraya shared the surprise her best friend expressed when she heard Soraya identify herself as white. When her best friend questioned her choice to identify as white, seeking some reasoning for this decision, Soraya explained, "I said, 'I don't know. I've just always have done that' and I know it's weird but I've never thought of myself as multiracial even though I *am*. That word has never been used in my head to describe myself, which is kind of weird. But that was the first time she put it in my head."

Up until that conversation, Soraya did not seem to question her own racial identity choices, but began to once she started to grapple with some of the contradictions created by her racial location and articulation of her preferred white identity. Being questioned by her friend heightened Soraya's awareness that racial identity is much more complex than a parental directive or presentation of race as a simple equation: "I'm white, so you are white." It is important to note that the absence of her father in her everyday life could account, in part, for the attendant absence of her Asian heritage in her self-identity. She discursively "disappears difference" by claiming singular whiteness. She illustrates my earlier point about the complexity of single race categories. Categorical whiteness accommodates her articulation of mixture, even as she fails to acknowledge it or even because she refuses to acknowledge it.

Participating in the interview conversation encouraged Soraya to consider these questions more deeply. The conversation invited her to arrive at her own self-understanding of race, rather than simply and uncritically accepting any well-intentioned but potentially misguiding parental directives. Her experiences growing up in a largely colormute and colorblind family, who only talks about race when it proves beneficial to securing the privileges of whiteness, were similar to several respondents' stories as well. I consider this approach to parenting as a kind of borderism: parental borderism. More specifically, when parents strategically avoid or engage in racial conversations to protect racial privilege, particularly for their multiracial children, I consider that action to be "beneficiary border patrolling." Soraya, then, is not unlike other respondents who reported minimally discussing race and identity in their families of origin.

Like most of the respondents with White and Asian heritage, Louise also had very few discussions specifically about race. Her experience mirrors much of Soraya's in its "white like me" dimension (see Gallagher 2004, 2000; Wise 2004; Dalmage 2004b). In a process Brown, Carnoy, Currie, Duster, Oppenheimer, Schultz, and Wellman (2005), as well as Andersen (2003), describe as "whitewashing," Louise detailed how she experienced this shifting from a white identity to a multiracial one:

> As far as I recall, I identified as white, I wasn't aware that I was half Korean and even if I was told that I was half Korean, I didn't really understand the concept behind that—that that meant that, "Oh, there's an Asian country named Korea, and these are the culture values." I didn't know, I knew nothing...I didn't have a schema for that. So I didn't know what that was. My real father, my biological father, is a hard-core racist, which people find really ironic considering he married outside of his race.... And I grew up, mostly white, with a mostly white racial identity. I went to school, and a lot of people used to make fun of me about my eyes, and you know the way I looked, and I never understood, I literally was colorblind. I looked at myself, I was like, "I don't see how I'm different." I looked at a white girl, "I don't see how I'm different." My hair is dark or whatever. You know? I didn't see the slanted eyes. "What do you mean, 'slanted eyes'? I don't know what you're referring to.' You know what I mean? I was like, "My eyes are just like *yours*!" You know? I had no comprehension of what they were talking about.

To be clear, Louise is not, in fact, "literally" colorblind. She is colorblind, figuratively speaking however, as she typifies the person who learned to rely on colorblind narratives to elide conversations about race (see Gallagher 2003b). She produces or relies on racetalk to refer to and reflect on shifting racial consciousness when she makes note of her "slanted eyes" (see Myers 2003, 2005). The term becomes a racialized code word for Asian as Louise advances the idea that Asian eyes appear this particular way. This idea essentializes race through the suggestion that "all Asians look alike" or that they share similarities in physical characteristics. These comments biologize race by locating difference in the body and not in the categories used to contain or organize those bodies. Louise's colorblindness also gets expressed in terms of what she sees as familiar (versus foreign). In her lived experiences, she is surrounded by whites. Korean people remain "foreign" or unfamiliar to her, despite the fact that her mother is Korean.

In her book, *Transformation Now!*, womanist writer AnaLouise Keating (2013) borrows from and builds on the work of Gloria Anzaldua (1987) to describe this shifting of racial consciousness. She refers to the transformative process of shifting, inviting readers to let Anzaldua's words ("now let us shift") resonate. What Louise describes above captures that shifting process and her incipient multiracial identity. She shares how she begins to see herself in racialized ways or differently racialized ways that are complicated by her in/visible mixture. As her consciousness shifts, she experiences shifting mixture from white to multiracial. She may not claim a "multiracial" identity, but she develops a better understanding of the term and how it could be applicable to her, should she so desire.

Her comments about her father beg the question, "How can a 'hard-core racist' marry 'outside of his race'?" As Dalmage (2000) suggests, many people in interracial relationships or partnerships make their partner the "exception to the rule." This makes it possible to accommodate or reconcile racist ideologies by recognizing one's partner as exceptional. This practice signals one limitation of the celebration of interracial relationships as the remedy of racism: the failure to see interracial intimacy as a site at which people reproduce racism (see also Roithmayr 2014; Spencer 2010). Louise's observations draw attention to that reality: that the very site of racial bridge-building and "loving" revolutionary acts can also be the site of profound cognitive dissonance and irony where racism and interracial intimacy tenuously reside (see Root 2001).

With a father who espoused racist ideologies and subscribed to colorblind racial rhetoric, and without her Korean mother equipping her with information about culture, race, and heritage, Louise had a blurry ethnic or racial road map with which to navigate her multiracial identity. She had few reference points for understanding her "multiracial" features (I put this in quotes to highlight the debate that race is not biological). Like many multiracial people who grow up without racial reflections of themselves in their immediate social settings, Louise may have wondered, "Does anyone else look like me?" (see Nakazawa 2003). Per her observation or estimation, her "double eyelids" and other "white" features betrayed her Korean-ness, marking her atypical appearance as more white than Asian (see Kaw 2003).

Louise's comments draw attention to the level of invisible mixture that may be another dilemma for "invisibly mixed" multiracial people. If they are negotiating an ambiguous appearance, or one that is not "clearly mixed," there may, in fact, be other multiracial people in their presence who are effectively hiding in plain sight. Without mutual recognition, they have little way of knowing that there are other people that look like them who share their racial identity. In addition, social settings that appear racially homogenous on the surface may have multiracial people present, who may be hiding in plain sight.

Like Louise, Lexie, another white Asian multiracial woman, articulated her own experience learning about race and identity within her ostensibly interracial family (see Ausdale and Feagin 2001). She described her father's nonchalance and reticence in response to her questions about race. Lexie provided this example of her father's colormuteness:

My dad, I remember one time, my dad was like, "Well, if it (a form or application) makes you pick one, just put white because I'm white.[2] My mother was like, "Whatever, it doesn't matter." And then later it was, "Well, you'll get more tax breaks if you don't put white." So you'll always put the other.[3] You'll always put Asian if you can. So that's the point of it now.... But I still put both. I still put both anyway.

Lexie later clarified that when her father said, "Just put white because I'm white," he likely meant, "It was more of a convenience thing. He said it like, 'Oh, just put that down.'" That he casually guided her to just check white instead of both while her mother guided her to check Asian is instructive.

Putting "the other" could easily be interpreted two ways: "the other" being "other than white" or "the Other," which equates multiracial with "Other" as it has commonly been presented in formal racial identification projects. This information ("just put white") contradicted the message her mother delivered, that Lexie should "opt for Asian" where possible. This also contrasts with evidence that suggests a tendency for white Asian multiracials to "opt for white" (see Rockquemore and Arend 2002). The implication of "affirmative action" associated with the comments Lexie mentions her mother making explains the emphasis on the "Other" status. This challenges existing evidence about white privilege. It obscures the intersections of race and gender privilege that white women are primary beneficiaries under consideration of the affirmation action policy (see Bonilla-Silva 2003a; Myers 2005). The motivations of either identity, as white or Asian but not both, suggest that the former two options hold more currency than the latter (multiracial) one.

What Lexie describes above also illustrates that her father may be participating in various forms of borderism, including protective border patrolling. As a white man, he may think of his daughter in a "white like me" manner. He may do this to protect her from any racial discrimination she would potentially face if she is perceived as a person of color. Much of the criticism launched at interracial families targets parents who minimize race or do not properly prepare their children for encounters with racism. A white father who attempts these "protective" lessons by simply reracializing his child as white misses the point about his multiracial child's racial reality. While Lexie may have a white experience socially, she may also encounter racism without even realizing it. She may falsely believe her white identity will buffer her from hostile comments, gendered racism, and the like.

Lexie's father may also want to preserve the privileges of whiteness and, thus, would need to socialize her as white in order to secure these privileges. This attempt to shift mixture towards whiteness is beneficiary border patrolling. The term recognizes the "invisible privileges of whiteness" as beneficial to white people individually and within families or other groups. Because multiracial children often learn about how they *should* identify racially and ethnically through significant others such as their parents and/or primary caregivers, the mixed messages embedded in racial socialization in/validate these identities.

As Gallagher (2003), Brunsma (2006b), and others demonstrate, many white parents of multiracial children socialize them to claim a white identity, where possible. This literature recognizes that parents' racial identification of their multiracial children works towards securing whiteness and white privilege, by proxy, for their children. However, in the literature, as in real life, little space is made to accommodate the agency of multiracial children. Rather than support the preferred racial identities of their children (see Rockquemore and Laszloffy 2005), many parents seem to be attempting to help their children access white privilege by proxy or by virtue of the child's white appearance. They do so even as their children resist, or claim what Woodfork (2005) refers to as shifting whiteness, or identities that are variations of whiteness including "off white" (Fine, Weis, Powell, and Wong 1997); "not quite white" (Lazarre 1996; Reddy 1997; Rothman 2006); "honorary black" (Twine and Steinbulger 2006), or what I call "black by proxy." As multiracial children grow into adulthood, and enhance their racial literacy, they may be better equipped to express their preferred racial identities in and on their own terms.

Any disjuncture between parental racial identification (imposed) and the preferred racial identity (chosen) of the multiracial child(ren) can result in invalidation. This disjuncture can create a gap between (parental) perception and (multiracial child's) reality. This validation and invalidation gets expressed through racial redistricting (Gallagher 2004) and what I call "beneficiary border patrolling." Beneficiary border patrolling intends to "expand racial boundaries" to envelop multiracial children into the racial group of higher social status;in most instances this means claiming white racial identification—the most privileged racial group (Bonilla-Silva 2003a) and envied social location in the US racial hierarchy.

This work restores the polyvocality of multiracial people, by showing the variation in their preferred racial identities (Rockquemore 2005), often in contradistinction to the racial redistricting many parents practice. That is, while some of the literature from the past two decades suggest a racial reconfiguration and shifting mixture in *white* members (mostly mothers) in interracial families, some of the respondents (with a white parent) described having more of a "possessive investment in whiteness" than their white parents (see Lipsitz 2006). This, coupled with colorblindness and colormuteness, encourages white parents to socialize their (multiracial) children as white and maintains white privilege for white-looking multiracial people (see Harris 1993 for discussion about whiteness as property).

The experiences above of Lexie, Louise and Soraya illustrate the phenomenon of "racial redistricting," by highlighting parental motivations to access white privilege by racially classifying their offspring as white (Gallagher 2004). This redistricting happens more often with White and Asian and White and Latino/s parents and less so with Black and Latino/a and White and Black ones (due to the persistence of hypodescent). As a result, parents invested in whiteness as property border patrolled their multiracial White and Asian or White and Latino children to claim whiteness (Harris 1993; Lipsitz 2006). However, not all parents participated in beneficiary border patrolling. Many Asian parents deploy discourses to discourage their children from forming interracial relationships of their own.

Even among Black Latino/a parents, beneficiary border patrollers worked to remind respondents of the important distinction between themselves (as "more than black") and those who were "just black." By promoting cultural maintenance, these parents actively celebrated their cultural heritage and signaled to their children the positive aspects of their cultural heritage. These messages often contradicted one another and emerged in the form of beneficiary border patrolling.

Feminist Cherrie L. Moraga (2002) offers a literary example of this type of border patrolling:

> No one ever quite told me this (that light was right), but I knew that being light was something valued in my family (who were all Chicano, with the exception of my father). In fact, everything about my upbringing (at least what occurred on a conscious level) attempted to bleach me of what color I did have. Although I was fluent in it, I was never taught much Spanish at home. I picked up what I did learn from school and from over-heard snatches of conversations among my relatives and mother (Moraga 2002: 25).

In writing about the precarious negotiation of being both brown *and* white, Moraga (1983) shares how she implicitly learned about the liability of brownness and the currency of whiteness through her brown-skinned mother. Much the same can be said by many of the participants in my research study.

In similar ways, Lexie learned about the valence of whiteness. Arguably, Lexie could still secure some or most of these privileges as an honorary white person, and her father, as a beneficiary border patroller, would believe that her assertion of a white identity would only enhance this effort (to access racial privilege). Lexie's father may, quite frankly, not want his daughter to be seen as an Asian woman (or a multiracial Asian woman) given the proliferation of positive and negative stereotypes about these groups. This paternal desire to protect his daughter could be read as paternalistic or it could simply be read as a father figuring out how best to protect his daughter. If he has insight into any of the racism that his Asian partner faces as his wife and Lexie's mother, in addition to her own social location, he would understandably want to shield his daughter from malevolent borderism.

Without blatantly doing so, each parent promoted his/her own race as preferable, encouraging Lexie to use her multiracial/ethnic heritage to her benefit in additive, not multiplicative, parts. In her interpretation, her parents never explicitly policed her behavior or offered directives. They reportedly never said "anything like, 'Well, around me you do this, and around her, you do this.'" These contradictions are not resolved easily during interviews or in the respondents' everyday lives. These contradictions support my earlier point that parents (or other family members) are not always racially literate in desirable ways. These contradictions allow Lexie to believe that her parents are indifferent to her racial identity although their conversations with her suggest otherwise.

Another example of parental beneficiary border patrolling is provided by Lexie again. While she could not recall her parents racializing her, Lexie nevertheless offered examples where they racialized her by pointing out (however humorously) behaviors that they felt were characteristic of her composite parts: "There's this Korean dish called kimchi. It's hot and spicy, the cabbage dish. And so my dad would be like, 'That's your kimchi Asian hot temper going through you. You got that from your mom.' There's stuff like that. And she (respondent's mother) does that, too. She'll be like, 'You have hairy legs because of your dad.' But that's about the extent of it." In what Myers (2005) might describe as a "caricature" of brownness in her discussion of "race talk," the "kimchi Asian hot temper" provides an example of an Asian stereotype. This discursively divides Lexie into halves: one part white, the other Asian. This gives her a fractional identity, rather than a whole one (see O'Hearn 1998). This divisiveness could be read as a form of border patrolling in that her father's race talk discursively differentiates her brownness from his whiteness, both recognizing and disallowing her "same/difference" (both/and, or either/neither).

In contrast to those who are limited in their racial literacy, other family members and parents in particular, may purposefully *mask* this literacy so that they and/or their multiracial children can explicitly benefit from white (or light-skinned) privilege (see Gallagher 2004; Campbell 2007; Brunsma 2006a,b). Without direct access to the parents of my respondents, I can only speculate that some of them have very high levels of racial literacy, and engage in various forms of border patrolling with their children to ensure that they can access as much racial privilege as possible, particularly if they publicly claim a privileged (white) racial identity. Not only do parents participate in this process, but so too do multiracial people, as I discuss in Chapter 5. Parents and multiracial children alike may blend racial borders when it proves convenient to do so.

Amidst the divisiveness of society exists a blurring of boundaries. The blending of interracial families occurs racially but also often on cultural and linguistic terms as well. People's connections to culture and language are mitigated by a number of factors including: proximity to relatives or various members of a cultural community, distance from other speakers of the shared language, and immersion (or lack thereof) in cultural groups or settings with similar linguistic background. Individual, familial, and collective patterns of migration also shape access to language and culture, with the gaps created by departure and distance from homelands often being closed by or managed in the technoscape (Appadurai 1996).

For some of the research participants, managing their multiracial heritage involved recuperating or attempting to access more of their cultural heritage to strengthen their cultural competence and self-understanding. By some appearances, people in interracial relationships are often regarded as having thick racial identities and a deep sense of cultural connection. However, this is not always the case. I discovered this in my analysis of narratives shared by respondents who desired greater knowledge about their cultural heritage and language. This desire often went unfulfilled in very Americanized and/or whitewashed families.

With an assimilated or "honorary white" mother, Lexie missed out on opportunities to learn about or be exposed to different aspects of Korean culture through her immediate and extended family. She was not able to cultivate that cultural competency or racial literacy that people gather through processes such as storytelling and the sharing of various traditions. Were she to learn these ways of life or gather that information, Lexie would have needed to assume that responsibility on her own. The process would become a formal one, not a casual familial one designed to share a wealth of knowledge or permit any cultural inheritance among Lexie's generation.

Lexie also noted the lack of literacy, in terms of fluency and familiarity, with the Korean language. Most of her immediate and extended family members who spoke Korean did not teach Lexie the language directly. They also did not speak Korean often enough for her to enjoy any vicarious benefits of this linguistic and cultural exposure or immersion. This point relates to my earlier suggestion that not all multiracial people are always born into already interracial families. Instead, some of the multiracial respondents I interviewed described having parents positioned in two different racial group categories but who shared colorblind ideologies and perspectives. This is a different reflection of shifting mixture as it captures the shift in racial consciousness among people in intimate interracial relationships. Over time, the bonds built between members of a couple can inform this change or motivate this shift. In "interracial" relationships, if the proximity between the white and honorary white (Asian) parent is close, then the "inter"-racial quality of the relationship could be called into question. If the gap between the "inter" is small, one could argue that "multiracial" children are growing up in families that closely simulate or approximate ones where all of the family members share the same or similar racial identities. This closeness or proximity is illustrated in Lexie's family.

Most of the white Asian respondents, like Lexie, lamented their lack of language ability and cultural connection. Lexie expressed both "a strong desire" to learn and a disappointment in not knowing Korean. Contrary to Kibria's (2002) work that suggested parents promoted and cultivated a racialized ethnicity in their second-generation Korean and Chinese children, Lexie possessed more of a distilled ethnicity, partly because she felt denied opportunities to successfully acquire Korean language skills (see Ang 2001).

With some frustration, Lexie asked her mother, "Why didn't you teach us?!" Out of respect or otherwise to her father, Lexie's mother ended the Korean language lessons she had started when her children were young. Lexie explains, "And from what I understand, it was because my dad didn't know Korean. He knew the basics, so my mom got to try to teach us. When we were of the age, the same age we were learning English, we would go to our dad, trying to ask for something in Korean, and he didn't understand, and my dad was like, 'I'm not going to *not* understand what my children are telling me, so stop teaching them.'" The lessons ended with their father's impatience once his own frustration reached its tipping point.

As I discussed above, parents may engage in racial border patrolling for a number of reasons. They may want to protect their children from becoming targets of racist hostility or they want their children to benefit from any racial privileges that they can access. Lexie's comments illustrate her parents' practicing a kind of beneficiary border patrolling, as they engaged in racial redistricting (see Gallagher 2004). This practice reinforced her whiteness and minimized her racial mixture (brownness and/or Asian-ness). Her parents' border patrolling worked to ensure that Lexie would more likely access (and enjoy) honorary white or white status. In other words, her "whiteness wins."

Not only did *not* learning Korean help keep her father content, it facilitated Lexie's connection to whiteness and her disconnection to (or dilution/thinning of) Korean language and culture. That Lexie expressed disappointment in not knowing Korean *counters* her parents' ostensible imposition of whiteness. This reminds us that multiracial people can resist racial border patrolling, despite the potential penalties to doing so.

Peg, an Asian American-identified transracially adopted white and Asian (Korean) multiracial woman, shared a similar experience around language and racial, ethnic, and cultural identities. She observed, "I lost the language. My mom didn't want me to speak the language anymore. There was more of an emphasis there to be more, without explicitly [saying so], like being white." Rather than be encouraged to explore her heritage and acquire information about her biological or birth family,

Peg's family, based on her account, practiced a generalized genealogical silence and secrecy around race matters. This racial reticence further disrupted her knowledge of her Asian heritage. The lack of balanced information, impeded by her adoption, inhibited Peg's immersion in racially mixed spaces; limited her access to Koreans; and, exposed her predominantly to whites.

Despite growing up in an interracial family that internalized external pressures to assimilate, Peg communicated to me a preferred racial identity that encompasses all of her known heritage. In feeling border patrolled by her family, among others, and wanting to explicitly disrupt the expanding boundaries of whiteness, Peg pointedly rejected white privilege by asserting, "I do *not* want to be like white." Her personal experiences involve challenging racial stereotypes about Asians and confronting racial discrimination. Often these stereotypes and racism were concealed by and expressed as racetalk; it confirmed that strangers viewed her as Asian, which compromised the "honorary white" status her parents had hoped she would enjoy. Once, a stranger told Peg that she reminded him of an Asian American comedienne/actress (Margaret Cho), she quipped, "Am I always going to be compared to Margaret Cho?" This stranger's observation suggests that, beyond the interchangeability of Asian women, Peg was perceived as Asian, not white, in that moment. Because she had not internalized a white identity, she arguably was better able to handle the racial slight otherwise, she would likely have been confused about being cast as Asian.

Both Peg and Miki described experiences that sound "whitewashed" (Brown, Carnoy, Currie, Duster, Oppenheimer, Schultz, and Wellman 2005). Miki mentioned growing up in an interracial family where her white (Irish and Scottish) mother and multiracial White and Asian (Japanese) father also did not discuss race matters much. Miki explained that she thought her father, who "identifies more with the white and that's why it's never come up as far as what I should identify as," embraced his whiteness more because "it's easier to be one thing." Evidence exists to support this notion: "It's easier to be one thing" when that one thing is whiteness (see Gallagher 2006).

Notably, Miki's comments reveal the way that parents may police their own multiracial identity, or self-border patrol; I turn to this topic in Chapter 5, as it relates to the respondents in my study. Here, I want to suggest that some multiracial people, like Miki, may learn important and implicit messages about their racial identity from their multiracial parents. When I asked what sort of conversations she had in her family, Miki suggested that her parents seldom talked about race. In many ways, the absence of these critical conversations inadvertently reinforces the importance and invisibility of whiteness. This was a lesson Miki learned through her family racial socialization, that race does not matter, and that "multiracial" can be collapsed, or almost disappeared, into whiteness. Her suggestion that her parents would *prefer* that she identify herself as white, even as she indicated that she "wouldn't change" being mixed since "it's not a bad thing," reveals the productive tensions that surround racial identity negotiations within families. While people's preferred identities should be respected, they may also be questioned. In other words, beneficiary border patrolling by parents may meet its limitations in instances where the multiracial person does not look "white enough" to access the privileges of whiteness or even honorary whiteness. Parents may pressure or encourage their multiracial children to "opt for white." Multiracial children (at various ages) may reject or resist that pressure, choosing to identify as they desire.

Miki's experience provides a few interesting examples: 1) the expanding boundaries of whiteness work to include not only her father, but potentially her as well; 2) that multiracial parents may "opt for white" and practice the colormuteness (Pollock 2005) often associated with whiteness (see McIntosh 1998, and Wise 2004 for explanation of how silence protects white privilege); and, 3) multiracial parents whose preferred racial identity is white may likely socialize their children as white as well.

Future research should examine these patterns and the motivations that multiracial parents have for the way they choose to socialize their children. The examples above, including Miki's, also highlight how "multiracial" does not always survive the next generation (Bratter 2007), especially if "multiracial" parents and children prefer to assert white racial identities in public *and* in private. This point is significant in its recognition of the racial mixture in the national population. While most people do not claim to be racially mixed, an increasing number of people do. How multiracial people manage their racial identities in public and private in part reflects the process of racial socialization that they experienced and will likely perpetuate with others. This racial inheritance can be negotiated, despite its powerful forces encouraging consent, so that families conform and experience cohesion and harmony. This is accomplished most clearly in interracial families where white multiracial children are guided towards whiteness as the ideal identity.

While some scholars contend that a pattern of "culture keeping" particularly exists within racial and ethnic minority families, my research shows this pattern can dissipate in some interracial families. Racial socialization that promotes intergenerational whiteness stands in contrast to the literature on culture keeping, because it illustrates how whiteness prevails. As some of the above examples illustrate, multiracial children who look white are encouraged to claim whiteness, as opposed to multiracial and/or multiethnic identities. Arguably, families can more fully "achieve whiteness" when their multiracial members claim whiteness for themselves, making the unit a racially cohesive one.

In her research, Nazli Kibria (2002) posits that Asian parents cultivate racial and ethnic pride, communicate cultural values, and attempt to preserve their language and other components of their heritage. Given the racial/ethnic thinning Yancey (2003) spoke of in relation to Asians and Latinos who interracially marry, the lack of racial socialization, or a tendency towards whiteness, makes sense. Unlike white mothers of black and white biracial children, white parents of white and Asian and white and Latino/a children often racially socialize through silence or colormuteness. Because whiteness remains central yet invisible, it remains ostensibly unmarked, unnamed, and unseen (see Dyer 1997; Frankenberg 1993).

Colormute practices may falsely convey to multiracial children growing up in households with at least one white-identified parent that whiteness is their default race. In the absence of meaningful conversations about race, multiracial children learn little about how to discuss race or why race matters. Instead, they learn this racial lacuna well, including how such silences protect the "property of whiteness" (see Harris 1983). These silences conceal any racial and/or ethnic multiplicity that exists in the family. It impedes the racial inheritance of this multiracial heritage and any knowledge or information that could be shared among family members.

When parents do discuss race, many tend to rely on colorblind rhetoric, minimize or ignore racism, or hope to racially identify their children as white. For example, Pilar, a light-skinned black white woman, related how she discovered more information about her mother, who she initially thought of as a white person. Through overheard conversations, Pilar learned that her white-identified Spanish and German mother was technically mixed, at least ethnically. Hearing her mother talk to her relatives in Spanish and prepare Spanish food at meals prompted Pilar to ask her mother questions about race and their family biography. Pilar learned that what seemed like a symbolic Spanish ethnicity entailed having Spanish relatives; this included her "full Spanish" maternal grandmother whose house she visited where relatives spoke Spanish and prepared Spanish food. Her new understanding of her mother and grandmother impacted the way she developed her own racial sense of self, since she primarily understood her identity until then as black and white biracial. Enveloping this new information into her racial identity shifted her mixture from black/white biracial to black/white Latina. This shifting mixture reflects a shift in racial consciousness altered by her acquisition of information regarding the rich heritage of her family. Had she not listened to those lessons or expressed much curiosity, she might have continued to overlook this connection to her Spanish family, culture, and heritage.

Another example was offered by Curlis, who noted that her family seldom spoke about its diversity. She regretted that her father talked little about being Puerto Rican[4]; she expressed disappointment about her parents' criticism of her preferred multiracial identity. She provided the example of discovering that her dad was Latino, even though "he never taught us Spanish;" "I didn't ever realize that he could speak Spanish until one day, I don't even know how old I was, we were in a Mexican restaurant and he goes to order and he's like, 'Oh, blah, blah, blah.' You know? He starts going on (placing his order in Spanish), and I'm like, 'Dad, what was that?!' and he's like, 'Oh.'"

Beyond some speculation, Curlis had little way of knowing that her father was "more than white." In the same way that others often "read between the lines" to decode racial and ethnic ambiguity in others, Curlis conducted her own ethnic/racial "reading between the lines" to figure her father out. Her discovery of her father's Spanish language ability initially puzzled her. So, too, did her parents' efforts to discourage her from learning or speaking Spanish and identifying as both white and Puerto Rican (or Latina). By claiming to be both, Curlis refused to be border patrolled by her family.

She provided another example of multiracial adult children asserting their agency around their racial identity:

> My parents and I disagree a lot about my race because, um, especially as I got older, like at the end of my high school career I was like, "Well, you know, I'm mixed." I told my parents, so "I'm mixed. I finally figured it out. I'm not just white. I'm not Hispanic. I'm mixed." And they were like, "But 'mixed' is mixed white and black." And I was like, "No, no. It can be anything" and uh, my parents were like, "No, you are white," and my dad, who is completely Puerto Rican, I was like, "But you are not even white." And he was like, "I am white. I'm a white Hispanic."

She also rejected the unearned privileges that inspire racial redistricting and parental beneficiary border patrolling in the first place. In claiming an experience akin to what Salvador Vidal-Ortiz (2004) considers a "white person of color," Curlis contested the whiteness bestowed on her. She resisted white privilege, attempting to reject the inheritance of whiteness (Harris 1993; Roediger 2003; Keenan 2014). In doing so, she arguably went from someone her parents wanted to perceive as white to multiracial. Given her parents' borderism, they likely did not validate the multiracial identity that Curlis claimed for herself. This rejection or invalidation of her identity shows the tensions that exist in families and how influential they can be in encouraging multiracial children to assert (or not) their preferred racial identities to everyone. The example Curlis and other respondents provide illustrates that even ostensibly interracially married or partnered parents of multiracial children may participate in border patrolling. When these parents misunderstand and invalidate their child's/children's preferred identities, they send powerful messages about the racial identity options available to multiracial children, suggesting that parents should make such decisions. One point I want to underscore is that this "parents know best" perspective is not always the case. When parents perpetuate colorblindness, diminish the reality of racism, or otherwise occupy a racial location and embrace a set of ideologies that may or may not align with that of their children, they do not know best. Instead, as evidenced by the narratives of my respondents, each individual knows his or her racial sense of self best. Parents can prove to be supportive guides on this journey but they should not overtly or overly determine their children's racial subjectivities or their sense of self.

The narrative that Curlis offered shows how she tried to resolve the tension stemming from her family's reluctance to openly embrace their racial and ethnic heritage. Instead of keeping her Puerto Rican-ness optional or symbolic, she incorporated it into her identity and presentation of self. Rather than straighten her hair or conceal her racial and ethnic mix, she preferred activating her mixture in social situations to form friendships and alliances with others. This public acknowledgment reportedly frustrated her father, and her family more generally; they wanted her to assert a singular white identity. In challenging her parents, Curlis countered their borderism and affirmed her multiracial identity. She refused to "inherit the entitlement of whiteness" (see Keenan 2014).

Her discussion exemplified the very power struggles that take place in families, as parental racial identifications of or designations for their multiracial children (even through adulthood) often differ from that of the multiracial person. This does not even fully begin to acknowledge the difficulty that might result from multiracial individuals asserting protean, or perpetually shifting, identities. That is, at times, the multiracial child may assert an identity that only occasionally aligns with the parents' way of seeing him or her. Resolving these disjunctures sometimes results in the multiracial child encountering identity invalidation because the family members prohibited or disregarded the multiracial individual's desire to assert this multiplicity. When her father says to her that "being Latino has nothing to do with your race" Curlis appeared hurt at his suggestion because she claims a multiracial identity that acknowledges both her Hispanic and white heritage.

What Curlis illustrates throughout our interview relates to the increasing likelihood that multiracial children are taking a more active role in the racial socialization process. Most discussions of racial socialization within families focus on parents as primary agents. My research reveals strong support for a more mutual process, one that I call "reciprocal racial socialization." This reciprocity is captured in the process of parents and children sharing their respective racial realities, particularly in families where all family members do not assert the same racial identity. Reciprocal racial socialization recognizes the agency of multiracial people throughout the life course.

Reciprocal racial socialization builds on, yet departs from, the typical top-down racial socialization that often occurs in families but often gets concealed or veiled through colorblindness and colormuteness. Just as Twine (2011) argued that white women in interracial families develop racial literacies from their family members, I argue that multiracial members of families can shape their family members' racial literacy. As multiracial children develop their own racial literacies, informed by their respective experiences, they can simultaneously enhance the literacy of their family. This process occurs as families share stories about their everyday realities. As families meaningfully engage in discussions, they gain exposure to the ways their experiences converge and diverge from one another.

An important point to acknowledge follows: racial literacy is not a default epistemology of multiracial people. That is, people with racially mixed parentage are not naturally equipped with this racial literacy. Instead, I argue, many multiracial people cultivate this knowledge through an accumulation of experiences that nurture various ways of knowing and being in the world. Multiracial people who grow up in families where colorblind and colormute rhetoric is encouraged may have a harder time developing this racial literacy. Colormuteness and colorblindness limit multiracial children's preparation for any potential encounters with racial discrimination, and their understanding of any racial privileges they enjoy. Nevertheless, the process of reciprocity recognizes that the experiential knowledge of multiracial people has value to families and society. For multiracial people growing up in whitespaces (Horton 2006), they often endure a shift in racial consciousness that allows them to begin understanding the complexity of their racial heritage and sense of self. As multiracial people learn how to share their racial literacy, they help counter any colorblindness and colormuteness that circulates around them. They can intervene in this mythology to expose how they really live race in America.

When multiracial people wish to assert their preferred racial identities in their families of origin, but encounter contestation, a possibility exists to reframe this invalidation as protection. I recognize that the contestation of preferred racial identities of their children may very well be a parental protective mechanism; a strategy for shielding their multiracial children from any harm or hostility directed at them in a racially divisive society. Parents may guide their children toward particular racial identities because they understand that this society may not easily accommodate shifting mixture or particular articulations of racial identity, depending on the person in question. As Curlis's example above illustrates, it may be that her parents wanted to protect her from racism by encouraging her to opt for white. This works to shore up white racial privilege for Curlis but ultimately denies her the opportunity to celebrate her multiracial and multiethnic heritage, as she desires. These contrasting viewpoints create tenuous moments and cognitive dissonance that multiracial children and parents must manage as they collaborate to create a cohesive and healthy social family dynamic.

Many of the multiracial Latina respondents describe similar experiences that illustrate this type of protective and beneficiary borderism. Jamila, an Italian Hispanic woman, communicates one example; although she asserted a racially, ethnically, and culturally mixed identity, a previous boyfriend collapsed it all into whiteness. He reportedly said, "I think of you as a white girl who speaks Spanish." Jamila lamented, "He sees me as one thing that does another. I am two things. I want to be two things." This also echoes Maritza's example of being a black Panamanian; she did not see herself (as others did) as a black woman who speaks Spanish. The two identities were woven together, as I discuss in further detail in Chapter 6.

Andrew, a black and white biracial young man, provided another. He expressed similar sentiments, noting that his friends (who identify primarily as white) "tell me I'm white." Though this assessment is not altogether inaccurate or false (he was adopted into an interracial family that consists of biracial siblings, white siblings, and white adoptive parents), it is incomplete. "I can't just pick one, when I am two. I have to pick two [races]."

In the same way, we can understand Curlis saying that she is mixed because she, like Jamila, wants to be "two things" together, at once, rather than a "white person who speaks Spanish." These respondents want validation of what David, another respondent, called "a blended perspective," or a blended identity that does not compartmentalize or dissect them into halves. They desire and deserve to be whole but instead encountered invalidation of their multiracial (and often multicultural) identities in the whitespaces they inhabit in their everyday lives (see Horton 2006). In being misidentified as primarily and singularly white, instead of more than white, these respondents endure the expanding boundaries of whiteness that envelop them as honorary whites (Gallagher 2004).

While parents may genuinely have their children's best interests in mind, they may be protecting their children in ways that are actually harmful. Parents may attempt to shield their children from racism, race talk, or other racialized attention by encouraging them to embrace and express a singular racial identity. From the evidence of respondents' accounts, however, this parental protective borderism did little to protect multiracial children from their everyday social realities. Instead, it had different, ostensibly adverse impacts in many cases: without much knowledge of or support of their multiracial heritage and identities, many multiracial people still encountered borderism from strangers; fell under the lens of racial surveillance; or, otherwise got asked any number of questions regarding their racial identity or any attendant ambiguity. If parents resist sharing biographical information and familial heritage with their multiracial children, the children will be ill-equipped to navigate these conversations with strangers in public. Moves to protect their multiracial children from racism may instead leave the children vulnerable to antagonisms or accusations that the multiracial person does not know who they really are, as evidenced by these authenticity tests. Failure to embrace their multiracial child's preferred racial identity then may compromise the very efforts to protect them.

Allison, a black and white biracial woman adopted into an interracial family, describes what seems like protective borderism. Her example also illustrates the synthesis or blurred boundary between that kind of borderism and beneficiary border patrolling.

> Well, I don't really so much talk to them about the racial problems. Mostly I didn't talk to my family about it [issues I was struggling with]. I mean I told them I was unhappy, like I couldn't relate to the people there. But like I really couldn't go into in-depth conversations with them because they weren't there experiencing it and you know, I could tell them about stuff and how miserable it is, but you know, if you're talking about those girls and how you don't relate to them, it's like, "Suck it up." You know, but I'd talk to my friend (who is Native

American and Latina), and she was right there living it with me, and we'd be like, "Argh. This sucks." We could definitely relate.

While her parents could "understand, across the board, the difficulty of being a college freshman," they had a harder time relating to her college experiences as a young, "brown" woman. They failed to comprehend the identity invalidation she also experienced as a biracial woman in high school where "you were either black or you were white." By befriending a diverse group of (brown) people who were also misread as "white with a nice tan," Allison formed friendships with peers who shared her "clearly mixed" appearance; she cultivated social networks to enhance her racial consciousness and support her growing (multi)racial literacy. Through her friendship circles, Allison increased her racial literacy, even becoming fluent enough to discuss race with efficacy and ease. Based on her account, the colormuteness in her family would not have strengthened this ability very much.

For Allison, having some biracial friends who could empathize and relate helped, as well as being in an area of the country that is "mixed up;" these friendships facilitated Allison's management of her mixed race identity. Her experience of being border patrolled as a "white looking," brown-skinned woman intersected with her parents' inability to share her racial reality. That is, they appeared to police her racially by adopting a race-evasive style (Frankenberg 1993) and not discussing her multiracial identity.

> My parents, it is hard to talk to them about the experiences that I go through because I'm brown. And my parents are awesome parents and I wouldn't want them to go through them not being able to give me...to prepare me for being brown in this world because they don't know what it's like. *That* was mainly a problem in middle school, not so much in college.

Allison sympathized with her white parents and their general inability to impart information specific to her racial reality; they are habituated to whiteness and navigated the world as white people, albeit in an interracial family with 3 biracial children. Because they moved through the world as white, and based on Allison's accounts, they lack the experiential knowledge of blackness that Allison would find helpful as a biracial woman in a predominantly white family and society. Her awareness of their racial differences prompt her to turn to her friends for insight into what she and others see as behaviors and cultural practices characteristic of black people.

Allison: But you know, all the cool people knew all about hair rollers and you know stuff like that. Getting a perm and going to the 'China store'[5] to get hair gel or something, you know. I didn't do any of that, like my parents are white, they didn't teach me. They didn't know black culture. They know M.L.K., Jr. and stuff. But the actual Southern culture that you have day to day if you're black, they can't teach me that.

Author: So how did you learn about it?

Allison: Well, I still don't know that much about it; I don't pretend that I do. I know that it exists but I don't know that much about it. It's things that you would learn from your black mom. Or your black dad. I don't know. It's hard to describe it but it's day and night, the difference between white and black. In middle school, there was so little mixing, it was hard...And I know, I know that I'm half black, but I'm not ever going to know everything. I mean since I'm half and half, if I could know half of everything about being black, that would be great. But I'm never going to know that much because I will only know what my friends teach me....I would pick up stuff from my black friends, pick up a few things from my Vietnamese friends here and there.

Allison traces the gaps in her racial literacy to that of her parents, or between their experiential knowledge and their shared knowledge; gaps also exist between her parents' whiteness and her brownness; and, between that and blackness. Her observations underscore how the lack of access or exposure to racial differences impacts levels of racial literacy within interracial families. If white parents of multiracial children cannot cultivate or access this knowledge, who can? If multiracial children need parents to improve their racial literacy, who makes this happen?

The absence of familial connections to blackness led Allison to feel as though she cannot immerse herself in black culture, but she does try to access it through her social network of peers and friends. Nevertheless, she cultivated a sense of blackness by absorbing what knowledge she could from her black girlfriends (and even Asian friends, interestingly enough). Her discussion suggests a few important points: 1) that she may consider her Asian friends to be "honorary blacks" or the "Latinos of Asia," thereby blurring their own racial boundaries in their own racial identity construction (see Bonilla-Silva 2002; Ocampo 2016); 2) that, by implication, white people do not have much racial literacy of their own or to offer as shared knowledge; and, 3) that her parents' perception of her may have been a "white like me" one, where they knew she was biracial but perceived and raised her as white. However, I think her parents might have wanted and worked to protect her from racial interrogations, especially in the context of questions about her adoption. While plenty of scholars have shown how white mothers raise black children (Lazarre 1996; Reddy 1997), white adoptive mothers raising black white biracial children (such as Allison and her brothers) may face different challenges related to race, family, and issues of belonging. All three siblings negotiated whitespaces (Horton 2006) with their protean, not white, identities. This suggests that, by avoiding discussions of race, their parents' efforts to protectively border patrol failed. The black and white biracial children in this family may not have felt fully protected or buffered from racism. (The parents' behavior could also be viewed as a form of benevolent border patrolling, underscoring that these categories of borderism are not mutually exclusive).

As Anthony acknowledged, "People will perceive me, I guess people will know that I'm at least mixed. Just because I'm pretty well-educated so I don't really talk like I'm ignorant, or use that much slang.[6] But I do to a certain extent. So I get judged, from black people. Like a black person would know that I'm not completely black I guess but a white person wouldn't really know." Here I would argue a few points: 1) Anthony relies on racetalk or racially coded language to complicate the conversation about racial authenticity; 2) his comments suggest a white person might speculate about his race but still choose colormuteness in any given moment; and, 3) Anthony's observation suggests that black people may be more likely to border patrol *and* have greater racial literacy than whites, in his estimation. Given DuBois's (1903) discussion about double consciousness, this logic stands to reason.

DuBois (1903) originated this idea of "double consciousness" to illuminate the necessity of knowing oneself and anticipating the actions of others. He described this as a survival strategy, much like Ta-Nehisi Coates (2015) does in his work. A contemporary discussion of DuBois emerges in Coates's work as he describes the paradox of being a country's "below." In order to protect your body, in its fragility and vulnerability, you cultivate sensitivities to threat. Perhaps much the same can be said for the choices multiracial people make regarding the management of their identities within families in this society. Given that Andrew and other respondents claim multiracial identities, and given where they stand on the color lines that DuBois discussed, they occupy an interesting position where they may rely on racetalk to articulate their racial identities. That is, Andrew appears to authenticate blackness through the tiresome trope of education. The "miseducation" of race advances the association of education and intelligence with whiteness; Andrew's suggestion that his education inauthenticates his blackness reinforces the stereotype, but at his own expense; for if he is smart or educated (and that is to be white), then by default, his logic makes claiming blackness tenuous and undesirable at best and impossible at worst.

While parents like that of Allison, Anthony, and Andrew may be able to indulge their children materially and socially, many are unable to fully bestow the racial privileges of whiteness to their racially mixed children. The narratives of these respondents suggest that, in recognizing this inability to transfer all of the benefits of whiteness to them, the parents likely protected their multiracial children by minimizing the importance of race (Bonilla Silva 2003a). These racial silences can conceal any of the hardships and adversity that parents of multiracial children face while simultaneously creating the appearance of an *absence* of these problems.

The minimization of racism could be interpreted as a disservice to some; I suggest that family members and friends who engage in border patrolling are simply not well-versed in how multiracial people experience and make meaning of their racial identities. Multiracial people, throughout their childhood and adulthood, can strengthen their own and their families' racial literacies by asking questions and exploring the development of their racial identity process with curiosity. Future research should address this lacuna in the literature to more fully explore reciprocal racial socialization and the ways multiracial individuals throughout the life course influence their (immediate and extended) family members' understanding of racial mixture. This points to one new direction in which to take studies on multiracial matters and family socialization.

The Thin Line Between Beneficiary and Malevolent Border Patrolling

As discussed earlier, many of the respondents reported having to challenge the racial connotations of activities, objects, and interests. Essentialist notions of race guide much of the (mis)perceptions that people have of one another or even what they think is possible for themselves. This racial imagination of "appropriate" behavior per each racial group reinforces the racial divide. What happens when people with racially mixed heritage disrupt or challenge these essentialist notions? Can they effectively stretch the boundaries of race to include themselves, or do they face further rejection in their futile efforts to so?

Julie, a black-identified respondent, who enjoys expanding the meanings and boundaries of blackness (see Brunsma and Rockquemore 2002) discusses this possibility. Using music and food as metaphors for race, she shows how much music has become a racialized form that people used to decipher and decode the racial identities of respondents:

> I don't just listen to rap music, soul music, rhythm and blues. I listen to classical...new age..."anger music" (punk, metal), I call it, when I want to blow off some steam, and that's not traditionally associated with blacks. I eat sushi, every now and then. And soul food restaurants? It's not my fault I don't like to go to soul food restaurants. I think they just don't cook it as well as they cook it at home. I like Thai. I've never had Indian foods. I'm afraid of it because I know it's spicy. I went to (this restaurant). I think it's Moroccan and it was so good to me, really good. So now I want to explore that type of regional food.

While her parents and partner regard her culinary choices as curious at best, seeing them as a metaphor for racial identity and loyalty Julie continues her explorations, literally and figuratively. Doing so helps her make sense of the mixed messages she receives: "I grew up hearing stories about my uncle moving to (a northern city) and passing for white but I guess I never internalized it until my mom said, 'Well, you know, you're part Irish.' So it's just kind of like—it's not something I've explored. What does it mean to be Irish? I'm black."

The question that Julie asked resonates with and corresponds to the narratives of other respondents. How *does* one incorporate newly acquired information (from family members or elsewhere) into one's identity throughout the life course? Julie interpreted learning about her Irish heritage as a "permission slip" of sorts to complicate discourses of race, and of blackness, by introducing the possibility to be what other respondents call a "different kind of black." She explained, "It's more so okay to have 'white qualities'[7] (i.e., speaking proper or "correct" English) within yourself because you have the right to have it because you're part Irish." Julie's comments echo those of Andrew and others, perpetuating the idea that whites are always already intellectual and educated and, presumably on the contrary, blacks are not. Often, these efforts at contesting and complicating race reinforce racism.

Because Julie is "the one to go outside of this box" in her family, she contrasted herself to controlling or stereotypical images of blackness (Collins 2005, 2004) by expanding its (blackness) boundaries rather than exploiting her aforementioned entitlement to "act white" or Irish. Julie's comments also raise a question about the embodiment and entanglement of race and ethnicity. It loops back to a variation of my question in the previous chapter: "Can 'white ethnicities' exist and be expressed by brown and black bodies?" Reframing the question means asking, "What does it mean to be Irish *and* black? Is Irish an always already "white ethnicity" despite, or in addition to, the fact that Irish people became white over the course of time and were not always already white?

Instead of feeling trapped by racial discourses that over-determine what is considered socially "acceptable" behavior, Julie challenged beneficiary border patrollers. She directly questioned familial and societal expectations of her, and self-defined what it means to be a black woman, on *her* terms and based on *her* experiences. Enjoying "all this stuff that isn't black" compromises Julie's blackness for significant others and makes it easier for others to border patrol her. Nevertheless, she views her choices as enriching her life with new and unfamiliar experiences.

Curiously, Julie's mother is the one who shared information about the family's Irish heritage, which Julie interpreted as her mother's desire to help her daughter benefit from this acknowledgment of mixture.

> I think she means it's important for me to know but to benefit from, for along some lines, some sort of white privilege. I want to go natural (hair) but my mom is reluctant, apprehensive about me cutting off my hair. Those are things that are hard for her to accept because for one, she came up in a time where the lighter you were, the better. So it's just her mindset, and I don't even think she's able to even see outside of that picture. Going natural would be nice for others to do, but not for me to do (according to her mother).

This contradicts what seems like her family's overall investment in blackness and their sense of black pride. While she accommodates the mixed messages from her family and knows that her family does not view her behavior as rejecting blackness, she challenges others who issue this critique of her. Like Julie, Sa feels a similar freedom to be rebellious of race rules as a means of disrupting racial expectations for "multiracial" individuals (especially black multiracial people). In taking the liberties to enjoy interests that seem to transcend race, Sa appears adventurous and pioneering. Perhaps this is a different sort of privilege that many multiracial people enjoy: the luxury of liking a variety of activities, events, music, and so on. These interests may be critiqued or contested, but eventually accommodated or pardoned because of the racially mixed status of the multiracial person.

Sa did not seem to recognize this ability to freely explore a variety of interests as a function of multiracial privilege. Julie, however, did.

She was one of the first black multiracial people in my research to acknowledge the social and material benefits of whiteness she could access to some degree. She noted how her mother sometimes explicitly outlined these benefits, and at other times, simply alluded to them. Her mother often might refer to white relatives in their family or speak about the currency of whiteness.

Julie's discussion of (white) racial privilege helped me clarify this category of borderism, as "beneficiary border patrolling" because it so clearly demonstrated the historical context and weight of the choice to racially identify as mixed versus opting for singular blackness. Our interview conversation also revealed the overlap between beneficiary border patrolling and that of malevolent borderism. Identity invalidation remains subtle in the former and more central in the latter. I turn next to examples where this invalidation, in the form of malevolent border patrolling, is more abrasive or direct, malicious, and insidious.

Malevolent Border Patrolling

Several respondents noted having their identity contested by family members. This contestation reflects others' invalidation of multiracial people's asserted, preferred racial identities. They also commented on facing antagonism from others in relation to any resentment over any unearned (multi)racial privilege others perceived them to be enjoying. Counter to the expectation that family and friends might likely be the source of social support for multiracial individuals, I found evidence to undermine that association. Rather than offering validation of the multiracial individuals' preferred racial identities, some family members and friends end up invalidating them. They do so in ways that confound or force confrontations with multiracial people. These contestations stem from unlikely places: the people who ostensibly know them well. In this section, I focus my discussion on this contestation, or what I consider malevolent border patrolling. Why do members of interracial families border patrol one another? Why would friends of multiracial people negate their multiracial friends' preferred racial identities?

For answers, I turn to the respondents and their narratives. Theresa shares an experience where she tried to participate in a maternal family reunion and attempted to blend in, but stood out and felt a sense of alienation. Because "everybody there is white...me and my little brother (not the older one), we always felt like outsiders." When asked if she felt that way or was *made* to feel that way, Theresa explained:

I guess a little bit of both...I mean, I think that my mom's side of the family...we just had looks, whenever we showed up at the family reunion.... And then again that could have been just my imagination...that I felt uncomfortable about it.... I love my mom's family, but you know the majority of them are not college educated, and...I don't want to say redneck, but they are, and proud of it.... They even admit that they're rednecks and they have the Southern flag in the back of their pickup trucks with their guns kind of thing.

What Theresa describes is what Phillip Brian Harper (2005) calls "felt intuition." Harper describes this feeling as personal and powerful, invisible and intangible, but no less real or meaningful. For Theresa, it is a feeling of not belonging, a sense of exclusion or marginalization, a lack of inclusion or a warm welcome. She relied on "looks" and other expressions to gauge her felt intuition and trusted her "body as evidence" of where she belonged or not (see Hobson 2012).

Theresa troubles the line between herself and these family members as borderists. By producing racetalk (they are "rednecks"), Theresa defends her marginalized position and replicates their exclusionary ideologies on the basis of stereotypes (see Myers 2003, 2005). To them, Theresa is not "white enough" (because she is also Asian) and to her, they are the wrong type of white ("redneck"). In the next chapter, I further illustrate the messiness that emerges in borderism. Just as people are targets of racial border patrollers, they too may advance some of the same racial ideologies as borderists themselves.

Another respondent shared her experience confronting borderism in her family. Grace was burdened by hypodescent and its peculiar Southern persistence. As a Black and Native American woman who was adopted into a black family, Grace encounters similar resistance to always claiming both. A friend teased her for "looking Ethiopian" but then told her "he had some Ethiopian...and Cherokee" ancestry. He later border patrolled her multiracial identity when she also claimed being Cherokee.

[When I said,] "I have it" [Cherokee], he was like, "No, you don't." And I was like, "I do." I have paperwork but I never bring it out because my mom keeps all of that stuff, so I don't even know where it is. But normally I'll just be like, the skin complexion, you know certain days I'll be more red than others, so it goes from there...Like a lot of people who look more Indian, um, most of them don't believe it, because they'll be like, "Oh, your hair isn't this way." Or "You're just not the typical Native American impression." Usually you have to refute it back and go back and forth. And just be like, I'm not just claiming because they'll be like, "All black people say they have that."

Rather than ignore these invalidating remarks, Grace contemplated and analyzed the border patrolling pratices; she attempted, perhaps futilely, to make sense of it. I imagine this process as particularly emotionally labor intensive for her, given that her adoption makes "proving" race more difficult for her. She explains, "My interpretation of why they say that is because they've probably just had people say they were mixed with everything. We're all not 'whatever.' So...I don't really know how to take that because how do you defend it when so many people are claiming it but they aren't or you know, don't know?" Grace describes these accusations as insinuations of her attempts to distance herself from blackness. If Grace has a racially "thin" black identity (Yancey 2003), it is both in response to immersion in racially mixed social groups and a desire to embrace her multiracial identity.

In my interpretation, they are malevolent because they denied her the agency or freedom to choose. This could prove doubly injurious— creating multiplicative trauma or injuries—to her point. As an adoptee, Grace does not know all of her heritage. Her point is a double entendre, one that recognizes that people in the African diaspora cannot know all there is about their heritage due to forced and involuntary migration and their enslavement by white slave masters. Her personal adoption story intensifies these mysteries of histories, and serves as a reminder of the racial kinship she may experience with black people whose knowledge of family ties is also partial (see Collins 2000).

Grace remained ambivalent about accusations and insinuations regarding her preferred racial identity, both agreeing and disagreeing that some people may be "trying to prove that they are a little more different or maybe just a class above, 'I'm more than just African, African American, or black or whatever.'" Her ambivalence stems from her own unique positioning in the debate and how her invisible mixture renders her "just black" in the eyes of many border patrollers.

> I don't think I'm distancing myself at all. But I mean, I guess I get confused a little bit, why they want to kind of force me almost to recognize, "You're just black; now stop claiming the other stuff."....
> Like I don't know who my biological family is at all, so it's not like I can be like, "Well, what else am I mixed with?" And am I to assume, I just always assume that maybe they just put the basic stuff that they claim, more than anything?

Not only does Grace embrace her known racial mixture, but also implies that, given her individual and familial circumstances, there "might may be more mixture" that she would also embrace upon her discovery of this information. Not knowing about other biological siblings means also not knowing about any phenotypic differences among them[8]. In addition to being denied these additional familial ties and information, this not knowing denies her the visual evidence that she craves when being border patrolled and prompted to "show and prove" that she is Native American *and* black, or what she considers a different kind of mixed. Grace explained, "I mean...I just get a little frustrated sometimes when people are just so demanding that you're just this. I'm not trying to downplay one or the other. I'm just saying this is what I am. This is what I represent." Border patrollers see Grace's naming the known "sum of her parts" as a way to dilute her blackness; she interprets her responses to the "What are you?" question as an opportunity to share the complexity of her known heritage.

Her experiences with borderism from some family members has reportedly discouraged her from participating in social clubs organized around Native Americans, which contrasts with Rachel's experience of *forming* such a club. This difference in experience speaks to differences or variations in racial privilege *among* multiracial individuals of different racial combinations. The malevolent border patrolling that Grace faced from her family[9] made her feel this way: "Well, here's the black girl just coming in and now claiming, and so, in a sense, in my mind, I know I belong, but...I just wouldn't join."

The already emotion-laden experience of adoption coupled with the contestation of her multiracial identity from significant others and strangers leaves Grace border patrolling herself. She questions her "right" to belong, using physical markers to disqualify herself. (She did so despite imagining how happy she would be in joining a Native American group, thinking "that'd be pretty cool," to have a place where she could talk about "this and that" with others. She inferred that such social groups could act as something of a support network, as she begins her adoption search: "And I've already thought about going to look for my biological mother so she could tell me about my great grandmother. I'm sure she knows more...And I'm sure my grandmother has a lot still in her, since my great grandmother is pure.")

Thus, being adopted complicates these racial negotiations with others, in this case with both significant others and strangers. Grace explained that learning about her adoption would help buffer her from some of the border patrolling she encounters. Having more information would equip her with details to serve as the "evidence" or "proof" that she is entitled to her black and Native American multiracial identity, even as her body does not suffice or serve as a legitimate source of evidence of her asserted identities. I have difficulty estimating the trauma exacted on Grace from her uncle's comment but I can only imagine its adverse impact, given the arsenal of questions Grace already has about who she is. Hearing such callous words from a close relative packs a punch that an individual already feeling a complex mix of emotions- ranging from anticipation, abandonment, anger, and otherwise- might have difficulty managing in a healthy way (see Delgado 2003).

Not surprisingly, Grace seems to have internalized this borderism and perpetuated some problematic racial ideologies of her own. For example, she admitted: "I like to hang out with black kids who I guess act more white than black, who don't really speak the slang." On the one hand, Grace could be seen as essentializing blackness in a problematic way that relies on tired stereotypes. On the other hand, this could be interpreted as internalized racism or a thinning black identity (see Bailey, Chung, Williams, Singh, and Terrell 2011; Yancey 2003). However, I argue that Grace appears to be attempting to escape borderism from blacks, rather than blacks themselves. This is an important distinction in its acknowledgment that many multiracial people who face constant contestation from family members are averse to border patrolling more so than people of particular racial groups. This "hate the sin, love the sinner" perspective contrasts the way border patrolling is often presented as a "hate the sinner, not the sin" matter.

Conclusions

Given the level of social and emotional intimacy that could exist within a family, its members can prove to be supportive and understanding of one another. In racially mixed families, this support can sound like affirmation of everyone's individual and relational identities, including, but not limited to, that of its multiracial members. For multiracial members of interracial families, this support works to validate their preferred identities, irrespective of any incongruity between multiracial people's racial identity, their appearance, and others' perceptions of them. That is, even if multiracial people approximate or look more like they belong in one race and not others, supportive family members affirm the preferred racial identities of these multiracial individuals.

In the absence of this support, borderism emerges, just as I illustrated in this chapter. With greater access to and knowledge of the identities and heritage of multiracial members of interracial families in general, family members are better equipped with information that they could deploy to racially police the borders of race that multiracial people often blur. This information may enable members of interracial families to question and interrogate the identity of its multiracial members. These lines of questioning or interrogation reflect a range of border-patrolling behaviors, from benevolence to malevolence, with protective and beneficiary versions intersecting or dovetailing with the others. Family members and friends engage in these various forms of border-patrolling practices for a number of reasons, but a desire to maintain the illusive racial divide and clear borders between racial groups is high. In addition, I found evidence that parents' comments and responses to their multiracial children's questions about identity and whom they should date and/or marry, can reveal where parents locate their racially mixed children. Based on the narratives of the multiracial respondents, this location is often singular and static, seldom shifting. This, in itself, can be experienced by multiracial people as a kind of borderism, especially if they experience their racial identities as fluid and flexible or their racial mixture as more malleable than not. Parents say, "I see you as I am." They encourage their children to "stick to your own kind," without much sensitivity to the complexity of multiracial identity. In other words, what does racial affinity look like for a multiracial person? Being asked to express this affinity, without opening up the possibility of encouraging racial border-crossing and blending, can also be seen as a border-patrolling practice.

In particular, the different dimensions of borderism from family members highlight an irony, as people in interracial families are believed to be mavericks and pioneers bestowed with skills of high racial literacy and sensitivity. In the absence of these purposefully developed skills, members of interracial families may fall into the trap of border patrolling their racially mixed members. Optimistically, this ironic situation confirms the seduction of colorblindness and the extent to which anyone can internalize this dominant discourse; it also exposes that everyone could benefit from an education on race, difference, and diversity, to enhance their racial literacy, and minimize their border-patrolling ways.

The patterns I observed in these border-patrolling practices suggest that even people perceived as ostensibly the *most* supportive of multiracial people's preferred identities may become border patrollers themselves. I showed how multiracial people manage this borderism and how they may respond to it as well. Because they have access to these preferred identities, some close family members and friends may use this information to socially relocate a multiracial family member in another racial group. This chapter continues to build the layers of borderism, pointing to additional possible sources from which it stems: family and friends. In the following chapter, I explore how some multiracial people may internalize borderism to the extent that they begin perpetuating this problematic action on their own. I consider why such individuals would work against their own best interest to support a racial hierarchy that often regards them as "out of place" or out of (the color) line.

Notes

[1] Patricia Hill Collins (1998: 65–66)

[2] Lexie later added, "When he said that, it was more of a convenience thing. He said it like, 'Oh, just put that down.'"

[3] Lexie's reference to "the other" could be understand as a double entendre, referring both to the other race she claims as a multiracial person, and also to the "Other"-ness of being Asian.

[4] The only Puerto Rican in the small town that he grew up in, her father assimilated into American whiteness.

[5] A good example of racetalk, the "China store" is a popular panethnic reference for any and all Asian business owners. While problematic in its underlying assumption that Chinese equals Asian, or Asian businesses must be Chinese-owned and operated, the expression has been normalized and continues to circulate without much contestation.

[6] The only exception he noted included using slang or swearing around friends, and "knowing better" than to do so around his parents, who brought him up not to, and whom he described as "two of the most upstanding citizens on the face of the earth."

[7] Julie disputed this term, highlighting it as problematic and flawed. In elaborating on these "white qualities", she clarified, "I guess it depends on who's looking at me and what they've been exposed to. I don't feel it's acting white."

[8] Grace speculated, "I mean, I could have a sister who's a lot lighter than me and whose hair is a lot straighter so it's just, it's just like I don't know....Like when my hair is out, like when it's longer, then it's like, when I wet it, it curls, but not tight curls, and it's really soft, and people love to play in my hair. Like "you're hair is so soft." But I just characterize it, like those are the differences between Native American, that's in me, but I still have black features because I have African American in me as well."

[9] Grace shared an example of this borderism: "My uncle calls me 'Niggichee.' So it's just like, "Oh, you're just a [the "n" word] claiming Cherokee.' It's just so bad."

5

Internalizing Racial Identities

Some people with racially mixed parentage or heritage experience great difficulty asserting their preferred racial identities, especially when others continue to police these preferences and choices. How is it that, at a time of increased freedom of choice, individuals with mixed race parentage and heritage sometimes reject this opportunity to choose all races that apply? Why do some invest in the racial hierarchy that divides yet feel forced to choose "one and only one" race rather than claim the sum of their parts? Why do some multiracial people buy into the false notions of racial realness, thereby effectively disqualifying themselves or believing that they are not "really" the races that they claim? Why do some multiracial people internalize the racial identities affirmed by others rather than the ones that they themselves prefer (if and when differences exist between the two)? When will be the time for multiracial people to freely choose their preferred racial identities without contestation? Why do multiracial people border patrol themselves?

That multiracial individuals support and uphold racial hierarchies and categories based in part on their own racial ideologies and actions means they are not immune from developing problematic, prejudicial ways of thinking and participating in discriminatory action. It may seem counterintuitive that many multiracial people police racial borders, including their own. Their borders stand in contrast to the border blending suggested by statements about multiracial people having "the best of both worlds."

One need only look at the ways that multiracial people encounter borderism from strangers, family members, and/or friends to understand auto-borderism, or a self-policing, border patrolling. Direct and indirect lines can be drawn socially between the border patrolling people encounter in society and their own perpetuation of that practice as directed toward themselves and others.

An observable pattern begins to emerge in which multiracial people experience resistance or opposition to claiming their preferred identities, thereby limiting their own choices (and those of others). In this chapter, I discuss the process expressed by some of my respondents who policed their own racial identities. I provide some explanations for multiracial people choosing to patrol, rather than blend, racial borders.

When Multiracial People Border Patrol Their Own Identities

In 1967, the *Loving v. Virginia* decision removed the ban on interracial marriages in the U.S. (see Alonso 2000; Noble Maillard and Cuison Villazor 2012). Ostensibly, the increase in interracial marriages and in the multiracial population can be attributed directly to this decision, as well as shifting social norms that accommodates interracial intimacy and families. What these effects of the *Loving* decision have revealed, and concealed at the same time, are the complexity and varied levels of mixture in interracial marriages and in individuals. That is, that historic moment, coupled with another (the Multiracial Movement of the late 1990s and early 2000s), amplified attention to the existence of racial mixture at individual and familial levels (see Dalmage 2004a). This legislation and the subsequent collective social action of the 90s made much of the previously "hidden" racial mixtures appear. This appearance seemed sudden, rather than a historical residue or a pattern that had been centuries in the making.

While multiracial identities are more easily accommodated in general, some of the research respondents noted the difficulty in expressing and having their preferred identities validated. Instead of being "racial border blenders," many respondents primarily opted for the ostensibly easier option: singular racial identities. Based on their accounts of borders, they felt unable to assert their preferred racial identities. Instead, they often chose to dissolve their complex, racial realities into tidy, racial categories. As the earlier chapters (3 and 4) reveal, asserting a singular racial identity publicly did not always prove a simple matter. Sometimes, it actually intensified the border patrolling these multiracial individuals faced.

Due to a lack of information about familial histories and racial genealogies; encountering invalidation or opposition from others; or, wanting to evade racial surveillance from others, respondents who border patrolled themselves seemed to internalize and perpetuate the policing of strangers and significant others. I acknowledge these connections between border patrolling from the outside-in, outsiders-within, and inside-out, focusing here on the last method of border patrolling—inside-out.

As discussed in previous chapters, I found that individuals managed their multiracial identities in many ways. Sometimes they internalized racial borders, imposing the rules of race and racial identity options on themselves. The ongoing process of racial socialization and the persistence of structural racism combined to inform multiracial identity choices and constraints; many multiracial people described how they policed their own racial identities. Rather than resist these racial rules and the racial hierarchy, they sorted themselves into socially appropriate and positively sanctioned categories. Many chose singular racial identities in response to these social pressures instead of enjoying "the best of both worlds." That is, many multiracial people managed social pressures surrounding their racial multiplicity by choosing singular racial identities. In this chapter, I discuss the way that multiracial people engage in benevolent, beneficiary, and malevolent border patrolling of their own. I begin with benevolent border patrolling.

Benevolent Border Patrolling: "All of My Life, I Was Socialized as an African American"

> "Black" is the umbrella term for minorities to kind of come together under because "black," as it has evolved, does not necessarily just refer to African Americans. On the other side, when you're saying that you're black, you're still keeping the dichotomy of black and white, which aside from not being fair to other groups, I think it's just not realistic as well. And it also causes some limiting there as well, because even though black is an umbrella term for minorities, it's still kind of rooted in some notion of an African American identity as well.
> (James, a black-identified Black and Native American man)

Throughout the interview, James complicated the concept and question of "blackness," interrogating the term, exploring its many meanings, and noting its expansive reach and inclusive quality. He also shared how specifically it applied to particular people, both including and excluding him at once.

I begin with the above quote from James because he grapples with the multiple meanings of blackness; his narrative attempts to answer the question posed in Brunsma and Rockquemore's (2002) article, "What Does 'Black' Mean?" In offering up his experiential knowledge of blackness, James shared ideas that echo the authors' discussion of what they call the "epistemological stranglehold of racial categorization."

These authors explore in their investigation of the meanings of blackness. Interestingly, as the category "black" continues to expand today to un/easily accommodate mixture, the category (to James's point) may reinforce a white/black binary. However, in ways that parallel the "expanding boundaries of whiteness" (see Gallagher 2004), a similar expansion of blackness continues. This draws attention to the mixture embedded in both whiteness and blackness. While this seemingly upholds these two racial categories as two-and-only-two singular and cohesive racial groups, I refer to them to simultaneously undermine the implicit and taken-for-granted singularity and cohesion within their categorical connotations. That is, this multiplicity and variability exists across all racial categories.

Racial multiplicity exists, and hides in plain sight, as "invisible mixture." Linguistically and socially, the terms "white" and "black" reinforce singularity, not mixture. The terms then make mixture situationally il/legible. Mixture largely becomes legible or visible through usage of the very term, "mixture," even as it exists in "single" race categories, such as "white" and "black." While these singular race terms suggest specificity, they also implicitly capture a multiplicity. That is, single race categories suggest just that, singularity, which reinforces the idea of "one-and-only-one" race. The myth of such a racially pure, cohesive, and coherent racial category convinces people that racial multiplicity only exists in people who claim more than one race. Thus, for most of the national population, this multiplicity often remains unnamed and resides under the veil of singularity. Mixture also disappears through the stories that families tell about themselves and their heritage. I discuss these "sins of omission" in the socialization that family storytelling makes possible in racially mixed families.

Mysteries of Histories

In attempting to sort out what I call the "mysteries of histories" in families, James asks "a lot of questions" to disentangle his heritage. He explores his family biography in an attempt to answer his many questions; to curb the curiosities about his identity and to solve some of those "mysteries of histories." He wants to more fully understand his Nigerian and Native American ancestry, especially in relation to his blackness. Recognizing both his African American and Native American ancestry is a practice that allows him (and other black and Native American respondents) to acknowledge "intermarriage further back in their family history" (Campbell 2007:926). This point follows Jessie Turner's (2013) work on historical and contemporary mixture and invites us to consider what constitutes the old and the new, with respect to racial mixture. To Jenifer Bratter's (2007) point, "multiracial" identity does not always survive the next generation. But when it does, it may take on new names with old faces, or maintain old names among new faces (see Dawkins 2012; Winters and DeBose 2003).

Despite considering the complexity of his rich heritage, James asserted what I understood as a singular black identity. However, he engaged in "problematizing blackness" by assigning expansive and inclusive meanings to the term, in its chosen (not forced) form (see Hintzen and Rahier 2003). Chosen blackness departs from the forced blackness historically mandated through the "one drop" rule of hypodescent; chosen blackness enriches and expands the meaning of blackness and recognizes more of its liberatory potential, a freedom to choose not fully afforded people with any known black African ancestry.

Other black multiracial respondents who identify as black engaged in this practice. That is, the term, "black," weaved together a multiplicity of races and ethnicities, as evidenced in other respondents like Jessica, a black and Asian Indian woman, opting for black as James did. In doing so, people can acknowledge historical and contemporary mixtures of blackness (see Khanna 2010; Turner 2013). In thinking about these complexities and contradictions of racial singularity and multiplicity, I draw from the experiences shared by another respondent. Abigail, an African American-identified woman (also of Native American [Cherokee] heritage), shared that she asserts a singular black identity in part because of her illegible identities or racially mixed heritage.

As one of the older respondents in my research sample, Abigail grew up in a time and place that more closely abided by the rule of hypodescent and, therefore, endorsed this "one drop" rule of blackness. That rule canceled out, or denied, her racial mixture, and informed her way of thinking about racial categories. Growing up in a white/black binary supported by society meant that her mixture remained relatively out of reach to her. She explained, "I'm not mixed race. I appear to be more African American than anything else, you know?" Because she believes others see her as black, or that others do not see or acknowledge her mixed race heritage, she claims a black identity. She minimized this mixture to adopt a black identity because she believes that it is her blackness that is legible to others. Abigail "thinks mixture" in traditional ways with history and family shaping her perspective; indeed, she has internalized the "one drop" rule. Abigail's narrative supports a "seeing is believing," or "believing is seeing" (Lorber 1993) approach to racial classification in the sense that she relied heavily on the visibility or legibility of race. Doing so invalidates her illegible identities, instead of challenging our collective reliance on (racialized) appearances to categorize ourselves and others by race.

Much like other respondents, Abigail offered contradictions on her own racial location, illustrating how she benevolently border patrols herself:

> I racially identify as African American basically but I remember that my mother told me when I was very young, she said, "Don't ever forget that you are part Cherokee, part Cherokee Indian, Native American." But all of my life, I socialized, was socialized as an African American or black child, you know, listening to R and B, and you know, dancing and everything was geared towards African American culture.... At the time, I didn't question it. It meant, as I got older, that there's something other than African American about me, something different about me.... That I just wasn't all African. That, you know, there's a part of me that was the "Other" if you wanna call it that. That wasn't defined. It made me intercept my thinking I was all black. Well, not all black, your DNA might come back saying you're all black. My appearance is black. Her words made me question that.

Despite questioning those "mysteries of histories" and her partial knowledge of racial mixture in her own family, Abigail continues to assert a black identity.

Similar to other black multiracial respondents, Abigail learned racial lessons, including that she should default to a black identity despite any "body as evidence" to the contrary (see Hobson 2012). Her story reveals what so many families work to conceal: racial mixture, then and now, and the stories that people speak or silence (see Nash and Viray 2014, 2013; Walters et al. 2011). These stories, and the silences that sometimes surround them, become part of the racial inheritance within all families, not exclusively racially mixed ones.

As Abigail illustrated, and in contrast to people with known Asian, Latino, and Native American ancestry who claim a white identity, people with known African ancestry may feel like they cannot claim a nonblack identity (Bratter 2007; Khanna 2010); otherwise, they opt for blackness as an assertion of their right to choose. In the latter case, the act of choosing is an expression of self-definition or an act of resistance to borderism. In the former case, multiracial people may sense some social constraints to available choices, such that the particularities of the geographies of race expand or limit their options; they may feel like they are "forced to choose" or effectively "passing as black" (see Khanna

2010), or they may actively choose a preferred black identity, experienced not as limitation but in terms of liberation.

The challenge in this choosing involves consideration of the history of individual and collective mixture; current and historical mixture; and, consensual and forced mixture. These considerations thus include acknowledgment of the variations of racial identity and claims to mixture made increasingly broader during the Multiracial Movement of the late 20th Century; they invite people to "think mixture" and reflect on how the concept of racial mixture and who is mixed changes across time and space.

In Abigail's example above, she thinks mixture through the lens of the one-drop rule. Although she acknowledges the familial mixture of black and Native American ancestry, she does not claim a black and Native American multiracial identity; her "opting for black" typifies the tensions between agency and the legacy of racial rules and paradigms that foreclose choice for people with certain racial combinations (see Campbell 2007). As Campbell notes, many African Americans in contemporary society remain reluctant to publicly make claims to their Native American ancestry, fearing racial invalidations and accusations similar to the ones described by respondents like Abigail. They worked to avoid the charge that they were falsely attempting to diversify or dilute their blackness with indigeneity. Respondents like Abigail opted for blackness but the kind of blackness that incorporates these charges with a positive spin. That is, if the common charge was that African Americans always try to claim Native American ancestry, then "blackness" in this context is always already mixed with Native American ancestry. Rather than risk naming both her African American and Native American ancestry, Abigail effectively wove those ancestries into blackness. This exemplifies my earlier point about the illusion of singular racial categories being cohesive. The narrative of Abigail and others provides evidence of racial multiplicity taking up residence in single race categories.

Another respondent shared the process of her racial identity formation and her experiences with benevolent border patrolling. Wendy, a light-skinned, black Hispanic, described moving from a northern city to a southern one, and navigating impediments to connecting with other Latinos. In that northern city, she felt her skin color and lack of fluency in Spanish disconnected her from other Latinas. During our interview, Wendy further suggested that her limited Spanish-speaking ability prohibited her from getting "that deep" with "the Spanish group" in high school because "every now and then, I wouldn't know what they were talking about" (when they spoke in

Spanish). She contrasted her lack of fluency in Spanish with otherwise being an "articulate person."

Unlike David (discussed later in this chapter and again in Chapter 6), Wendy does not experience, or admit to, this lack of Spanish language literacy and fluency as a source of tension that generates "imposter syndrome" (see Moore 2015). In contrast to him, she expresses much less awareness of the way the social construction of race and ethnicity are shaping these social dynamics, even as she discusses these and related issues. Instead, Wendy offered up a narrative framed by colorblindness, which minimized the significance of race and racism:

> You know, when you're asking me [about race], it's weird. I'm trying to think back and I don't really ever remember race being an issue, whether it was both of the races or either one of them. I mean, I guess I would more relate to being black because I don't speak Spanish fluently and a lot of the things that I was put into as far as a child were mostly minority-oriented or black-oriented rather than Latino [said with an emphasized Spanish accent]. So I guess I would relate more to black but I mean there wasn't really any like you know, "You're black and Puerto Rican," and I mean "You're biracial." I don't remember ever asking, I don't think I had an identity crisis or a race crisis about who I was. I remember I said to my mom one time, I um, I said, "Mom, I'm not black; I'm peach." But that was, you know, like...the extent of it. I didn't really think about it like that, I think.

Arguably, if race and ethnicity did not matter, it would not matter if Wendy knew Spanish, as people of all racial and ethnic groups have varying language literacies and skills. Ostensibly, she would be able to make connections to even a few other Latinos or to any and everybody based on her logic. However, if the expectation is that Wendy—as a multiracial Latina—know Spanish well (which she admits she does not), she may feel or be disqualified on some level; any markers of blackness may serve as further disqualification to some, or conversely, qualification and authentication to others. That she is read as black, but not necessarily Latina, offers partial explanation for the disconnection she experiences. She conveys a narrative that suggests that she is not allowed to be both and, therefore, border patrols herself.

What Wendy's experience highlights is the lacuna, or the silence surrounding the racial and ethnic socialization she received in her family. She points to this silence as an absence; in that void, the term "biracial" does not exist. Hearing such a term might have affirmed to her, or signaled, that "black" and "Latina" are not mutually exclusive terms. Despite not learning the language to refer to her black and Latina identity, Wendy does show how she is able to intercept—and correct—the language others use to describe her: "I'm not black, I'm peach." Despite noting that she does not think about race and ethnicity, she obviously does. She offers an awareness of her embodied reality, as she experiences the "multiracial" as "multicultural." Wendy's innocent and simple description of her color, as it contrasts with the language that speaks only to her "legible" blackness, allows her the agency to contest this and to recognize her reality as a multiracial and multicultural one.

The shift between "black" and "peach," therefore, is not only a nominal and discursive one but also an important agentic one to the "names we call home" (Thompson and Tyagi 1996). These names are a colorful expression of embodied hybridity and multiplicity of life in the borderlands (see Anzaldua 1987; Canclini 2005). Wendy makes space in her family that the ampersand between being black *and* Latina creates. The ampersand acknowledges and accommodates her mixture, making space for complexity in her racial identity, and what some see as a contradiction, instead of the identity composition or sum of Wendy's parts. While she may claim to not think about her life in racialized ways, she is clearly impacted by these dynamics in her family and in society, as they shape her sense of self and the social interactions she has with others.

Other respondents negotiate the ampersand differently. In contrast to Wendy, whose peach-colored skin could locate her in "white," "honorary white," and "collective black" categories, darker-skinned black Latinos reported different experiences as individuals more definitely located within the racial category of "collective blacks." For example, Sanchez, a black and Latino Puerto Rican man, confronted the realities of borderism as a darker-skinned man. This reality includes recognizing the racial hierarchy and classification system that inform people's perceptions of others and themselves He explained how he embraced the categorization to arrive at a singular racial identity. Growing up in "basically black or white" spaces (schools, neighborhoods, etc.), Sanchez noted how the absence of Asians or "any other race" created a white/black binary that meant he was defined as a black person. "I was like, 'Okay, I know that I'm a black person. I mean my skin color is dark, so therefore I'm a black person.' And I never really, to tell you the truth, when I was younger, I never really thought about race as much as I do today." Sanchez's understanding of his social location within the U.S. racial hierarchy supports Bonilla-Silva's (2003) contention that darker-skinned people are sorted into a collective black category.

Similar to Sanchez, Frank, a 21-year-old man describes how he arrived at a singular black identity and what I interpreted as benevolent borderism:

> I identify racially as African American or Black. Now ethnically, I consider myself a mix and I'm a mix of different races—I mean different groups of people. Ah, Native American; as well as Spanish and oh no, not Spanish. Sorry, Um, German and French. My African American identity is dominant. It's almost like chromosomes. You have dominant and you have recessive. So the Native American history, the Native American heritage or ethnicity, they're all the same; they're all related. The ethnicity is sort of recessive.... I experience being African American. In all honesty, I don't think it has much to do with how I identify because even if I didn't identify as African American, I would still be treated like an African American.... Because that's how I look. I look African American. I guess I'm not light enough or um, of the consistency or what not, or whatever the case may be, to be considered mixed, so when they, for example, see me, the first thing they think of is black. The first thing that comes out of their mouth is "black."

In borrowing from the language of natural sciences, Frank refers to the "dominant" and "recessive" genomic matter ("chromosomes") which becomes a metonym of race, though in reverse (see also Bliss 2012; Dawkins 2012; Hochshild 2014). Frank observes that his "African American identity is dominant" in this society which means that he sees his African American parentage and heritage as phenotypically dominant, a point that inadvertently reinforces the one-drop rule to some degree. It suggests that because it is most visible (among his racial mixture), blackness trumps any other race, and that said racial mixture must be visible in order for it to be claimed.

In contrast to this dominance based on physical features or appearances, and based on the racial hierarchy in the U.S., the opposite proves true about social and structural dominance. In terms of power and privilege, whiteness, as a group position and ideological framework, dominates (see Blumer 1958; Feagin 2009). The taint of "contaminating" black blood (see Douglas 2002), borrowing from the biology of race discourse and racist ideologies about the polluting qualities of this blood, has historically been used as evidence of black inferiority; this discourse also supports false notions of race as biological, effectively essentializing and naturalizing it (see Spencer 2010; Bridges 2011).

Frank contrasted his self-image with others' perceptions of his race, pointing to the pattern in which others see him as black. Because of his (dark skin) appearance, Frank (like Abigail) believed that asserting a mixed identity would prove arduous, a point echoed in the work of Khanna (2011) and others. The absence of discernible markers of mixture dissuaded Frank from incorporating mixture immediately into his identity.[1] He regarded visible mixture a requisite criteria for claiming a mixed identity, despite discursively recognizing a "multiethnic," if not multiracial, heritage. He explained his rejection of the label "mixed," citing these reasons:

> The diversity is not allowed to exist. That's why it's recessive. The resistance is everywhere. It's in institutions, with your peers...Institutionally, for instance, you, until recently, weren't allowed to identify as anything more than, either, you're African American, you're white, you're not European American, or you're Asian American and so forth. Even if I put on (forms), considering that I have Spanish and German, Native American, African American, I could put on there "white" but if I get stopped by a police officer, shoot, no matter what, pick one, no matter what happens if, they'll look at you, and you say white, they'll say, "Yeah, right. Yeah, stop lying." You know. You could have a black person immigrate from Germany to America and they say, "Okay, you're German. You're black. You're African American." Which they don't know how far back you have to go to get to Africa in this heritage but it's got to be back there somewhere because you're black. And "African American" to my peers is devalued. It is considered an insult, like you're denying yourself or you're insulting your race or your heritage to say, "Okay," that you're not just black because you have the oppressor and you have the oppressed and the oppressor.

Frank's comments illustrate what Audre Lorde (1984) discusses in *Sister Outsider*, that we are all the oppressed and oppressor together, at once. Because he has encountered borderism from others, Frank opts for black:

> I mean, I like the African American ethnicity. I think I identify with it. I think I would also, however, at least identify with my Native American heritage, I'm not so partial to my German and French heritage in that, it's basis is on people being forced to come. It's not like they had a choice in the matter. If you get over here and you don't like it, there's a chain and you get whipped up. I mean, so, granted I am very much an admirer of Germany's brilliance and France's, you know, medical and scientific advancements, as well, you know, in that I have great respect for them.

Frank recognizes his Native American ancestry, respects his German and French ancestry, and connects to his African American ethnic heritage. He also decidedly interprets race and arrives at his own racial identity on the basis of hypodescent (Khanna 2010; Brunsma 2006a). During our interview, Frank rejected the possibility of a person's mixture being "clearly invisible" (Dawkins 2012; see also Buchanan and Acevedo 2004), which ignores the number of multiracial people "hiding in plain sight" because they do not appear to be what I call, "clearly mixed." In a way, this logic upholds the racial hierarchy and system of racial stratification. By doing so, he border patrols his racial identity choices. This creates a chain of events, reflecting others limiting his racial identity options and illustrating his own imposition of that limitation; this potentially extends to how he supports or denies others in their preferred racial identities. That is, as he is denied choice, he likely internalizes that constraint and, in effect, denies others with invisible mixture their own freedom to choose. Frank also overlooked how many visibly multiracial people face similar kinds of identity invalidation, if they too, like him, do not look sufficiently mixed or are not clearly ambiguous.

Like Frank, Kelly (a black-identified woman with French Guyanese, French, Asian Indian, Blackfoot Indian, Black American, German, and a "splash of Irish" ancestry) racially identified as black or "Black American because...that's how the general public perceives me." Both felt that they would be treated as black by the public and in public; this implies that 1) they anticipate or fear facing antiblack racial discrimination and devaluation (see also Yancey 2003), alienation, or differential treatment because of their perceived blackness, and/or 2) they would benefit from collective conscience and experience black solidarity and racial kinship if and when perceived by other black people as sharing a similar black identity.

Though Kelly thought she "would claim a multiracial identity if society allowed," she made clear her satisfaction and "comfort with being black." Rather than adopt an "anything but black" position (Bonilla-Silva 2003b), Kelly and others actively challenged such antiblack ideologies by purposefully opting for black. Despite persistent antiblack racism, that includes maneuvers away from blackness in this society, Kelly, Frank, and others moved towards blackness by embracing African American racial and ethnic identities.

With racial mixture in her family that was "more distant...not direct (since) it's not like my mom's one mono-race and my father's one mono-race," Kelly described the intergenerational negotiations of race. This accounts for both mixture shifting as well as a change in racial categories and the meanings attached to them across generations. In socially constructing her parents as having singular races, while recognizing their racial mixture as "distant," Kelly conveyed the way that distance made claiming a multiracial identity feel inaccessible to her. This distance, however real or imagined, made multiraciality that much more off-limits given the absence of immediate, visual markers of racial mixture. Although Kelly's mixture is both contemporary and historical (Turner 2013), she remained ambivalent about claiming a multiracial identity.

Kelly's reluctance, much like Frank's, rested on her perception and understanding of what counts as mixed; it also illustrates Bratter's (2007) concern about the survival of multiracial identification to "the next generation." It may also relate to the construction of a black family. To some, the maintenance of a "black" family may be predicated on *all* its members asserting black identities versus departing from that expectation. The implicit concern is that a single departure would signal a departure from blackness (or be read as antiblackness) as opposed to a problematizing of blackness, in recognition of its richness and categorical complexity, across the diaspora.

Having grown up in and been socialized as part of a family that collectively asserted blackness (or whose members individually and/or collectively asserted black identities), Kelly did not exactly view herself as a "first-generation" multiracial (Daniel 2002) and felt she would not be able to claim a validated border (mixed) identity (see Campbell 2007). In fact, one-quarter of the respondents (with black heritage or parentage) asserted a singular black identity, evidence that supports existing literature indicating that a very small portion of blacks claims a multiracial identity (Lee and Bean 2004).

Notably, Kelly mentioned others' interpolating or hailing her (Althusser 1971) as "more than black" (Daniel 2002). "I mean I've had people ask me, 'So, what are you?' And…for simplicity sake, you know, I say, 'I'm black.' 'No, but really, what are you?'" That some people see her in this way suggests that, should she choose, she *could* assert a multiracial identity that others might validate in those moments (rather than fear imminent invalidation and contestation). Nevertheless, Kelly seemed to resent and reject the intended "compliments" others provided in presuming her to be Brazilian (mixed, not black); or, when saying, "'Oh, you don't look fully black.' Or 'You know you have…a little bit of oh, something *else* in you.'" She suspected that others may have intended their comments as compliments but she failed to see them as such. Instead, she implied that she saw them as sociologist Heather Dalmage (2000) describes: "racist compliments."

Had her parents' looks contrasted each other more, such that they were more "obviously interracial" or visibly mixed, and/or had they chosen multiracial or black identities, Kelly might have felt more compelled to choose such an identity for herself. I suspect this might be the case for other black multiracial people. Without these verbal or visible markers of mixture in significant others, those who get to claim such a validated multiracial identity remain on exclusive and contested terrain (Morning 2000), a point Khanna (2011) also makes in her book, *Biracial in America*.

For Kelly and others, choosing blackness also serves as an expression of racial solidarity and/or an explicit rejection of "multiracial" privilege. As some black multiracial people move towards, not away from, blackness, they challenge the antiblackness that prevails in the U.S. Many black multiracial respondents expressed views similar to Kelly. They found that the "absence of a presence" (Fine 2002), in this case a racial presence, or a "clearly mixed" phenotype or physical appearance, denied them the chance to choose a "mixed" identity. The absence of racial mixture in the form of a visibly recognizable or legible interracial family (nuclear or extended) remained present in their lives. They negotiated this absence by expressing their desire to explore more of their family heritage and racially mixed ancestry. Their choosing blackness then can be understood as both constrained and concerted: their "too dark to *not* be black" skin color marked them as black, because of the one-drop rule (Khanna 2010), but also allowed them to actively, positively embrace blackness.

In the next section, I consider the ways in which multiracial individuals make strategic identity moves to increase their mobility and facility in the world. I illustrate the ways that some multiracial people curiously produce colorblind narratives or deny the reality of race, yet appear to be managing their multiracial identity in ways that ensure their access to some racial privilege.

Beneficiary Border Patrolling: A Matter of Choice, Convenience, or Privilege?

For some of my respondents, acknowledging a racially mixed *heritage* proved easier than asserting their own mixed race *identity*. Naming a multiracial heritage enabled them to preserve the privileges associated with the identities they chose. Unlike benevolent border patrolling of identity, beneficiary border patrolling involved respondents generally claiming a singular race that ensured greater social status than the races not embraced or acknowledged. Most examples of beneficiary border patrolling came from white-identified individuals (including White and Asian and White and Latino respondents, and one White/Native American respondent). In these cases, I saw these respondents as avoiding a multiracial identity (based on the perception of its lower social status and value in the racial hierarchy), and opting for white (based on the perception of the benefits that accrue from whiteness).

Sociologists such as Mary Waters (1999) found that white people reveal and conceal their ethnicity as they so desire. They may claim one ethnicity based on its popularity in a particular historical moment, social setting, or context; or, they may reject or deny parts of their ethnic heritage. They claim or reject contingent on a set of variables including the popularity of an ethnicity, or any animosity directed at certain ethnic groups in particular social settings or historical moments. In my research, I discovered that some multiracial people engage in practices parallel to exercising their "ethnic options" by making a series of racial options. This ongoing process of negotiating identity involves revealing and concealing the composite parts of their (multi)racial heritage.

Consistent with the ways a white person interprets their "ethnic options" (Waters 1990), Dakota, a white-identified white Asian multiracial woman, treats her racial identity similarly. She explained: "I do identify as Korean when it is convenient,[2] I guess...I always say that I am White on the standardized tests and things like that but, in social situations when I am talking to people, I always say that I am half Korean. I guess it makes things more interesting and I don't feel that I am a boring White girl." This last observation suggests that Dakota was "thinking the border" strategically—opting for white and/or Asian, depending on which identity benefits her. As she suggests, she benefits from being "half Korean." Being able to brighten the borders of race, she highlights her Korean identity to spice up what she might see as "vanilla" whiteness.

Formally identifying as white on applications can prove materially beneficial for white multiracials, as evidence suggests "opting for white" (Rockquemore and Arend 2002) is a currency in today's racial hierarchy (Bonilla-Silva 2003a,b; Hunter 2005). These and other sources show the material benefits of and the possessive investment in whiteness (see also Lipsitz 2006; Harris 1993; Roediger 2003). Consistent with discussions of the emergent multiracial "identity grab bag" (Rockquemore, Brunsma, and Delgado, 2009), Dakota defaulted to whiteness because her physical appearance does not deny her that option. Alternately, one could interpret that she formally opted for whiteness, while having her ("half Korean") mixture operate as an added "flavor." However, some people read her as ambiguous, which places her in white and honorary white categories (and accounts for the different groups to which others perceive her as belonging to). The identities she chooses remain contingent on the situations she finds herself in and the perceptions of others.

As a general observation, I noticed that this and other white Asian multiracial individuals situationally employ their racial literacy to strategically shift their mixture to acquire the most privileges—the social and material benefits—attached to whiteness and increasingly to multiraciality. This ability to shift mixture operates as a material benefit not only of whiteness then, but also of white- or light-skinned multiraciality. That is, visible mixture affords some multiracial individuals material benefits comparable to white privilege in white-looking multiracials (see Bonilla-Silva 2004; Doane and Bonilla-Silva 2003a,b; Gans 1999).

Finally, Dakota's convenient deployment of her Korean parentage and identity allowed her to spice up her vanilla existence and reaffirm her whiteness. This speaks to the point that cultural theorist and literary critic, bell hooks, makes in her work; this "illustrates a commodification of the racial otherness as 'a spice, seasoning that can liven up the dull dish that is mainstream white culture.' The white woman does not seem to seek a broader cultural appreciation, but rather a brief cultural appropriation...She can perhaps have the fun of pretending to be black for one night, but can soon return to her privileged white appearance and style" (hooks 1992:21). Specifically among white Asian multiracials, many of them "spice" themselves up with their Asian "Otherness," which reaffirms their predominantly white racial identity and white privilege. They normalize their choice for whiteness through these "Othering" discourses (Frankenberg 1993) and Orientalizing moves (see Said 1978), which fetishize rather than respect and celebrate difference. This fetishism of difference can also be a self-Orientalism when the "Other" is the self. This became evident in Dakota's interview, when she said the following:

> I see really cute Asian girls and sometimes I do wish that I looked Korean because, I don't know why, but I just think they are so cute. But there is nothing I can do....I look at myself and I don't feel like really Korean a lot, other than my hair color and a little bit my eyes. You know, like typical Korean girls have really small bodies, too thin.

By using language that supports the fetishism of Asian women, apparent in her reference to "really cute Asian girls," Dakota could be viewed as admiring and/or creating a racialized spectacle of them.

Though not mutually exclusive categories, these ways of seeing Asian women dislocates Dakota from sharing that identity. In my interpretation, it not only dislocates but distances Dakota from the category, "Asian American woman." Perhaps as Dakota continues her education, she will consider ways of seeing herself as a part of the group of women she finds cute. How she constructs or imagines racial boundaries, specific to Asians, will reveal where she positions herself over time accordingly, be it at the margins or the center.

Some respondents, reluctant to embrace a mixed identity, also illustrated that they were transitioning into an incipient multiracial identity, much like Dakota. By learning more about their family's racial diversity and starting to solve their family's "mysteries of histories," some of my participants began to more readily recognize their own multiraciality. They cultivated these nascent identities, growing their dimensions as they acquired knowledge of their family's racial mixtures.

During our interview, Dakota stated, "I always feel White." She experienced the feeling of being disqualified for not looking "Asian enough," and described a disconnection to Korean culture, language, and people (resulting from being border patrolled by significant others, as previously discussed). These feelings of disconnection and encounters with borderism partially explain her racial identity options. Rather than reject Korean culture altogether, she seems ambivalent towards it: "I mean, it's not like I am trying *not* to engage my Korean culture or anything like that. But I just think it's that my mom didn't really force Korean culture onto me...I mean I feel strange going to the Korean market." Because she looks more white than Asian (and Korean specifically), Dakota feels out of place in predominantly Korean settings. Were she to be both darker and smaller, Dakota noted, she might feel more entitled to actively and publicly claim a Korean identity. This is so largely because people essentialize ethnicity and race, proscribing what counts as Korean or not. Believing that she fails a variety of authenticity tests, Dakota instead opts for white.

In ways that echo traces of Dakota's narrative, Rose offered some of her experiences as a white-identified white and Native American multiracial woman. Rose readily acknowledged some Native American heritage and partially did so by recognizing the racial differences between her grandfather (who she described as having dark skin and being part Cherokee) and other relatives (who she described as white). Registering this racial difference discursively distances and disconnects Rose racially from the physically or phenotypically different relatives, thereby keeping her "whiteness" intact. Such discursive practices stabilize the category of whiteness without compromising its mythical purity, despite the acknowledgment of racial mixture. That is, Rose asserts and maintains a singular white identity comfortably, though she "spices up" her vanilla whiteness with the difference of "Otherness," in this case, her Native American ancestry[3] (see hooks 1992; Rubin 1984). She offers different details than other respondents who see their multiracial heritage as a flavorful addition to their chosen whiteness, although Rose effectively does the same. Rose offers, "My mom's dad, he was a quarter Cherokee. They didn't have a good relationship. I never knew him. I think he's dead. I really couldn't say. There's no documentation [proving his Indian identity], it's just what they're telling me." At once, Rose remains skeptical of her family's "mysteries of histories," and diminishes any connection she feels toward her maternal grandfather. Her discourses work to do what I call "disappear difference." She disappears difference in herself by erasing mixture through the speculation (instead of certainty) of her grandfather's death, and then by questioning his racial identity in life.

Because her family socialized her as white (rather than multiracial), Rose learned to identify as white. At some point, her mother "just kind of brought up that there was Indian blood in us," and said, "'Oh yeah, we have some Indian in us....I think it's Cherokee. Yeah, it's Cherokee.' And I've always been interested in Indian heritage. I think it's neat. I don't know how else to put it. I don't know the 'P.C.' way to put it." Like Dakota, Rose employs language that infantilizes and fetishizes difference not in whites, but in Indians or Native Americans. In fairness to Rose, she acknowledges her limited racial literacy when she admits to not knowing the socially appropriate expression.

Following Bonilla-Silva (2003a,b), I wonder if Rose would regard her whiteness as "neat" as well. Her ways of describing "difference" in relation to whiteness reinforces the spectacle that so often surrounds Native Americans and other racial groups of color, and normalizes the centrality and invisibility of whiteness as well (see DeLoria 1999; Dyer 1992). Concerns about people "playing Indian" surface in instances where Native American people and culture are regarded as more interesting than white people and culture (DeLoria 1999). This is another way of understanding hooks' concerns of "spicing up" whiteness with "Otherness." This is especially notable in instances where multiracial people who choose whiteness regard their "Other" racial identity as something of an accessory; this Otherness can be put on when desired and disregarded when not. This fashioning of race speaks to the "optional" quality it takes on, as I discussed earlier (see also Goldberg 1997; Waters 1999).

Amidst her curiosity about her "one-sixteenth" Cherokee "blood," Rose indicated, "I think I would still identify as white, depending on the situation." Because of this, and the fact that she knew precisely what "fraction" Native American she was, she appeared to me to be a beneficiary border patroller. The border patrolling that she experienced from outsider within (significant others) partially related to her own border patrolling of identity. This is not indicative of the racial treason that scholars have described (see Segrest 1994; Wise 2008). Instead of having traitorous identities that reject "whitely scripts[4]," Rose and her family embraced white privilege and engaged in racial redistricting to remain race evasive and privileged (Fischer 2006; Frankenberg 1993; Thompson 2001; Warren and Twine 1997). Her uncertainty concerning her grandfather's mortality and identity exposed racial ideologies that partially explained his peripheral position in her family and memory.

> I can't exactly remember...I was just looking at pictures, and I saw a picture and apparently it was my grandfather but he didn't look related to me at all, like he was very dark skinned, with dark hair. His nose was a little bit bigger, I guess. And just looked mean to me. He just looked angry, but my grandfather and grandmother weren't together for very long so it could have been likely that he was really mean....You know, he drank too much; he was not necessarily physically abusive but definitely verbally abusive, and um, kind of a slacker. Wasn't around, didn't want to work.

One can speculate that the rocky relationship between Rose's maternal grandparents colored and contaminated her perception of her grandfather. The negligible relationship that Rose had with him seemed soured by others' unfavorable accounts of his personality. This illustrates the importance of the stories people circulate within families, that "our stories matter" (Nash and Viray 2013), in terms of how they shape and support our identities.

Additional interpretations of Rose's narrative and experiences exist. One possible interpretation of Rose's attitude towards her multiracial heritage draws attention to her inability (or reasonable unwillingness) to recognize herself in her grandfather. While it is difficult to say whether or not her perception of differences in terms of gender, color, physical features, and other characteristics largely stems from the disparaging remarks of others, I do think Rose's discussion of these differences dances around the idea of "real" racial differences, as evidenced through her description of her grandfather as "only" one-quarter Cherokee. That Rose indicated that it would be easier to opt for white in any (casual or professional)[5] situation, suggests her desire to possessively invest in whiteness (Lipsitz 2006). Her narrative reveals both the relative ease with which multiracial people with whiter or lighter skin can assert their whiteness, and some of their reasons or motivations for doing so.

Rose implied that others might not take much of an interest in the details of her mixture and, that in those inquiring moments, she would not "want to overstep my boundary of information." She suggested that sharing information with strangers would be contextual, restrained, and relevant to the social situation or particular interaction (Waters 1999). However, it is more instructive to consider what information Rose *is* willing to share about herself racially, namely that she is white. Interestingly, when she mentioned lacking evidence of her racial mixture, she did not feel this dearth in relation to proving her whiteness. That is, she did not speak of the need to prove whiteness in ways that contrast with her need to prove her Native American ancestry. It is as if she has internalized government requirements to "document" or legitimize her identity, not only to herself but to others as well. Rose shared:

> I think, you know, if I found out undeniable *proof* then I would probably say White and Native American, just that I would give an explanation. But if I couldn't prove it, then I wouldn't want to give false information. I'd just say White. I wouldn't want people to be like, "Oh, well, tell me about your history." Like, "Gasp."... I think it's also, I don't know, I would sort of be proud if I was a part of that history that's been pretty much demolished. I'd be proud to have the opportunity to carry on some part of that because I know that there isn't a whole lot of it being passed on. Um, I don't know.

Rose's example suggests that when people lack racial literacy in a general sense, they often still possess enough working knowledge of the racial hierarchy to understand the wages of whiteness (Roediger 2003). They experientially know the material and social benefits of whiteness which require little proof of light- and white-skinned multiracial people. White (looking) skin becomes proof enough, with the body as evidence, but how does one prove something one ostensibly cannot see? Rose's comments expose the differences in racial group membership status and socialization. What seems apparent is that she was likely socialized, through colorblindness and colormuteness, to maintain the "invisibility of whiteness" while recognizing her indigeneity as the "Other." Consistent with white racial socialization, she claims whiteness, while remaining ambivalent about her "authority" to claim any indigeneity. As a result, she reinforces both the idea of whiteness as property and her invisible mixture.

Another interpretation of Rose's identity articulation relates to any fear she has of facing further invalidation as a white-looking person trying to acknowledge a racially mixed heritage. As a multiracial woman with white skin color, Rose knows that asserting a mixed race identity marks a risky proposition; doing so jeopardizes any white privilege that Rose accesses and enjoys, which also runs the risk of inauthenticating her mixture. As with other respondents, Rose reported that her phenotypical whiteness motivated her singular white identity. Negating her mixture and affirming her whiteness could be her way of border patrolling herself for her own benefit and, as I discuss shortly, for self-protection.

Unlike those White and Asian multiracial respondents who opted for white or tentatively claimed more of an incipient multiracial identity while enjoying their honorary whiteness, Peg rejected her honorary whiteness by increasingly attempting to assert a validated Korean identity. As a white Asian multiracial woman who was adopted into an interracial family of the same racial mixture (white and Asian), Peg increasingly embraced her Asian identity, even as she wrestled with not knowing much about her birth family.

In the South, she found relative ease in emphasizing her Korean heritage. She had no "concept of, like, being identified as white." However, her move away from her adoptive family and from one part of the country to another facilitated some of these changes in her racial self-perception. She noted that her racial sense of self shifted, such that she no longer saw herself as primarily Korean. Peg tired of others' inability to *not* see her as Korean. As she moved away from and became increasingly ashamed of being Korean, she remained bothered by this misrecognition.

This moving away from being Korean did not translate into intentionally moving towards whiteness. As Peg explained, she was essentially becoming white; the white culture, and mostly white friends in their "completely white world," made being Korean "different" but also "honorary white." Even though she "blended in very well" into these whitespaces (Horton 2006), Peg described feelings of racial alienation. Though "it was understood that I was Asian because I was different," many of the white people in Peg's life treated her as white. This behavior included making disparaging comments about other (than white) races. This exposure to how her white friends felt about her as an Asian solidified her honorary white status but also caused her to feel alienated from these friends. The ease with which they revealed ugly truths concealed in their race talk (Houts Picca and Feagin 2007) drew a wedge between them and Peg. She felt increasing dissonance over her friendships with whites, who accounted for and then effectively denied, her preferred racial and ethnic sense of self. By not expressing criticism of their racism, Peg maintained her honorary white status with them, using it to her advantage.

Following the rules of racial etiquette, or the "polite silences" of colorblind racism, none of the multiracial individuals admitted to wanting to access white privilege. This, however, does not mean that they do not want to *enjoy* the privileges of whiteness. Denying white privilege allows the beneficiaries of this "invisible knapsack of privilege" to continue enjoying earned advantages while maintaining the view of deserving them (McIntosh 1998). The literature on white privilege echoes this point by illustrating how whiteness and its invisible knapsack of privilege remain sights left unseen.

Many respondents who claimed a white identity also spoke of the nonwhite (or part-white) parent as highly assimilated. Also, they espoused a rather colorblind view of society and centered whiteness throughout the interviews. In that way, many of the part-white respondents engaged in beneficiary border patrolling of their identities because they knew they could access or had already accessed, the unearned privileges of claiming a white, honorary white, or multiracial identity versus a singular or collective black identity. This strategy reaffirmed the new racial hierarchy (Gans 1999) in which most multiracial individuals enjoy honorary white or white status in society. That is, respondents with part-white parentage or ancestry could and would more easily acknowledge their partial whiteness and its attendant privileges, while those with part black parentage or ancestry were more likely to claim a biracial or black identity than a singular white, Asian, or Hispanic one.

Protective Border Patrolling: Choosing "Black" When Others Don't Understand "Biracial"

Prevailing racial hierarchies and ideologies shape the choices people make regarding their racial identities and romantic partners. These forces inform many differences between the public and private presentation of their racialized selves. When people encounter opposition to the racial identities they choose, they may become increasingly self-protective. They opt for public identities that differ from their preferred (and private) identities to minimize this invalidation. They also do so anticipating that it will make more facile the social interactions with others (including strangers, family members, and friends). This does not always prove true.

In order to buffer themselves from reactions, including surprise, amusement, rejection, and so on, many respondents reported expressing public identities that they could convincingly "get away with" (see below). This observation underscores the performative aspect and expectation of social interactions (see Goffman 1963, 1967). It also highlights how much those interactions are racialized (see Khanna and Harris 2014). Not all multiracials felt they could give a convincing performance of their preferred identities. Consequently, they opted for simpler, often singular options, in an effort to achieve this legitimacy (in their own eyes and that of others).

As Gloria, one black and white biracial respondent recognized, whiteness was out of bounds or out of reach for her, despite her golden skin and curly blondish hair (as affirmed in people's comments about her appearance). Her experience illustrates that the boundaries of whiteness seldom expand to include black/white multiracials, a point made by Gallagher (2004a); Lee and Bean (2004); and others. This explains why she asserted a protean identity (black and white, biracial, "Other" [her term]), but never a singular white identity.

The identity grab bag that Rockquemore, Brunsma, and Delgado (2009) discuss does not afford all multiracial individuals the *same* number of racial identity options. In part, the racial hierarchy privileges whiteness and, thusly, allows multiracial individuals with white parentage an arguably more diverse range of options. Ironically, as my research illustrates, multiracial individuals often reinforce the racial hierarchy and the current racial classification system by border patrolling their own identities. While many multiracial individuals expressed a preference for shifting mixture, others preferred to collapse their complexity into singular categories. However, multiracial individuals with white and black heritage/parentage, for example, did not feel that they could choose whiteness, in the same ways that some white and Asian multiracial participants did. Despite the relative ease with which the latter may claim a white and/or Asian identity, most respondents of this combination chose to assert a mixed race or white racial identity, not a singular Asian identity. No respondents claimed a singular Asian identity.

This contrasts with Gloria's observation about the limitations to racial identity choice. She felt the option of whiteness was socially denied her, as exemplified by her response when asked about it (if she ever opted for whiteness): "I don't think I could get away with it (whiteness)." "Getting away" with whiteness involved looking white, not simply having a white parent, or claiming a white identity and having others affirm and validate such a choice rather than regard it suspiciously or dubiously. That Gloria has "never thought about that, honestly" shows the extent to which whiteness expands selectively, careful to exclude part-black multiracials in the process. Her reportedly having never thought about this issue could also be read as "not *having* to think about that." That suggests that Gloria either enjoys enough white privilege to not have to think about race and racism deeply or meaningfully, or the option to claim to not notice race through the twin discourses of colorblindness and colormuteness. This colorblind and colormute kinds of explanations exemplify the dominant patterns of people seeking to avoid conversations about race and any acknowledgment of racial difference.

Deploying colorblind explanations deflects attention away from any unearned privileges she enjoys as she approximates whiteness. Her comments that directly engaged racial matters in the interview contrast with some of her colorblind narratives. For example, she communicated that she claims a protean multiracial identity and has thought about that enough to equate whiteness and blackness combined with mixture. A more likely explanation again rests in the racial hierarchy that places Gloria more centrally in the collective black category, and more decidedly *outside of* categorical whiteness.

Chloe, an African American and Native American-identified woman (with Irish and Italian ancestry), also discussed how she defended her racial identity to family members. When some of her black relatives made disparaging comments about whites, Chloe, "out of defense," reminded them of her Irish and Italian parentage (mother). Chloe recognized her behavior as a "defense mechanism" when she took those comments personally because of her white mother. She observed, "If you [relatives] think this about white people, well then, what do you think about me, or my mother, or her side of the family?" Despite her understandable agitation, Chloe acknowledged that she mostly asserts a black or Native American identity. Doing so replicated others' invalidation of her racial mixture, making her identity align with how she appears to others: "more black" than any other race(s). Chloe's choice captures the reverberation of invalidation.

Even as she recognizes her multiplicity, she asserts a simpler or singular identity. This illustrates how many multiracial people may choose racial identities that reflect borderists' logic, or may become border patrollers themselves, in these cases, of their own identity options. This also illustrates the impact that border patrolling from strangers and familial others has on multiracial individuals and the identities they choose (or do not choose). When multiracial individuals internalize this borderism, they begin to perpetuate it themselves.

Though not her intention, Chloe (in opting for a black identity) also alienated some white relatives who saw her as multiracial and not black. She chose blackness to "uncomplicate things" and challenge the societal devaluation of blackness. However, doing so confused others' ways of seeing her, even as these other family members worked to *affirm* her multiraciality.

The above example underscores the predicament that places a burden on multiracial people who have to manage both the luxury and the liability of racial identity options (in contrast to people who feel altogether denied this choice) (see Rockquemore and Lazloffy 2005). Despite having more luxuries, in terms of choices or racial identity options, Chloe highlighted one limitation of that choice: opting for white. She offered:

> I definitely don't think I can get away with saying I'm white. "What? Did you just come back from vacation?" But yeah, I mean it's not something that I'd do. But you know, I'd love to say, I'm Italian, too, but what Italian community is really going to accept me? And the rest of the world, you know, maybe one community might accept me, but the rest of the world, when I step outside, they'll be like, "Italian?" Yeah. "She's Irish, you know?"

Chloe also linked how she arrived at her racial identity in relation to the racial socialization she received primarily from her father who "definitely wants us to identify as black" because of "decades of conditioning." Chloe's father prepared his children for the possibility of facing racial discrimination resulting from others' misperceptions of them (as black and stereotypically so):

> He definitely wants [us] to know that…when we step outside, nobody really cares that our mother's white…. He's done it subtly you know? He hasn't actually sat us down, and said, "Well, you do know that you're black." Or "There's some things that comes along with being black."…. He's subtly reminded us countless times that we can't expect the rest of the world to, like, buy into this biracial wonderland that we have at home, maybe.

In her "biracial wonderland," Chloe expressed a dichotomy between the public and private selves (Goffman 1967) or what others have called "public identity" and "internalized identity" (Khanna 2010). In Chloe's public presentation of self (Goffman 1963, 1967), she performs blackness yet, while in the comfort of her wonderland, she can more easily claim her racial mixture (though not without occasional contestation from some relatives) (see Brunsma 2006b).

Chloe's description of the backstage into which she retreats, or perhaps luxuriates, connotes the comfort she experiences there. This comfort eludes her in public in instances where others question or even challenge her identities. Like many other multiracial women with black parentage or heritage, Chloe draws this distinction to show the racework that many multiracial individuals engage in, during these public interactions with strangers; Steinbugler (2012) discusses this in her work with lesbian, gay, and straight, interracial relationships. These circumstances and social conditions reveal this racework and also make more visible the extent to which multiracial people manage their racial identities. The management of these identities involves auto-borderism, a self-policing of one's racial presentation of self in public and, sometimes, in private settings as well.

Opting for black for simplicity's sake did not, in fact, always simplify social interactions. Instead, they sometimes created productive tensions or intensified conflict between multiracial individuals and others, including strangers, significant others, other family members, and friends. Vanessa, a black-identified woman, explained why she too asserted a singular black identity as a protective mechanism: "I say I'm black because it's easier. I don't get a lot of questions that way." Opting for black enabled her attempts to evade borderists' racialized attention or the racial panopticon (Foucault 1977; Mirzoeff 2011) on the visuality and spectacle of bodies (see also Markovitz 2011). In a way, her choice to collapse her multiracial parentage into blackness can be interpreted as a kind of self-border patrolling. Her choice also shows how "multiracial" does not always survive to the next generation (Bratter 2007).

> My father is Cherokee Indian and African American. He identifies himself as African American. My mother is Caucasian and African American, and she identifies as African American....My family also identified us as African American because that's how we are seen by society and that's how they see themselves. They feel like they'd be able to relate to, they can deal with issues they are given by identifying as African American instead of something else.

Similar to other black multiracials, Vanessa gets asked if she is "anything besides black." People often say that they think she looks "different" and "exotic," as if there is "something there that I don't see." I suspect that they see signs of racial mixture (Cherokee Indian, African

American, and Caucasian) that Vanessa only partially acknowledges but does not incorporate into her identity. Her mixture is her habitus and thus it remains, relatively speaking, "clearly invisible" to her. To others, her mixture appears always already visible.

Her desire for privacy and simplicity does not always dissuade others who continue to wonder about Vanessa's racial identity. Identifying as black then backfires to the degree that it does little to deflect these inquiring and curious gazes. What Vanessa draws attention to here contrasts with her desire to *not* draw attention to herself. The legibility of race—the in/visible mixture—relates here to racial literacy and betrays the way people ignore, deny, or minimize the continuing significance of race (Feagin 1991).

Another black-identified multiracial woman respondent, Juanita, explained her own complicated racial parentage and reasons for choosing her preferred racial identity:

> I say that I'm black but I'm not really sure how to say *it*, like when people ask me that question because I don't know how to include everything and so I just leave it (she laughs). "Everything" is of course African American, Native American, Creole, Puerto Rican, I think that's it. There's maybe something else…Some Caucasian but it's just further out (generations back).

Like Vanessa, Juanita opted for black, to elude attention and evade others' (un)spoken expectations of her to elaborate on her racial identity. She strategically employed this tactic to manage public interactions with strangers but effectively erased her racial multiplicity, or at least attempted to, when she is in public. She suggested that opting for black proved easier than elaborating on her racial mixture to strangers, "because I get less questions that way." Eliding inquiries and evading racial interrogations is possible by collapsing her multiracial identity into blackness. That way, Juanita avoids comments claiming that she is "confused" or a modern day "tragic mulatto" who struggles with what she called "the Tiger Woods problem." This persistence of a problematic narrative, the troubled, confused "tragic mulatto," must be managed by many multiracial people even those who claim a singular racial identity and even if they are not the ones experiencing confusion over their racial identities.

Juanita collapsing her racial complexity into a single category is a variation of Rose's practice of "disappearing difference," as I discussed earlier. In my estimation, Juanita does not work to deny or avoid her mixture but rather simplifies it. She displays knowledge of the social interactional rules; the ones that nudge her to abbreviate her responses to strangers' questions (see Goffman 1967, 1963). This contrasts with Rose, who appears to intentionally "opt for white" to avoid any penalties she might otherwise incur for naming her Native American heritage (despite her discussion of how interesting this detail of her heritage makes her).

Like other black multiracial respondents, Jessica, a black-identified young woman of black and Asian Indian parentage, discussed having a black habitus[6] which largely influenced and explained her singular black identity. She shared her negotiation of the space in between (feeling and "acting black") and the way she patrolled her own identity:

> I've always felt black but I've always identified myself as biracial so it's kind of weird, you know what I mean? Like I—I know it's not proper to say this: I act black, you know, because that's how I grew up.... That's kind of what I identify with, you know, but if like, I'm filling out a form or something, you know, I'll put multiracial. Whereas when I was younger, I'd used to always put black.

Jessica's response captures the conflict of racial identities in tension with one another and in flux over the life course (Doyle and Kao 2007, 2004). Though Jessica wanted to "recognize both parents," she opted for black. Jessica's border patrolling worked to both affirm and problematize blackness (Hintzen and Rahier 2003). In celebrating her pride in being black and her love of black people, Jessica overshadowed her Asian Indian identity while deferring to it in order to nuance her black experience. As with other respondents, Jessica had not thought about or noticed any unearned privileges she enjoyed because of her multiraciality and racial ambiguity. In not noticing, Jessica enjoyed her singular black identity in ways that preserved her occasional colorblindness. This colorblindness and colormuteness prevented her from registering how her skin color and beauty operates as a currency in this pigmentocracy (Bonilla-Silva 2003a,b).

Like Jessica, Jamie also asserted a black identity even though her light skin tone piques others' curiosity about her heritage. Based on Jamie's accounts, people interested in her racial identity and ambiguity often confrontationally commented, "No, you're not black. You're black and something else." These comments troubled Jamie because she grew up in a small Southern town and in a community and a family where people abided by the racial binary: a person is either black or white. She dogmatically denied the racial mixture that was the result of a white man's sexual exploitation of a black female relative that occurred generations ago. Here, her denial of mixture is actually a refusal to acknowledge mixture; a strategy or stance mimicked in her family, who worked consciously to preserve blackness by negating and erasing the trauma of rape (and the forced inclusion of whiteness into families) (see Gray-Rosendale 2013; Spickard 1989; Walters, Mohammed, Evans-Campbell, Beltran, Chae, and Duran 2011).

When I asked her to elaborate on her reasons for choosing "black" over other options (i.e., "white," "mixed," "biracial," etc.), Jamie replied: "Because it wasn't a choice that they (black female relatives) slept with them, slept with the white people. It was rape. It wasn't by choice.... To be honest, if I could pass for white, I probably would say that I'm white but I couldn't pass for it, so I wouldn't say it." Since Jamie felt too dark to be white, she resented relatives who passed as white and enjoyed "the advantages you get just by being white," or what Peggy McIntosh (1998) refers to as "white privilege." She recalled having heard stories of white-looking black relatives trying to assert black identities and encountering resistance and invalidation: "They told her (a relative), 'No.' That she wasn't, they told her that she wasn't black. That she was white.... Oh, I have some pictures—they look exactly like white people but they're not white. They're black."

While Jamie acknowledges why her family actively preserves blackness by denying and eliding the painful racial reality of how whiteness was incorporated into the family, she remains conflicted over racial identity choice. Her narrative captures the ways that the meanings people attach to racial categories often encapsulate or get informed by the messiness of historical traumas. Claiming anything other than blackness could be a trigger, resuscitating past individual, familial, and collective traumas. Sensitivity to these matters involves attending to the historical residue of trauma, and the traumatic residue of history, as Jamie acknowledges and alludes to in her narrative (see Walters, Mohammed, Evans-Campbell, Beltran, Chae, and Duran 2011).

Curious about her conviction to reinforce the black-white binary, I asked Jamie to reflect on the term "biracial." We shared this exchange in discussing her views on the term:

> Jamie: I don't like it. I don't think there's such a thing (as biracial). It's either one or the other. Because you can't be *both*. You just can't; I just don't see how you can be both. You're either black or you're white, whichever is more *prominent*, that's the one you are, to me.

> Author: If one is *more* prominent than the other, then that means that the other still exists?

Jamie: It exists, but you don't have to acknowledge it. You can't identify with both. When somebody asks you what race you are, you can't say, "Oh, I'm multiracial," or "I'm mixed."

Author: Why not?

Jamie: You're just not. I just don't see it. I don't understand how you could say that. Like I have a cousin and my uncle, he's very light skinned, green eyes, and he's black but identifies either way though. But he had 2 kids by a white lady and they look white. Like you couldn't tell they have any black blood and they don't say that they're black or mixed. They don't say that they're black or mixed. They say that they're white. Because if they say, "Oh, I'm mixed," or "I'm black," people gonna look at them like they're crazy.

Jamie regarded racial mixture as impossible, relegating it to the body (but not something that should be socially claimed in reality, as a possible identity). She found multiraciality largely incomprehensible. She lacked an awareness of the social construction of race, failing (or refusing) to see how her community and family reinforced a black/white racial divide in her life and mind. "Where I grew up at, you're either black or you're white. No in-between. And those are the only two races: black or white." Although some scholars argue that members of the same family are of different races because of the ways we socially construct race in this country (Ferrante and Brown 2001), Jamie rejected that reality. Instead, she insisted on her black identity.

This insistence was compromised by some of her classmates ("white girls") who considered her white. Once on a class trip, one classmate commented, "I wanna get a tan like [Jamie]." Stumped by this white girl's perception of her, Jamie thought to herself, "White with a tan?" She explained her conflicted feelings about racial passing and the politics of skin color:

Skin tone is a big thing for me; I'm just getting over it.... I don't want to be *dark*, like this is too dark for me. I don't know, I don't think that dark skin's pretty. [I got that idea from] my grandmother....She always used to tell us not to be out in the sun, and you know, that's not pretty. You don't wanna get *black*. There was some saying she used to say, I don't even remember it." (Emphasis hers).

Even though her maternal grandmother was light-skinned enough to pass as white, she chose not to do so. Despite her choice, the grandmother conveyed the importance of lighter skin to Jamie, who observed that "they were seen to be a little bit better than the other black people...and it was mainly because of their skin tone." Jamie's mother also emphasized the importance of light skin and discouraged her daughter from darkening by similarly admonishing her and advising her to stay inside (see Golden 2005; Rondilla and Spickard 2007). While Jamie's mother cleverly couched her advice in gendered terms, "Don't go outside, or you'll get dirty," and initially deflected attention away from a racial hierarchy, Jamie's reflection on her mother's (and grandmother's) comments suggests that despite these attempts at racial displacement, she knew better than to ignore the significance of race in these narratives.

In order to avoid or minimize this border patrolling from strangers, black multiracial respondents asserted a singular black identity. In part, they hoped to elide this attention (Frankenberg 1993) and avoid being a racial spectacle (DeBord 1995), however benign the racialized gaze (Foucault 1977). Choosing blackness as a means of circumventing interrogations and the usual inspection, or what Gloria Wade-Gayles (1997) calls "eye questions," then could be interpreted as protective border patrolling.

A few "honorary white" respondents had similar experiences. David, another respondent (white Hispanic) discussed his blended experience in terms of a "two-ness." In borrowing from W.E.B. DuBois (1903), David described himself "racially as white and culturally as bicultural." In his elaboration, he explained how being both white and Hispanic meant enduring authenticity testing from various sources. In feeling these pressures, David works to protect his multiracial, bicultural identity.

> Because I grew up identifying as biracial but as I came to explore what race means, it became more and more evident to me that um, it's, it's much more of an identity that's assigned by the outside rather than a sense of self and it's, it's linked to um, how I've experienced the world because of privilege and things like that, and so, of my siblings, I'm the whitest one and, and I, you know, came to realize at some point that perhaps this was not just, "Oh, I worked really hard." That I'm the only one with a Ph.D. and the other two, one just has H.S. and she's the darkest of us, the one that's most immediately recognized as Spanish or "spic" (he says with a Southern accent; imitating a Southern accent) or Latina, however she's clearly recognized as something other than white and my youngest sister is kind of in the middle. And so I identify racially just sort of out of my awareness of um sort of oppression dynamics, power, privilege issues and my lens, my outward-looking lens, that's pretty impossible for me to define. I, I realize that, I know that I do not see the world as, um, people that I know that are white from both parents, um. It's very clear to me that,

that I see the world very *differently* than they see the world. Even those who have had more awareness around racial constructs and things like that. And so it's a cognitive distinction that I'm easily able to make and in terms of Latino people, I, I don't experience a sense of belonging from the inside but as a legitimacy I guess is a better word. And so I clearly don't see the world from the perspective of people who are completely Latino because, or even Panamanian specifically, because my whole life, I've, I've sort of been given that, that sort of, you know, reminders that I'm the gringo, that I'm the white one. So I have no idea how I would, you know, describe.... my racial identity from the inside, because I can't, I can't—to me I can only say there's . something about this blended perspective.

For this and other white Hispanic/Latino/a respondents, being blended offers a unique vantage point for experiencing the world. While they situationally enjoyed the privileges of whiteness, they also experienced social life as "optional people of color" (Gonzalez 2016) or "white people of color" (Alvarez 1998). As such, they may be read as "a different kind of white" due to their Spanish language ability, but they are also often read as "not quite Hispanic enough" and disqualified accordingly. Having many of his white American father's physical features and appearance, David endured authenticity testing throughout adolescence and young adulthood as others evaluated his legitimacy as a "real" Panamanian. He even appeared to internalize some of this disqualification. He said:

It was a strange reverse because the power dynamics of our, the racial dynamics of our society were reversed in my family. My mother, the Latina person, was the dominating figure and I grew up in a household that devalued white people. Everything from "Their food has no rhythm" to "They're imperialist bastards." You know? And so, I grew up in a world where white was the bad guy, and um, for me, you know, I was never, you know, I was adored but it, it and so the bad guy didn't apply to me, um, in any of those ways. It applied to me in, "[He] doesn't like mangoes." I don't like mangoes. (Here he enunciates, mimicking/mocking whiteness through "hyperarticulation"). "Mango," (pronounced with noticeable or emphasized Spanish accent, presumably the "proper" pronunciation), whatever you wanna call it. And you know dancing, I can't do salsa.... I dance like a white guy. Yeah basically, that kind of stuff. And um, my older sister, has the, in addition to her physical features, she also had this notion, she was actually born in Panama, and so she is a "real" Panamanian and I am not. And so since my mother was the idolized figure in the family, I have her personality traits, but I, I was raised with the notion that I got stuck with my father's physical traits.

As a point of clarification, and in my estimation, the comment, "There food has no rhythm," loops back to my discussion of vanilla whiteness, and (stereotypically) speaks to this point by casting whiteness as boring or bland. It endorses a different stereotype, that of "spicy" or exciting Latino culture. As Dalmage (2000), people reinforce race and police racial borders through the use of stereotypes. The narratives that circulated in the interviews, and in the daily lives of my respondents, make this clear.

The extent to which David participated in performing his racial and ethnic identity intentionally at some points and unintentionally at others is interesting, particularly given his geographical location: the South. Khanna (2010, 2011) discusses the ways in which multiracials form and perform their racial identities in the South. As someone living in the South (at the time of our interview), David was not only reflecting on his experiences forming and performing race from his blended perspective but also within the particular geographical context of the South. The bifurcated system of race that prevails there does not easily accommodate his "two-ness" and keeps his mixture relatively invisible to others.

Throughout the discussion of disqualification and authenticity testing, he deploys his cultural knowledge and capital in a way that authenticates the very identity that others have disqualified. When he pronounced certain words such as "salsa," and "mangoes" he used a decidedly Spanish accent as if to stamp these words with his identity, to inflect them in ways that native Spanish speakers would, to solidify his position as a "real" Panamanian who speaks Spanish well. His hyperarticulation, the deliberate enunciation of both syllables, offered up whiteness as hyperbolic and hegemonic, as well as a reference with which to contrast his Panamanian identity. When he said, "I don't like mangoes," he was almost mocking whiteness, and himself, as he recognized that he is white and not white; his tone of voice also inferred that he is not the kind of white that others suggest he is. He tentatively embraces whiteness or reluctantly identifies with what whiteness connotes to the people who see him as only white. Another possible interpretation of this enunciation and interaction is that he may disidentify (see Muñoz 1999) with this kind of hyperbolic whiteness.

To make his whiteness visible, David makes his performance of whiteness intentional and recognizable in its clichéd form (starchy, "proper English" speaking). Doing so comfortably centers him in the interstices or the borderlands and affirms that he is both white and Spanish (see Anzaldua 1983). This affirmation results from his ability to "do" race and ethnicity well (see Khanna 2011 for more on forming and performing race). He can "sound" both white and Spanish in its most recognizable essentialized, even hyperbolic, forms. This racial (and cultural) performance not only validates his knowledge of both but cements his position in-between. This performance also begins to explain the blended perspective of which he spoke in the interview.

> It wasn't so much liked or did, because I liked and did. It was more of just the way I was; the most vivid example that comes to mind, I haven't thought about this, and I'm realizing there's some emotion in all of this as I am talking about this. I haven't talked about this in a while. Um, ah, I, I did not drink when I was a teenager, you know; I wasn't getting laid with as many women as possible. I wasn't you know, I wasn't a tough macho guy. I played the piano and so... I still, I remember my cousins, because I lived in Panama when I was in high school, and I remember my cousins you know, on the balcony of their, of their porch in Panama City, you know, and they each have a glass of scotch and soda and they say, "C'mon, you have to drink. You cannot be a Gonzalez unless you drink." I remember distinctly thinking, "Shit." You know. "Now I'm even more white because I don't like the taste of scotch and soda." And um, it wasn't until later in life that I looked back on that memory, which is a vivid memory, but it wasn't until later that I realized, you know, they were linking being Panamanian, um, with drinking, and toughness, and things like that. My cousins, every once in a while, would could home, like with a black eye, because they got into a fight. And I could hear my mother— "Over a girl!" and yeah probably, you know, or because they stood up for themselves, talking trash to some larger guy; and you know, I remember my mom contrasting, "[David] would never do that; he's smart; he's going to college" and all of that stuff. And so the very traits that were different were also somehow linked to the fact that I was going to achieve. And the only positive things my mother ever said about my father, um, there was a lot of playful, um, insulting as I was growing up, at him, she was, the most repeated thing was, "I only married him because he had blue eyes and fair skin." And that was a big accomplishment for a Panamanian woman in the 1960s.

As the lightest sibling in his family, David stood out as different. His skin color made him a target of ridicule and teasing, but also made him a symbol of "potential," a sign of inevitable success. For him and other respondents, protecting one's preferred racial identity proved important. While most were recognized as mixed, they were not always validated as such. In maneuvering around and manipulating mixture, they opted to protect this mixture. For many of the black multiracial respondents, especially those with darker skin color, they attempted to protect themselves from racial interrogations and identity invalidations by choosing blackness.

Some portions of David's narrative suggest a more insidious or condemning tone than he registers. In some of his examples, he notes the way people use humor to defuse the charge of some racialized comments and observations. If one could understand this practice as a kind of "racetalk" (Myers 2005), one might consider how this discourse impacts others. What is the impact of these discourses on multiracial people like David? Does the existence and circulation of these discourses link to the kinds of border patrolling behavior of multiracials themselves? In the next section, I discuss malevolent border patrolling, drawing particular attention to the patterns that emerge in terms of people policing their own identity choices.

Malevolent Border Patrolling: Black, but Not *That* Kind of Black

Many people, including multiracial people themselves, believe that multiracial people cannot express individual racism. This section challenges that view, offering up many examples of multiracial individuals negotiating their participation in racism and precarious positions of privilege in the racial hierarchy. As multiracial people internalize racism, they participate in malevolent border patrolling when they express any variety of problematic stereotypes that situate them as "better than" other groups of people. In addition, malevolent border patrolling insists on a singularity. It reifies racial categories and generally denies mixture and, thus, racially mixed identities.

Some respondents who confidently asserted a multiracial identity deployed somewhat stereotypical thinking in affirming multiraciality. Take Sanchez, a black Puerto Rican man:

> I'm not one-sided on my race in any degree. I'm basically like in the middle. I like Spanish food, like paella. Stuff like that. Platanos are really good. Reggaeton. Merengue. And stuff like that. I love that music. And of course, I'm black. I love hip-hop and all that other stuff, like hip hop, rap, R and B, and of course fried chicken. And all those stereotypes.

Here, Sanchez presented himself as a divided (versus composite) self, enumerating his mixture as one part Hispanic, the other black. Each part obediently follows what hegemonic culture dictates. These discursive practices cement the idea that to be black is to like rap and hip-hop or that to be Hispanic is to eat paella. Interestingly, Sanchez acknowledges how his friends were affected by the policing racial discourses of their parents, who held stereotypical views of blacks as violent, criminal, "shacking up," uneducated, incarcerated sex fiends (see Davis 1981; Collins 2005).

Jessica, who engaged in both protective and malevolent border patrolling, explained that growing up around black people both prompted and pressured her to identify as black because "that was really all I was exposed to." She continued,

> I identify with black culture. I listen to, you know, traditional black culture, stereotypical music, you know, hip hop, R and B, all types of music like that, and I mean, I guess just being around all black people helped me identify more with that side of me.

Jessica also described not knowing "a lot about Indian culture," since her mother, who "you can't tell is Indian just by talking to her" and is "pretty much fully Americanized," has "assimilated toward it, regular culture." In addition, "She cooks American food. She doesn't cook Indian food." With both sides of her extended family in the Midwest, Jessica noted that she has little contact with her parent's relatives and other extended kinship networks.

Jessica's reference to "regular culture" speaks to the way that "American culture" becomes the dominant reference point, despite her growing up in a multicultural family (see Takaki 1993). Her logic extends to matters of race as she relied on troublesome tropes of race to situate herself in society (see Gates 1986). Jessica deployed similar stereotypes in explaining how she arrived at a black identity. Her contradictory comments above suggest that blackness was imposed on her (the racial identity to which she should default), even though she was aware that "when people see me, they don't see a black person because I don't look black. I look like I'm mixed." She actively chose and embraced blackness "because I love black people." She did so amidst being teased by other black people:

> If I say...an urban comment, you know..."What's up??" or something that's really urban, people will make fun of me and they'll be like, "You ain't black. Stop acting black.".... Like my boyfriend. He's black. Um, he grew up a certain way. Of course, he grew up with the mom who used to punish him, and beat him whenever he did something wrong. And he knows that the way I grew up, it wasn't like that because I didn't have a black mother, so you know I didn't get punishment all the time.

Here, Jessica participates in racetalk. Following Toni Morrison, Myers (2005) describes racetalk as permeated everyday life with "racial signs and symbols" designed to oppress black people. In earlier work, Myers (2003) contends that racism is always already present in social interactions, whether or not black people are present; racetalk is "symptomatic of a racial structure in which some racial/ethnic groups enjoy more privileges than others."

In some ways then, racetalk allows Jessica to deploy racial stereotypes of black people, despite her own blackness and her admission, "I love black people!" The deployment of these stereotypes (that black mothers physically punish their children as discipline; or that "real" black people "have it rough" growing up) is a curiosity in that Jessica used it to both mark blackness and differentiate her blackness from the recognizably stereotypical form. Much like Sanchez deployed racial code words, tropes and stereotypes, so too did Jessica. To Jessica, to be "urban" is to be black; it is to grow up a "certain way" (which included examples associating verbal and physical punishment and discipline with black people). This racetalk reflected the troublesome tropes that persist which can be used to perpetuate racial stereotypes and to authenticate race.

Others seemed less aware or equipped to deal with their own stereotypical thinking about race and racial identity. For example, Toni, a young African American-identified woman with Black, White, and Native American ancestry, also faced invalidation of her racially mixed heritage. "When I say I had a white great-grandfather," some refute her assertion by saying, "Everybody did. Who doesn't?" Toni explained, "I acknowledge that (mixture) because that's just my history." Ironically, while confronting the racial ideologies of others and elaborating on others accusing her of "acting white," Toni reified many stereotypes about blacks:[7] that they "go around with nails and hair" [presumably long and loud]; and look "ghetto" and expressed some problematic ideologies of her own.[8] When I asked her to clarify what "acting white" meant to her, she offered the following:

> People think I "act white" because I don't act like *that*. (Emphasis hers). You know what I'm saying?.... Well, I know I'm very reserved. I guess by the way I speak, that I don't speak slang, I guess. The way I carry myself.... The way I dress; the things that I wear.... And also because I, I've never, I don't hang around just black people. I've never gone to an all-black institution, like schools. I've always been around whites (attended racially diverse schools).... Except for one. I started off at an HBCU (Historically Black Colleges and Universities), and it was a culture shock for me.... Because they were African American

through and through. They weren't like me.... They were a little bit wild, more outspoken.

By "wild," Toni meant "just flying off the handle about everything; cursing." Her comments about being "African American through and through" suggest an authenticity or "realness" about blackness. She knows these authenticity tests from experience yet supports them in her observations of "real" black people. She also suggested that many had "strong personalities, not saying that that's a black thing. But it was just different than what I'm used to." After a year, Toni transferred to a predominantly white university. Her experience "wasn't as bad as at the HBCU [because] everyone acted like they were supposed to." Toni's comments illustrated that not only do some whites subscribe to racist ideologies but often blacks do as well. The comments also contrasted blackness by differentiating between "good" and "bad" blacks. Toni was not alone in her deployment of these discursive practices.

The racetalk that Toni engages in supports the point that Bonilla-Silva (2003a) makes in his work, *Racism without Racists*. He argues that blacks increasingly adopt the style of colorblind racism many white people rely on in this society. Bonilla-Silva (2002) also addresses this covert operation in his article, "The Linguistics of Color Blind Racism." This article details the new face of racism—the softer, subtler kind. While some people continue to keep racial epithets in circulation, they have recently introduced a gentler style of racism into their repertoire. The stylistics of this new racism have begun to seduce not only whites, many of whom feel "outnumbered" or otherwise crowded out by immigrants and/or people of color, but also by some of those very immigrants and/or people of color. In an ironic but perhaps not altogether surprising pattern, members of the honorary white and collective black groups have coopted whites' styles of racial discourses, which replicate and reproduce dominant racial discourses and racial hegemony.

Toni's comments suggest some internalized racism which provides a partial explanation for her perception and description of some black people as "wild." The result of this internalization of racism could also offer explanation as to some of the contradictions that emerge in her narrative, relating her contradictory admiring and disparaging comments about black people (see Bailey, Chung, Williams, Singh, and Terrell 2011).

In contrasting shades of blackness, these respondents promoted themselves as having ostensibly "better" kinds of black versus "not *that* kind of black" identities by juxtaposing themselves with the more mythical, hyperbolic blackness. Alternately, black-identified respondents with multiracial parentage may experience border patrolling as an attempt (by others) to dis/qualify their blackness. Invoking stereotypical images of blackness can position one as an insider because it suggests an intimate familiarity with such mythologies. Conversely, circulating these stereotypes discursively could position one as an outsider, thereby compromising their blackness even further. Perhaps one could argue that a little bit of both are at play here. Toni, Jessica, and others show how racial ideologies in a post–Civil Rights Era remain contradictory at best.

That Jessica performs her blackness by getting "a little ghetto" or "putting a little accent with my speech" suggests that she is both a racial insider and an outsider to blackness. Her racial performance remains problematic in her evocation of or reliance on stereotypes to express her blackness publicly. Feeling pressured to prove her blackness (versus both her black and Asian Indian identity), Jessica border patrols herself. To alleviate some of the pressure of this border patrolling, she notes that increasingly she acknowledges that she is mixed, with plans to travel to India "to try to learn a little bit about that side of me."

Jessica's narrative deviated slightly from that of Sa, who pointedly felt a sense of entitlement to freely explore a number of experiences and cultures that her Black, Brazilian, and British relatives introduced and exposed her to throughout her life course: "That's why I'm kinda like dipping into every little thing because it's just like from one side I have my (white British) grandmother showing me this (etiquette; tea parties; 'ballet, opera, classical music...and museums') from the other (black American) aunts and cousins introducing me to rap music and stuff like that ('jazz' and 'Luther Vandross')."

In describing this freedom to choose, Sa not only contrasted (and racialized) the interests of family, she classed them as well, at least implicitly, with references to the "ballet" and "opera" signifying high culture and "rap" signifying low culture, in the dominant imagination. The class connotations intersect with race to suggest that ballet, opera and the like are "white" pastimes while rap music and jazz are "black" pastimes. On a related note, respondents like Sa expressed an appreciation for being able to blend racial borders by exploring their interests cross-racially ("dipping into every little thing"). Ironically, as they did so, they described different activities in bounded and race-specific ways. This reified the racial connotations (and their attendant limitations) of various social and cultural activities such that they equated ballet with whiteness or jazz with blackness (see Steele 2011). These dichotomies are false but, paradoxically, when mixed, they can signal blending, border crossing, and affirm multiracial mixture. Indeed, they signal mixture.

Respondents who were border patrolled by significant others did not seem to be as easygoing about border blending. In general, they appeared more tentative and policing of their own interests as a result. Respondents whose families encouraged border blending, then, more easily seemed to embrace their racial composition. Unlike respondents who felt regulated and disciplined by others' borderism, Sa, for example, felt unrestricted. Since she had not internalized others' borderism, she felt free to explore her interests without being a docile body pressured to follow racial scripts (Foucault 1977).

Another expression of borderism involved respondents articulating antagonism about or frustration with being misread or misrecognized racially and ethnically (see Harper 2005 and Harris-Perry 2011 on misrecognition). While some respondents regarded such misreading as complimentary because it facilitated their ability to blend into different racial groups, other respondents responded less favorably to this misreading that they felt was pejorative. This ambiguity sometimes increased their social access to more groups of people.

Zach, a white Asian multiracial man, revealed more interesting, almost incitable ideas about his reactions to being misread as Hispanic. Because he jokingly referred to himself as a "flip," which some Filipinos do (see Francia and Gamalinda 1996), I considered his experience in transitioning from "'flip' to 'spic'" a provocative way to draw attention to his ostensibly internalized racism and the white privilege he enjoys as an "honorary white" or "not fully Asian" person. Bailey, Chung, Williams, Singh, and Terrell (2011) discuss internalized racism or racial oppression as it relates to black individuals, but one could argue similar patterns may be observed in multiracial individuals of various racial combinations. The aforementioned transition from one racial location and consciousness to another occurs when his friends fail to grant him honorary whiteness by problematically pointing out Zach's difference through "jokes." They do not make fun of his Filipino identity, notably, but rather the racialized ethnicity for which he is often mistaken. Speculatively, Zach's friends tease him about this, knowing of his displeasure in being mistaken for a Latino. He expressed this displeasure in misrecognition to me at various points in our interview conversation. He provided this explanation and observation of the humor his friends deploy to deal with the differences between them. Note their use of the diminutive, "little," to describe a Mexican person; this is indicative of what Eduardo Bonilla-Silva (2003a) argues is one of the primary styles of colorblind racism:

It seems like it's just a big joke, like my friends that are white, they're like, "Ah, you little Mexican, come here." I mean, they don't mean any harm by it. I know they're just kidding; they're just messing with me. Like I have one friend who's, he's a white guy, and I call him fatty, because he's a big guy. And he's like, "Come here, you little wetback. Will you come cut my grass?" That kind of stuff, and it's all fun and games so I don't take any offense to it. Like the thing that really irritates me though is when I go to a Mexican restaurant or someplace and like a Mexican, or a Latino generally, will come up to me or my girlfriend and just assume, right off the bat, that we speak Spanish. And I'm like, "Dude, I don't speak Spanish" and they have this look like, "Why not?" and I'm like, "Because I'm not Latino. I don't have to know Spanish."

His racial attitudes about Latinos are insensitive, if not abrasive. They are not, however, altogether uncommon, particularly in the national and local context of intensified public debates and discussions regarding the (legal and/or illegal) presence of immigrants, especially Mexicans in the South (see also Schuman, Steeh, Bobo, and Krysan 1997). His vehemence becomes more visible and striking in opposition to the racist jocularity he exchanges among friends, most of whom identify as white.

Rather than enjoy the multiple honorary memberships he is granted because of his ambiguity (that some mistake him as Hispanic), Zach reacts with frustration. Ironically, he remains tolerant, if not accomodating, of the racist jokes and race talk his friends casually deploy in his presence (see Houts Picca and Feagin 2007; Myers 2005). Arguably, when he joins in the joking, he might even be viewed as encouraging their behavior. Whether he forgives them for joking or actually does not even seem to find any offense in this type of humor, he takes obvious offense to strangers misperceiving him as Hispanic or presuming that he knows Spanish. He appears insistent on distancing himself from Latinos or Hispanics, so much so that he disregards that others may see him as multilingual (a speaker of Spanish and English), rather than Spanish-speaking only. So palpable is his aversion to this perception that he rejects this possibility and firmly celebrates that he primarily knows and speaks only one language.

This, in some ways, exposes not only how his white friends view him as "honorary white" or "not really Asian" (except for the "good food" his Asian mother is able to prepare), but also suggests that he 1) may see himself similarly, as "honorary white," and 2) may harbor potentially prejudicial views of different racial/ethnic groups (except whites and Asians).

What is ironic about Zach's opposition to honorary Hispanic membership, or more generally to being perceived as of a group to which one does not claim membership, involves the lack of information that people have about the very groups to which they *do* or *could* claim membership. For example, because one could understand Filipino as a mix of Chinese and Spanish (Root 1997; Espiritu 2001, 2003, 2004), one could read Zach's frustration with or rejection of being misperceived as Spanish as a form of internalized racism—or a lack of literacy or knowledge about the complexity of multiraciality among Filipinos. One might suggest he is border patrolling himself, except that he appears unaware of what Filipino mixture includes (historically and in contemporary society) (see Ocampo 2016).

To not know the composite parts of his identity prohibits him from seeing that disliking or distancing himself from Hispanics/Latinos could be interpreted as disliking or distancing from himself. While I cannot draw this conclusion, I share part of his narrative as an example of how easily some multiracial people can access white privilege, revise their own family histories to maintain this privilege or enjoy "honorary white" status, and reinforce socially constructed differences between racial and ethnic groups. His example also reveals a certain fragility or precarity in that honorary position.

Zach's experience echoes that of Tracy whose friends reportedly directed a lot of racetalk at her as well. As I discussed in the last chapter, Tracy also enjoyed an honorary white status in her mostly white friendship group. However, because she reportedly ate rice and "Chinese food, or Asian food, everyday just about," she faced a similar set of insensitive and racist remarks or "jokes" from her friends. In both examples, Zach and Tracy espouse colorblind narratives throughout the course of our interviews yet these moments they offer punctuate, if not rupture, their colorblindness. Their narratives reveal a far messier negotiation that they must make, as they may want to preserve their honorary white membership in the friendship circles and their integrity. Reacting "too strongly" could easily jeopardize their status and reinforce racial divisions that otherwise get ignored or minimized. Their experiences suggest that these negotiations can much more easily be framed through humor because that interpretation is more forgiving. To interpret the jokes as more malicious, or racist, would require emotional work and communication that multiracial individuals and their mostly white peers may not be prepared to handle effectively. This sobering reality suggests that more work must be done to equip people with the tools to talk more openly and honestly about race, racial difference, and racial discrimination on individual and institutional levels.

Just think about the impact and injury that these "jokes" have on young people crystallizing their racial identities (see Collins 1998b; Myers 2005). Is it any wonder that multiracial individuals engage in racial border patrolling, denying parts of their parentage to blend in, instead of blending borders?

Conclusions

What many of the narratives of multiracial respondents revealed is the sobering reality of racism. That is, as some multiracial individuals acknowledge the way that they are targets of racial discrimination and differential treatment and that they are positioned at a disadvantage in the dating and mate selection process, others participate in and produce what Kristen Myers (2005) calls "racetalk." Sometimes, the same individuals may be targets of discrimination and also participants in perpetuating it individually. This participation upholds and circulates the problematic racial ideologies of members of various racial groups. As multiracial individuals negotiate their potentially shifting mixture, they may manage their multiplicity by border patrolling themselves.

Policing or constraining their own choices, instead of enjoying and exploring these choices, reflects a trend that reinforces Bonilla-Silva's (2004) contention that anyone living in a racial pigmentocracy and hierarchy will learn to participate in the process. Multiracial people may choose to present themselves in ways that bring them better access to racial privilege, positioning themselves in closer proximity to some color lines and further from others. Doing so also upholds the antiblack racism that persists in this country and the dis-privileges that collective black members experience.

In Chapter Six, I build on my discussion of borderism to show how people who are policed, in terms of their racial identities, produce new ways of seeing race. Through their own literal and figurative journeys, many multiracial people cross racial borders as well as geographical ones. What does this multiracial movement do to our collective conceptualizations of race when we are encouraged to take into account different racial paradigms? How do these migrations facilitate racial transformations and reconfigurations in the racial classification system and the way people locate, dislocate, and/or relocate themselves within this system, in this society, and others?

Notes

[1] He held this belief despite saying, "Almost everybody's a mixture of the oppressed and the oppressor because when you look at how many children were the children of sexual, I mean, I hate to say it but, sexual molestation of the white master on the black slave. A lot of kids came from that. And so you are a mixture of the oppressor and the oppressed."

[2] Dakota revisits this term and provides the following elaboration: "My mom's best friend is also Korean and married to a White man. They have two daughters which are half Korean and so when we are out, we are like whatever, but when they are at home with us and mom, and they are speaking Korean, we can start to be like little Korean girls or whatever, but only when it's convenient like that. That's what I meant when I said 'convenient.'"

[3] More evidence of this "spicing up" of whiteness occurred with Rose's discussion of exploring more of her Native American ancestry: "I think it would be fun, something to learn, about my culture.... Um, I think I would try to promote the heritage more, if I could, I'm not saying that I wouldn't promote it, I think it's great to promote other cultures but I think if I knew I was definitely a part of it, then I would try to participate in more things that were culturally from that sect of Indian culture."

[4] Rosalind Fischer (2006) described these as "rules and roles that support and maintain the domination of people of color."

[5] "I think if it was like in a class, where people were asking about it, I'd want to share more about it, but maybe professional situations where they don't want to know details, just they want to know, 'What are you?' Okay, move on. I would probably just say white."

[6] By this, I mean that she mostly grew up in predominantly black neighborhoods and "black settings"; and established black friendship networks.

[7] Toni also reified stereotypes about whites, noting their reserved demeanor, proper speech, and polished appearance and dress. These examples illustrate racetalk (2005).

[8] Bonilla-Silva (2003a,b) discussed how some nonwhite groups possess more prowhite attitudes than whites themselves. The converse, then, involves blacks having anti-black attitudes that match or exceed that of whites.

6

The Changing Geography and Demography of Race

Throughout this book, I have attempted to show some of the variations in people's ways of seeing race. In that discussion, I have illustrated how people's perception of race and ways of understanding race differ, in part, because of the lenses through which they view themselves and others. Sometimes, these competing perspectives result in the racial negotiations that take place in the form of borderism. It is during the process of borderism that people wrestle with the multiple meanings attached to race. They attempt to resolve possible tensions between competing racial paradigms; they do so in order to make sense of the racial paradigm upon which they rely to understand the social world.

In many ways, borderism reflects how firmly people hold their perceptions of race, while also opening up the possibility of seeing race less rigidly and more openly. That is, as more and more people express and encounter borderism, there are increased opportunities for sharing, listening, and learning. People who express borderism can listen to the stories of people who encounter borderism, by inviting them to share their racial realities, including their preferred racial identities, as a way of opening up a border-patrolling person's perspectives on race. As I suggested in the previous chapter, some multiracial people might find these experiences opens up their own perspectives. This point recognizes the potential in everyone to both engage in borderism and to learn from it. Together, people who express and encounter borderism figure out ways to tell their own truth; the challenge thus far is doing so without contestation.

In this chapter, the story I want to tell is a variation of this contestation. More specifically, though, it is one of racial transformations, migrations, and reconfigurations. It builds on the race and immigration scholarship, by extending the reach of this discussion globally, to consider how the movement of multiracial people, socially and geographically, shapes and reshapes their identities, while influencing the ways we collectively and individually conceptualize race. In addition, the social and geographical migrations of multiracial people can potentially reshape their own ideas about race and systems of racial classification. This could influence ways of seeing race at individual, collective, and national levels.

My interests here are in how the migration of multiracial people in my sample impacts the way they understand the social construction of race, where they situate themselves in a racial classification system, and how they talk back to or challenge these racial constructions and classifications. These topics put the work of Wendy Roth directly in conversation with mine. In her book, *Race Migrations*, Roth (2012) describes how immigration facilitates new ways of understanding race. As people forge new connections across geographies and communities, locally and globally, they often maintain social ties while building new ones; this helps bridge home and host countries for people enduring or choosing these migrations. Roth contends that the connections people create and grow influence their views of race. When people move from one country to another, they not only learn new words for the old ones in their existing vocabulary, but they many learn that there are sometimes no easy translations for race across time and space. Two of examples of this that will relate to some of the respondents who I focus on in this chapter follow: Consider the term, "Hispanics." G. Cristina Mora (2014) argues that the term reflects a social, cultural, and political construction of a "new American." While the term has increasingly gained resonance in the United States, to Mora's point, it holds less meaning or relevance elsewhere. That is, the term ostensibly makes more sense in a country of immigrants, than in any respective country of reference. Roth (2012:30) explains, "As a racial category, 'Latino' is not very useful for distinguishing one person from another in Puerto Rico."

To her example, "Puerto Rican" arguably holds more meaning than "Latino" or "Hispanic" in Puerto Rico, as "Panamanian" holds more meaning in Panama than "Latino" or "Hispanic." Although individuals from either country might likely be classified as "Hispanic" or "Latino" here in the U.S., they might be classified differently in their home countries. Secondly, the racial classification system in each country might differ, such that the term, "Negro," the Spanish word for "black," might mean something altogether different in Puerto Rico than in Panama. The unique specificities of each country, and their national demographic population characteristics, differentially shape these understandings of race (see also Landale and Oropesa 2002). An individual categorized as "black" in the United States might find herself categorized as "moreno," or brown in Puerto Rico, and "blanco" or white in Panama. An individual people consider "white" in the United States might find himself categorized similarly in Puerto Rico or Panama. However, some verbal displays of cultural identities that unveil his connections to a place, through language or local cultural knowledge, might offer up additional cues that prompt a reclassification of him as "brown" in either Puerto Rico or Panama.

As people migrate around the globe, they discover many dimensions to a singular race, which potentially experiences its own shifting mixture. For people who claim multiple races, they may experience moving in and out of racial categories frequently, with or without intending to do so. They may find that a racial descriptor applies to them in one national context but not others; alternately, the same word or descriptor may have different meanings and connotations contingent on the geographies of race. For individuals settling into one country for a longer period of time, they may find themselves challenged by these inconsistencies, and the complexities of race. Multiracial individuals may also find that others use a number of different terms to describe them. Depending on the other person's ways of seeing race, a multiracial person might look different to any number of people. That is, the same racial mixture can elicit a different racial designation or classification contingent on the person's perception of the multiracial individual in question, and his/her understanding of race.

Some of the people perceiving multiracial people may be multiracial and/or immigrants themselves, given the existence of and increase in both of these populations; thus, it important to acknowledge that some shared knowledge of race in different settings may exist. People can communicate this understanding during social interactions, where they discuss these real and imagined racial differences across geographies and societies. As Roth (2012:32) observes, "Different nations and cultures often have their own ways of dividing the world into racial categories and deciding how to assign people to each one... [I]ndividuals can change which set of categories or rules for sorting people they use, and while there are many factors that may influence this change, immigration is a significant one. Do immigrants to the United States come to adopt an 'Americanized' way of viewing race? Or do they change American notions, like a racial melting pot, to create new concepts out of the immigrant experience?" Through these questions, Roth (among others) draws attention to the ways that immigrants shape and reshape the national landscape, creating new racial meanings and new expressions for capturing these changes. As people develop new connections to a land and its people and cultures, they experience shifts in this sense of connection, which informs their action or behavior.

Words used as a descriptor in the United States may not have the same resonance abroad; by extension, a word—as a racial descriptor—may have a certain register in the U.S., while its meaning shifts in another setting (or national context). People develop their own ways of referencing race, as "there are many different ways of classifying race" (Roth 2012:31), and create their own system of classification, or cognitive schemas, for race. Migrations, or movement, from one country to others, prompt some people's reconsideration of race. This partially answers Roth's (2012:31) question, "How does immigration affect the way people thinking about race and classify themselves and others?" Roth continues to argue that immigrants potentially change others' ways of thinking about race, introducing their own racial reality and cultural complexity to individuals who have never experienced such migrations.

These migrations impact individuals within their familial and social environments, such that some must learn the "racial rules" that operate in this country. They can teach new ways of seeing race to others, in the process of learning the status quo at the same time. However, multiracial people making these moves within and/or independent of their families of origin also influence others. As I have illustrated throughout this book, borderism reflects this negotiation of meanings, an attempt to crystallize the borders of race. But what does it mean to be multiracial if one is born outside of the U.S.? What does a multiracial person look like in various parts of the globe? Revisiting the "What are you?" and "Where are you from?" questions enables recognition of the many faces of multiracial identity around the world, or of "global mixed race" (King-O'Riain, Small, Mahtani, Song, and Spickard 2014).

Global Mixed Race, the work of the aforementioned authors, speaks to this more directly. What these scholars call "global mixed race" recognizes the geographic dispersal of racial multiplicity on a global scale. It grapples with the tensions produced by the term, and invites us to see this population as both something old and something new. In the latter case, the new speaks to the ostensibly increased choices that people have available to them, whether they exercise these choices or not.). Interviews with people who claimed connections outside of the U.S. drew my attention to the importance of understanding how race operates for multiracial people in the U.S. who also know how race is lived elsewhere.

This topic is of interest to me personally, as a woman who migrated from a U.S. territory (USVI) to the "mainland" over 20 years ago. As a newly arrived, already American citizen by birth but an "immigrant" in the sense that I traveled from another country to arrive in the U.S., I wrestled with the questions people freely posed to me. I know the "What are you?" and "Where are you from?" questions well. What I thought then was that I would further "assimilate" enough that those types of inquiries would cease, or at least dissipate. Instead, I have found, they remained constant, if not increased. That the quality of these interactions or these questions has not dramatically changed suggests how little racial curiosities and the system of racism have changed.

These interactions now make me wonder why, when the social landscape of society has changed so much in many ways, are people still asking the same "What are you?" question (since the words are seldom modified). The stagnant place that this question occupies is quite telling in terms of our collective racial literacy. The question is a loaded one at best. I always tried my best to answer honestly while protecting my privacy, yet often felt I had provided "interesting," even if sometimes disappointing, responses.   Scholars including Sanchez and Bonam (2009) have studied the strategies people deploy as a way to manage their public presentation of self as multiracial; they determine whether or not to disclose their racial identity.

The persistence of the "'What are you'?" question speaks to the similar persistence of the problem of racism. In my youth, I underestimated the duration of this problem or the endurance of this question. When I indicated that I identified as biracial, then people pressed on with, "Well, where are you from?" "The Caribbean." "Oh, that explains it." "That explains *what*?" My dubious visage said more than enough, but I then posed a question of my own. "What *exactly* does it explain?" (I was convinced that my biography is much more complex than can be conveyed in a short exchange with a stranger, or through my racially and ethnically ambiguous appearance). Rather than provoke strangers, I opted for the "less is more" approach. "Okay. Have a nice day." I would politely curtail the conversation before the use of "exotic" or "different" was deployed to describe me or fit me into another ill-fitting box.

It was only in retrospect, and after I began analysis of my research data, that I began to fully consider conversations like these and the multiple meanings produced and negotiated within these social interactions. As anyone who has visited the Caribbean knows or has witnessed the human variation there, people come in a variety of skin colors, and it is neither completely common nor altogether unusual to see "white people of color," or people with brown skin and blonde hair (Vidal-Ortiz 2004). The latter may not identify the ways the "brown-skinned white girls" in Twine's (1996) research did. Their body as evidence speaks to the possibility of many generations of race mixing, and to the plethora of ways this mixing shows up in the body.

In a small place colonized by a number of European countries, the mixing of races, through colonial conquest and also by consent, coupled with waves of migration to this tourist destination, produced much of the observable human variation in the local population. And yet, demographically, the territory's population has been described as "predominantly black," with that portion of the population hovering over 90% (see U.S. Census 2011). But what exactly does this "blackness" look like? Does it look the same as blackness in the U.S.? Where do multiracial people fall categorically and do people largely agree with or contest, these racial designations? In this chapter, I primarily consider two examples of respondents who claim connections to countries that demographically and socially differ from that of the U.S.

On Racial Migrations, or a Different Kind of "Multiracial Movement"

For a handful of my respondents, who had connections to family outside of the U.S. (primarily in Puerto Rico, Latin America, and South America), they reported growing up with different racial realities, when compared to participants who did not describe these connections or acknowledge them as significant. These different racial realities reflect variations in family biographies and individual experiences, as well as different historical forces and events that shape race in specific geographical contexts.

As respondents shift from one national context to another, they learned that whiteness (in the U.S.) was a privileged position, even though they grew up with alternate perspectives. Some grew up outside of the U.S., lived in other countries in their youth, or studied abroad in young adulthood. This early exposure to other racial contexts gave them more points of reference when considering race in the U.S. Many of them learned to challenge the supremacy or superiority of whiteness, having heard, over their lifetimes, racial discourses that openly critiqued, scorned, or disdained whiteness.

Respondents may have experienced their racial identities in particular ways within their families in other countries; these experiences may align with (or overlap with) their experiences in a variety of public settings (in school, work, religious institutions, etc.). That is, there may be racial heterogeneity in these other national contexts, and there exists potentially different racial hierarchies. Where respondents fit within these national contexts informs their sense of self, their sense of belonging, and their various identities.

For respondents who were in a (nonwhite) racial group that occupied a dominant position in their home society/country, their migration to the U.S. might have facilitated a shift in their mixture. That is, the individual may begin to have experiences in which others regarded them differently than they racially regard themselves. The categorical assignments to racial groups may not align, or the experience of migration does not translate to the U.S. context.

Here, I primarily focus on the experiences of two multiracial respondents, David and Maritza, both Panamanian by birth or by heritage, one who appears to others as "just white" (David) and the other as "just black" (Maritza). I bring their narratives into conversation with one another to compare and contrast their experiences, and to suggest that David is "more than white," and Maritza is "more than black." With subtle but sharp intelligence, both elucidate the dimensions of diversity within the category, "multiracial." Respectively, they embody multiracial whiteness and multiracial blackness (see Joseph 2013), which complicates our understanding of those terms when we consider global mixed race.

The two recognize differences in national histories and racial hierarchies. By making apparent their own multiple perspectives that pull race, ethnicity, nationality, class, and gender together, these two respondents illuminate what being multiracial means in two national contexts. Into their stories I weave that of other respondents who were born and/or raised in another country (or countries) or spend considerable time in other countries. Tracing these transnational journeys and linking them to the ways respondents understand their own racial subjectivities support my discussion of the transformations made possible by these migrations. I also attempt to illustrate how the assertion of identities that fall outside of others' expectations grows the racial literacy of everyone involved in these social interactions. The assertion of these identities also encourages a reconceptualizing of race, or at least a reconsideration of current understandings of race. It begs the questions, "Do other ways of seeing race exist? If so, what are some new visions[1] people might enjoy?"

David's Narrative

Readers may recall David (who I discussed in previous chapters) claiming a bicultural experience: "I identify racially as white and culturally as bicultural." From this liminal yet privileged position, he developed a curious feeling about what he described as his "two-ness," an idea he noted borrowing from W.E.B. DuBois (1903), who popularized the term, "double consciousness." This concept captures the conflict of someone inhabiting an oppressed position in society, who has two thoughts, his own and that of the oppressors.

As a light-skinned Latino white man, David explained that he was not idolized or idealized in his Panamanian family (as he might have been in the United States). Instead, he was often teased, and put through ostensibly playful authenticity tests. His "two-ness," or racial and cultural multiplicity, made the playful more painful. In his observation, negotiating his white racial privilege in a bicultural family that "devalued white people" contrasts with the dominant ideology pervasive in most of the households of other white multiracial respondents in my sample. In their households, as in society, whiteness was valorized, desired, and exalted.

In contrast to his experience in Panama, David's experience in the U.S. differed. In general, his light-skin-color-as-a-liability there registered as light-skin-color-as-a-currency here in the U.S. He effectively passed as white despite feeling and wanting to be a white multiracial, multiethnic, and multicultural man. He resented the imposter syndrome his invisible mixture, or illegible two-ness/difference enabled, as I discussed briefly in the previous chapter. He witnessed his Panamanian mother making fun of her white husband, his father. She conveyed the value of having a white husband ("I only married him because he had blue eyes and fair skin."), her actions reinforcing the importance of a white man as marital partner to a brown-skinned woman (see Hunter 2005; Rockquemore and Laszloffy 2005). The social structure of a society that valorizes white men contextualizes their importance in the mate selection process (see Childs 2005). Scholars speak to the social phenomenon of brown-skinned women "marrying up" when they legally and romantically partner with a white man (see Nemoto 2009; Steinbugler 2012; Twine 1997, 1996). Espiritu (2001) and others argue that whiteness is idealized worldwide, enhancing its currency even in places where rhetoric of resistance to whiteness and white domination prevails. The discursive contradictions of white idealization and domination in a society as contrasted with its devaluation elsewhere informed David's thoughts about his own partner choice (including who he envisions as "ideal"), which created a productive tension for him.

David explained that his father accommodated the "playful insulting," and did not really react to that. For David, his own "whiteness as a phenotype has always been, you know, sort of on me in my home." This contrasts with other social settings, such as school, where people unfamiliar with David's bicultural, blended identity express curiosity about his ambiguity. At once, David must manage his white appearance and his multiracial, multiracial, and multiethnic identities. As discussed in Chapter 4, people make guesses about his identity. The external pressures to sort or figure out David's ambiguity heightened his awareness of his racial and ethnic locations in the U.S. He explained that he remains aware of power and privilege, as it organizes social life. "I define race as a power and privilege construct, not a cultural construct, even though people with race have a cultural experience." This underscores the idea that everyone has a race, or racial group membership(s), as well as an ethnic and cultural heritage.

Despite his own increased awareness of white privilege, and his efforts to resist this privilege, David confronts others' challenges to his invisible mixture. He described what I consider a kind of "situational" acceptance and/or rejection contingent on appearance (phenotype), and other people's perceptions of a multiracial individual's racial location. David emphatically describes facing this acceptance/rejection "all the time. And, and I have two things that jump out: A lot of them just assume that I'm white, um, unless I say otherwise. And some have that, 'I'm not sure what you are.' I think that's just, some people look more closely.... But I remember, in my doctoral program, how the white students shifted the way they talked with me once I started speaking up in classes, around cultural and race discussions." This comment reveals the "two-faced racism" (Houts Picca and Feagin 2007) that the authors document; the book provides evidence of the shift in racial discourses that white people will make when they think they are in "like company" (among other white people), versus when they are in "mixed company" (pardon the pun).

David's comments reveal the racial rules of etiquette that whites are expected to follow: do not *publicly* participate in race and cultural discussions, as doing so may reveal troublesome (racist) ideologies. As David observed, "It's fascinating, because what happened was exactly what I see happening when whites talk to people of color. They preface half the things they say with, 'Now, I don't want you to think I'm racist, but,' whereas they weren't doing that before, until I identified myself as, as either speaking about racism, or speaking about my identity as *also* a Latino person, or a Panamanian person. So that's one way that I see shifts all of a sudden. When, "Uh-oh, I have to regroup. I have to regroup on how to relate to him."

Once David made his "two-ness" or mixture visible to other whites, he jeopardized the white racial kinship that allowed his white classmates to presume an alliance with him (see DuBois 1903; Houze and Weberman 2001; Vaca 2004). His invisible mixture shaped his peers' perception of him as racially white. With that came a set of connotations and expectations, including his agreement to not discuss race, or draw attention to matters of white privilege and power. Doing so made his invisible mixture more visible, and also compromised the racial loyalty his white peers felt they had established with him, simply by virtue of being (perceived as) white. This alliance was not founded on shared values, as David's comments revealed. While many white people presume an alliance with him, David does not automatically presume this alliance with them. "I never experience myself as being one of them to begin with." This prevents David from feeling excluded from whiteness, even if these white peers are effectively saying, "You're not one of us." David's comments challenge the expanding boundaries of whiteness, in that his racial literacy and consciousness disrupt the colorblindness and colormuteness that many people prefer, particularly white people, and practice in their everyday lives. Actively participating in critical racial discourses actively challenges the kind of whiteness to which David does not want to belong; this critical whiteness enables his rejection of its attendant white privileges. Richard Delgado and Jean Stefanic (2001, 1997) explore critical whiteness in their work, as a way of "looking behind the mirror" of whiteness, much like David does.

David discussed the ways in which he managed his invisible mixture in graduate school, as both a student and a teacher. While others might likely read David as only white, David described experiences that suggest he walks through life as a "white person of color" (Vidal-Ortiz 2004). Despite his invisible mixture, students often express curiosity about his racial and ethnic identity. Students eventually confess to him their curiosity about his social location. "'Before we go on, can we ask you a question? It's a personal question; you don't have to answer it, if you don't want." And the question is always, 'What are you?'" The students debate David's whiteness, in part because they believe a white person would not issue criticism about white privilege and power in the way that David does. His precarious position as a white person of color troubles some students' understanding of who can engage in discussions of critical whiteness and who can practice antiracist work, including liberatory pedagogy.

Once David reveals his "two-ness" to his students, he notices that "from that point on, the white students are much more cautious…They suddenly feel vulnerable. They suddenly feel vulnerable because before I was a white guy who was talking about this stuff so it was easier for them to be white, because, 'See, white people can talk about this stuff.'

But then, the second I become Latino, all of a sudden, even though, when I say exactly to them, I identify racially as white and culturally this way, the white students immediately lose somebody that they can say, 'Not all white people are nothing but racist.' (Not all white people are racist.) Because by that time, I've gotten the credibility that I'm not this overt racist, even though I say I participate in racism, as we all do."

David drew a connection between this point, and some of the internal conflicts that he admitted having with regards to romantic relationships. During our interview conversation, I asked David to discuss his relationship history, and specifically how his invisible mixture might inform "who's attracted to you romantically, and who you're attracted to romantically." He sighed audibly, and replied, "Um, that's a loaded, loaded question." He explained that other people's perception of him, and their misrecognition of him in particular, has caused relationships to abruptly end or otherwise "come to a sudden stop when the realization that I am not Jewish happens." David clarified that, when he attended school in a northeastern city, he was mistaken for Jewish "all the time" in part because his last name is a "very Jewish name." He even joked that his friends "fully, fully believe that I am Jewish and have gotten me to the point where I'm saying, 'Maybe I am...'"

David describes a painful tension between idealizing white women with blue eyes, and darker-skinned women with brown eyes. He seemed to be caught between these ideals, as he respectfully considered which women to date. The dilemma of his dating prospects related to a shifting or wavering attraction to the ideal, and a rejection of that ideal. Who he idealizes links to how he identifies. His comments capture this ambivalence: "There definitely is this part of me that will grieve if I don't end up with someone who's Latina." He succinctly stated, "There's a part of me that doesn't want the white to win." By this, David observed the pattern of marital partner choices not only with his Panamanian mother, but his sisters as well. Both of his sisters "married white, blue-eyed men." David also expressed an awareness of the intersection of race and gender on partner choice for people like him and his sisters. "My mom definitely said she wanted me to marry a Panamanian girl, but she absolutely did not want her daughters to marry Panamanian guys. And, I agree, because culturally—culturally, the sexism is just tremendous...And you're practically gay if you're not having affairs."

David related his dating anxieties to his anticipation of others' potential disappointment in him not being "Latino enough." This fear links back to that discussed in Chapter 3, where he described the dread of being exposed as Latino. This strikes me as similar to white anxieties about discovering otherness within, or seeing the Other as self; in addition, it differs from this because he is not afraid of not been seen as white or Latino. Rather, he is anxious that he will not be seen as white or Latino enough. The imposter syndrome that David admits to feeling can be linked to his comments about being "outed." Typically discussed in relation to sexualities, the "coming out" process pertains to the disclosure that a person makes to reveal a potentially socially stigmatized identity. For David, imposter syndrome encourages him to selectively and strategically manage his blended identity. Managing disclosure involves making decisions about revealing his identity in ways that remain comfortable and appropriate to him, or conversely, concealing the complexity of his identity.

Being "outed" or identified by others as Latino provokes these imposter feelings. David does not feel that he is passing or trespassing as white, since he has "been granted membership in that community" even if he does not always desire such membership. However, because he has had his Panamanian identity and loyalty challenged and contested by family, friends, and strangers, he is less sure about others' reactions. In some ways, he expects some invalidation, which explains why the disclosure remains so fraught, fragile, and tense. As he recalled, he has managed this invalidation since his childhood, and that invalidation offers the context of this "deep, deep-seated fear." Despite some fleeting feeling of validation and embrace of his identity, David can only momentarily enjoy the feeling before it is countered by an "intense fear" that follows, a fear of invalidation.

David reveals the pain of invalidation and invisible mixture when he confesses: "I mean I'm always aware that, at some point, I'm going to get accused of being ashamed of my Latino identity, and that's why I'm not involved in that when that's so ironic to me, because it's not the shame of being Latino. It's shame of not being 'Latino enough,' and I'm always afraid it's going to be construed the other way around, and if that happens, I imagine I would get tearful. And, like I said, that cuts really deep for me." David highlights the layers of complexities involved in or associated with making mate selection choices. His comments directly speak to the ways in which some multiracial people must manage feelings of invalidation in terms of their individual identities, feelings that their partner choices can intensify, alleviate, or some combination thereof.

The irony of David's predicament involves the persistent anxiety he feels in choosing a partner, particularly a Latina woman, and being disqualified by her family. He clarified that he does not fear being rejected because of his whiteness, but because he imagines or anticipates others "rejecting me because I'm not really Latino." He enumerated his fears, including these: "I won't be able to dance salsa; I won't be able to speak with the grandparents; I won't be able… In reality, I probably can do both, but it's just all fear. It's all fear." While David feared disqualification of his Latino identity, having some generalized anxiety about real and imagined rejection, he revealed an experience that contrasted with darker-skinned respondents. His experience illustrated the way that the white women to whom he was attracted, and their families, worked to protect and preserve their possessive investment in whiteness (Lipsitz 2006). His fears about invalidation from Latino families contrast with much of what darker-skinned multiracial respondents described. When put in the context of the racial hierarchy, these examples lend support to the racial sorting that occurs in social situations, in the process of mate selection or relationship formation, and the border patrolling that upholds the current racial hierarchy.

David's example illustrates the importance of being able to express identity complexity without contestation. He lives with white male privilege, and the contradictions or irony of accessing that privilege from this position of ambivalence. As someone who is critical of social inequalities, he is unable to fully "enjoy" white privilege, but rather observes how it operates in his family and in this society. He knows he is not favored in his family of origin (nor by many extended kin) the way he is generally favored in the U.S., simply by virtue of his white appearance.

Having this awareness arguably better positioned him to be an ally, and to do the social justice work he finds necessary. His racial epistemologies allow him to compare two different racial structures in two societies, to see how vastly differently they operate. He is also able to recognize contradictions in both systems, as they continue to inform his own contradictory ideologies and behaviors. His example links to that of Maritza, another respondent from Panama. While he suggests, despite being teased, that being a white Panamanian makes more sense to Panamanians or can be accommodated there much more easily than in the U.S., Maritza makes a similar point, except from her position as a dark-skinned woman. I focus on her experience next.

Maritza's Narrative

To begin, I want to consider Maritza's experience as a Panamanian woman with dark skin. During our interview, Maritza described having Latin American familial roots. She described the incredulity others expressed when they learned of her Black Latina identity and heritage (as described in Chapter 3). Growing up in a diasporic family created a different racial habitus for Maritza than other families who see their roots as more localized. Her perception of race suggests that she makes more distinctions between whiteness and blackness, which upholds a white/black racial binary. This departs from the contemporary racial hierarchy that triangulates race into whiteness, honorary whiteness, and collective blackness; it also departs from any other racial classification system that gets beyond the binary. Maritza illustrates her own racial logic, when she explains that she considers an "interracial" relationship one that involves a white person and a person of color, as opposed to two people of color. Sociologist Brenda Gambol (2016) provides an example of the latter in her examination of intermarriage among nonwhite individuals. That Maritza appears to rely on whiteness as her reference point for understanding intermarriage helps to contextualize her understanding of racial mixture on individual levels, in addition to these relational levels.

As someone with ties to another country, Maritza initially found it difficult to understand why others expressed confusion about her multiracial identity. In her home country, her having dark skin color and being Panamanian are not at odds. What others misunderstood, Maritza understood as her home base. Being both black and Hispanic was her truth and lived reality rather than an "impossibility." She shared her experience negotiating the ampersand, as well as ambiguity and racial multiplicity:

> Pretty much everyday at work, someone asks me, "So, where are you from?" No, no, no, not, "Where are you from?" (She corrects herself here.) "How did you learn how to speak Spanish so well?" And then I say, "I'm from Panama." And then they say, "Oh, okay." Now regardless if I don't know if they know where Panama is, and if they don't, maybe they'd be ashamed to say, "Well, where's that at? Do they speak Spanish out there?"

During social interactions such as the one above, Maritza shared her heritage and national identity with others. She doubted that people asking her these sorts of questions actually had much knowledge about her home country of Panama. People puzzled over her invisible and shifting mixture, in part, based on their limited literacy, or knowledge of Panama, demographically and geographically. If, in people's imagination, an absence or a void (nothingness) surfaces about a particular nation and place, they have no framework, besides their own, to understand others. This lack of knowledge impedes their understandings of people like Maritza, whose body blurs racial lines by crossing racial and geographical borders.

As Maritza and others illustrate, this utilization of one racial frame in place of others does not always suffice. The result, in my observation, is border patrolling. In other words, if a person who has lived in the U.S. and has never heard of or learned about Panama, geographically, socially, or demographically, that person will likely rely on their own racial frame to situate the multiracial person into their schema. This may mean that when people see Maritza's (dark) skin color, they locate her in the (collective) black category. While she may place herself in this category, she *also* sees herself as Spanish or Latina, or in her terms, a Black Panamanian. That she offers such specificity echoes Roth's (2012) point about the range of descriptive words used to label "Latinos."

When Maritza speaks Spanish, she creates cognitive dissonance for people who believe black people do not typically speak Spanish, or at least not fluently. That she speaks Spanish well because she *is* Spanish, not just knows Spanish, creates a hiccup in many people's racial logic. Many people learn that Spanish people are brown but not necessarily black. That Maritza has dark skin throws off this association of a particular (lighter) shade of brown being synonymous with Latinidad, a term used to refer to Latino pan-ethnicity (see J. Rodriguez 2003). There is little room in the dominant racial frame in the U.S. to hold these two categories—black and Spanish—together easily, given the tendency to create either/or options and enforce binaries.

What further complicates Maritza's experiences with others involves her family of procreation. She reported having a child with a multiracial man of black and Asian ancestry. She described the small but significant Asian (primarily Chinese) population in Panama, and that people in her family have a "thing for Asians." Because people often rely on the social groups and/or partner of a multiracial person in question to decipher racial ambiguity, Maritza's African Hispanic identity, her Black Panamanian Asian son, and her (former) multiracial partner who is Asian and black, blurs versus brightens racial lines. Her chosen family exemplifies how multiracial people, in general, may be more comfortable blending borders as they grew up in familial contexts that created a racially mixed habitus.

Her experience also reflects how living in a country in Central America, exposed her to different racial groups and dynamics, and thus different ways of seeing race. In Panama, a smaller place than the U.S., race is lived differently across settings and depending on one's particular racial mixture, identity, and group location. What she reports as normative in Panama—being black *and* fluent in Spanish is less so here, outside of particular states, such as New York and Florida. Other people's limited exposure to these possibilities can feel like borderism to a person accustomed to these variations. These interactions between borderists and respondents provide chances for increased racial awareness for all involved. The borderist learns of the actuality of Black Hispanics in Panama and the U.S. They can choose to incorporate this information to enhance their imagination about a location; it strengthens their understanding of im/migration geographically and racially. The respondent learns how others see them and where they are locating them in the racial hierarchy. This location is typically not fixed but more like a moving target. As the example above illustrates, relationships also demonstrate shifting mixture, such that borderists might be further confused about Maritza's racial location, when she appears in public with her multiracial Asian, Black, and Latino child, and/or his Asian Panamanian father.

Her example captures shifting mixture in all of the fluid and flexible ways race is lived. Her example also illustrates how geographical migrations, in her case from one country to another, made her shifting mixture more of a curiosity abroad (in the U.S.) than at home (in Panama). This reframes or shifts the center. As her experiences suggest, these geographical migrations can initiate or facilitate racial migrations. That is, Maritza might find moving from "multiracial" to "black" easier to articulate in these conversations. However, she might not get away with claiming a black identity, nor does she want to do so. Instead, she prefers to embrace her African Hispanic heritage.

Discursively, she moves away from blackness to preserve her preferred Black Panamanian identity. She does not want to be viewed as "just black" or as African American. As I see it, Maritza wants to articulate the specificity of her blackness, without negating that blackness. She appears to be drawing different parameters around blackness, so that she may be included, and have her blackness authenticated, but not at the expense of her Panamanian identity. In this way, Maritza wants the "best of both worlds," but not in the cliché way; she simply wants to articulate and authenticate all of who she is and knows herself to be. She does not want one part to cancel out, erase, or disappear any other.

To her dismay, she discovers her proximity to blackness when others negate her preferred identity. Despite this perceived proximity, Maritza maintains some social distance by speaking Spanish, which ostensibly works to linguistically, and by implication or extension, characteristically differentiate her from blacks. She also maintains a putatively privileged position in differentiating herself in this way from native-born blacks in the U.S. While some might argue that she could be penalized as an "immigrant Other" for her social location and bilingualism, she maintains her multiracial identity to honor her family heritage.

When taken together, we see a few commonalities between David and Maritza. They grew up in families and societies where people openly discussed race, racial identities, and racial politics. They observed alternatives to societies where whiteness was privileged, revealing ways in which multiplicity (versus singularity) could be acknowledged and where blackness was valued, if not privileged. Thus, their relationship to privilege and disprivilege differ based on their own standpoints, and gets informed by their exposure to different racial hierarchies. In part, Maritza and David have developed what Nestor Garcia Canclini (1992:32) called "hybrid transformations generated by the horizontal coexistence of a number of symbolic systems." That is, their respective multiracial blackness and whiteness call into question cultural and racial signifiers of race; they create the appearance of racial singularity while embodying multiplicity, making the terms, "multiracial blackness," and "multiracial whiteness," both useful and meaningful, but also redundant. Their blackness and whiteness are always already multiracial, and their migrations facilitate hybrid transformations that reflect what Jose Muñoz (1999) called "disidentification," a topic I turn to next.

From Racial Migrations to Disidentifications?

In his work, Jose Muñoz (1999:4) introduced the term, "disidentification," positing, "Disidentification is meant to be descriptive of the survival strategies the minority subject practices in order to negotiate a phobic majoritarian public sphere that continuously elides or punishes the existence of subjects who do not conform to the phantasm of normative citizenship." Muñoz envisioned disidentification as a technique or strategy for navigating dominant or hegemonic culture and society. Muñoz clarifies, "Disidentification is *not always* an adequate strategy of resistance or survival for all minority subjects. At times, resistance needs to be pronounced and direct; on other occasions, queers of color and other minority subjects need to follow a conformist path if they hope to survive a hostile public sphere. But for some, disidentification is a survival strategy that works within and outside the dominant public sphere simultaneously" (Muñoz 1999: 5).

I chose David and Maritza's narratives because of the thick description they offer that illustrates this term, "disidentification" (see Geertz 1977). They exemplify how individuals may remain knowledgeable about the dominant frames of race, while undermining them through their lived experiences and assertions of multiplicity. That David and Maritza respectively look white and black puts so much of the social interactions others have with them into that context. They both contest or speak back to these locations, by expressing how they are not "just white" or "just black." Adding nuance to these racial categories allows them--and others who act accordingly--their agency. They are able to reclaim difference or variation that is denied by the labels of whiteness and blackness. Their invisible mixture partially accounts for their relationship to these racial categories, and explains their desire to maintain their multiplicity and liminality.

On the one hand, David knows that people perceive him as white, even joking, "I catch myself, you know, saying, 'If I didn't know me, I would just swear I was white.' And so, that, I have a bicultural lens and I can shift those, and so, the term 'bicultural' fits me; that's the only label that fits my two-ness; um, racially, I'm aware to me it is more of a political statement that I recognize that I have experienced some advantages mainly as the result of how I am identified by others, even though I don't see, um, see the world, the way I see most people see it." On the other hand, David struggles to make his multiplicity recognizable or legible in ways intelligible to others.

In my interpretation, David is exemplifying a disidentification with whiteness, or perhaps with what could be described as hegemonic whiteness (see Gramsci 1971). I also believe that this disidentification extends to his Latino heritage, where he rejects the myopic stereotypes of Latinos and embraces the parts that enable him to be atypically Latino, in his own way, on his own terms. He is disidentifying with the troublesome tropes of Latinidad, and tries to update its meanings to make space for him to claim the culture and identity as his own (see Gates 1986). He wants to be both without these claims to whiteness and Latinidad compromising the other. He feels, or is made to feel, that his whiteness dilutes his ability to be a *real* Latino, and claiming his Panamanian identity seems to foreclose a *real* white identity. Thus, being both white and Latino seem illogical or incompatible; they are seemingly disparate parts, regarded as mutually exclusive, rather than inclusive in a way that recognizes generations of such mixture throughout history and the world.

Optimistically, disidentification opens up the space for him to offer racial articulations that are true to *his* reality, his unique combination of races, ethnicities, culture, and experiences. This combination complements, rather than competes, with itself. It celebrates such mixture, rather than denigrating it. The quintessential bridge built between groups is in him, and he wrestles with this reality daily. However, he also can utilize this bridge to make connections to people who appear similar to him on the surface (whites) and those who appear different but that he may have more in common with culturally or ethnically (Latinos, or people of colors). Here, I borrow from AnaLouise Keating (2013) and Reanae McNeal to describe the significance of this bridging across socially constructed and reinforced racial categories, and across the color continuum (see also Espiritu 1992). This bridge helps to form a link between the experiences of David and Maritza, and others who share their realities.

David's story is somewhat like that of Maritza, whose narrative also reflects disidentification. When people ask her how she can be both black and Hispanic, they too are perpetuating the myth that these categories are mutually exclusive. As she problematizes blackness, she moves toward and away from the category. She both distances and differentiates herself from singular blackness. As a young woman with two black Hispanic parents, Maritza socially identifies similarly to them. However, she also vacillates between a formal identification[2] that is both "Black Hispanic" and "African American." Viewing the two terms as relatively interchangeable, Maritza defers more to the former than the latter. "If I was to be asked what I am, I would automatically say 'African Hispanic.' Like if we were talking, that's the first thing I would say." Although she arrived at this choice in part by feeling that her parents gave her the option to identify as she liked, Maritza noted, "They've always said, 'You're not a Black American. You're a black Hispanic because your parents are from Central America and you're bilingual.' So that's where—now they said if I wanted to racially identify as African American, I can totally do that but that's what they would identify as, so I just took that."

Maritza draws distinctions between the two names for herself, African American and Black Hispanic: "I guess you could say it's (African American) not necessarily accurate. 'Hispanic' would be more accurate but it just depends on why am I actually choosing, for what, you know? Is it a job? They look at whether you're Hispanic or black. They say they don't discriminate against race or anything, but they definitely look at it." This discourse reflects how Maritza situates herself within the US frame, to acknowledge how race shapes employment opportunities for her. Her observation that they (prospective employers) "look at it" (race) indicates her awareness of how others' perception of her (as Black and/or Hispanic) matters because race matters.

Maritza feels encouraged by her parents to disidentify as African American and to embrace a black Hispanic identity, a common strategy that darker skinned new or recent immigrants adopt to distance and/or differentiate themselves from native-born blacks (Yancey 2003; Waters 1994; Foner 2000; Hintzen and Rahier 2003). Despite this socialization from her parents, Maritza chooses a different approach. She asserts a protean identity. This shifting became clearer to me when she said the following during the interview: "I mean I've always kind of just chose whatever just came up to my mind. I never really said, 'This is what I'm going to stick with.' So if you were to pick five different (job) applications that I've filled out, maybe three out of five of them would be different. And it's not depending on the job. Or you know, wherever I'm at, or like if I'm at the social security office, you know?"

Her comments speak to the degree that social setting can influence one's racial sense of self, such that individual's racial identity can be fluid and unstable. This explains why she might not look like the same person on paper, but in fact this multidimensionality marks the fluidity of racial identity and identification. Unlike previous generations, this one arguably offers Maritza the very choice she feels entitled to exercise. About this fluidity and choice, she said, "It doesn't bother me at all. I just feel like, like I have that option."

While she appreciates having this choice, Maritza was unable to articulate-during the course of the interview-what influences this choice, or explain why she chooses differently from one setting, or job application to another. "I mean, even in high school, I took a reading test, and they ask that question at the end. And I don't even know; I couldn't tell you what I chose. It was probably African American. Why? I don't know. But maybe because I was in high school. I don't know if it makes a difference, but to me, none of that matters....I never looked at it that deep." Her comments suggest that, as she has matured, had a multiracial (Black, Hispanic, and Asian) child of her own, and experienced more freedom to choose, she does choose her public identity seemingly haphazardly. That is, for her, the choice appears arbitrary, inconsequential.

Again, this contrasts with previous generations that felt different pressures to publicly maintain racial categories that largely excluded "multiracial" (see Wallenstein 2002). Maritza's occasional colorblind comments contrast with her awareness and discussion of race; the former works to minimize race, while the latter reveals her race cognizance, as evidenced in her discussion of the racial (ethnic and cultural) identities of her family members, including her child and her siblings. To this point, Maritza described birthing her multiracial son, noting that his father is a black and Asian man whose "mother is Japanese and his dad is black." Maritza wondered: "Now ask me what my son will be? Or is? He's everything. We call him, he has two nicknames: 'Papito' and 'Chino.' I mostly call him 'Papito' and most of my family calls him 'Chino.'" She might doubt that she understands the language of race because she tenuously negotiates both the borders and the geographies of race, but she does have some racial literacy. The monikers that Maritza endearingly employs mark her son ethnically and culturally, and gently draw attention to her own version of the "What are you?" question and to other types of literacy that Maritza possesses. That she expresses her own curiosity about her son's racial identity ("Now ask me what my son will be?"), Maritza reveals an openness to this question, which contrasts with some of the comments respondents shared about their own parents. Rather than engage in beneficiary, protective or malevolent border patrolling, Maritza simply shares her speculative knowledge that "he's everything." That is, Maritza does not make demands on her young son by attempting to maximize any racial privileges attached to his Hispanic and/or Asian ancestry; she does not deny his black and/or multiracial identity, but rather appears affirming of his identity complexity. To me, this suggests that she recognizes in her son a reflection of her own ability to negotiate the borders of race, and strategic attempts to transcend them when necessary. This provides partial explanation for Maritza attempts to maintain a relatively race-neutral perspective. Doing so allows her to discursively dismissing racial divides while simultaneously blurring boundaries typically erected between racial groups in her own life. Her narrative adds complexity to the black, Asian, and Hispanic categories, teasing out how boundaries are regarded and protected, and still socially porous and penetrable or malleable. This contrasts with a strategy of simplifying identity, to manage difference by diminishing it or collapsing its complexity.

While Maritza may feel that she does not completely understand "how race is lived in America," she does offer a multilingual example that exemplifies life on the borders of race. When she posits, "He's everything," Maritza may be falsely, I would argue, read as resuscitating racial tropes about the superior valence of multiraciality. Instead, I read her assertion as an affirmation of his multiracial, and multiethnic, multicultural, and multilingual reality. Perhaps it is a mother's wish for her son and a transcendent racial future that prove hopeful and successful, rather than "tragic," as the trope about multiracial people suggests (see Manganelli 2012).

Negotiating Borderism Through Disidentification or Simplification

The narratives of David and Maritza offered up so much richness, in terms of really exemplifying racial migrations, the "cultural transformations of race," and the flexible "nature of race" (see Roth 2012; Morning 2011, 2003). That is, both of their experiences speak to broader social phenomena about the negotiation of the borders of race. Maritza's question about how her son will or already does identify racially connects to the question Jenifer Bratter (2007) poses in her work, "Will 'Multiracial' Survive to the Next Generation?" These questions around racial identity and intergenerational conversations about race reveal individual, familial, relational, and communal struggles with and celebrations of identity. However, as many of the narratives among my respondents revealed, much like with geographical migrations, there are "push/pull" factors enticing or dissuading multiracial people from making claims to particular groups or identities. For as much as Maritza might encourage her son to claim that "he's everything," will she continue to celebrate his racially (ethnically and culturally) mixed heritage? Will he choose to cross the borders of race differently, such that he opts for singularity instead of complexity? In this section, I want to return to David's narrative as an example, to explore the persistent questions that linger, perhaps more so for people who cross racial borders and geographical ones as well. What unfolds here is a discussion of the interplay between people's racial identity choices, their family socialization, their relationship formation, and their migration experiences. Any potentially contrasting or conflicting social environments, cultural norms and social values all shape these migrations of race, space, and place. They reveal a complex set of decisions some multiracial people make, about claiming and maintaining their racial complexity, or opting for more simplicity.

As I discussed above, the term, "disidentification," captures an intentional, critical movement away from narrowly defined or myopically viewed racial and ethnic categories. I contrast that here with another identity articulation I observed emerging in the data: simplification. Instead of asserting protean identities, or otherwise maximizing the ostensible range of choices in their "racial identity grab bag" (see Rockquemore, Brunsma, and Delgado 2009), many multiracial participants opted to simplify their public racial identity. I argue that this process of simplifying one's rich racial ancestry could be experienced as a form of borderism; alternately, as I mentioned earlier, this could also reflect optional races in ways that parallel or meet with optional ethnicities.

David provided an example of this kind of borderism during our interview conversation. What he described illustrates what Gloria Anzaldua (1987) refers to as "la facultad," and what Keating follows thematically, in terms of shifting ways of seeing, thinking, being, and connecting. AnaLouise Keating (2013) engages this theme of shifting in her book, *Transformation Now!* She elaborates on the importance of this shifting, or the embrace of unfolding possibilities for new ways of thinking and being, and of connecting to others. David began by discussing how he experienced a shift in ideals. He also related that shift to his own fluid identity:

> David: With respect to Latina women, it totally parallels my own sense of awareness; I vividly remember, it was the Grammy's one year when Linda Ronstadt sat next to Olivia Newton-John and I literally remember the point at which something shifted inside of me from "blonde, blue eyes, fair skin is beautiful" to "big brown eyes and, you know, olive skin or dark skin is beautiful."

> Author: Did it have to be either/or?

> David: Well, it wasn't so much either/or. It was how, how I would describe my ideal. And that was purely, I assumed at the time, that was purely on a physical level, um; it's not until the past 3–5 years that I experienced a lot of pain about that issue of—because I do remember vividly, being aware that I didn't, um, I didn't want to be with a Panamanian girl or a Latina girl because I didn't find them attractive and Olivia Newton John was attractive.

Throughout his early childhood and adolescence, David had valorized white femininity, learning to associate white women with beauty. Though he did not initially see his attraction to "everybody that looked like Olivia Newton John" as a racialized preference for whiteness or as ideologically supportive of white superiority, he later developed that awareness. Developing this critical lens continues to trouble David, and create cognitive dissonance for him. He noted, "I'm not attracted to (this white woman) and I'm becoming aware that a lot of that lack of attraction is because she's white with blue eyes. And that there's something going on with me, and I have yet to figure out where I'm supposed to be."

In wanting to protect and preserve his heritage, David confided in feeling a sense of connection "when I hear a woman, you know, speaking Spanish." He described longing to keep that sense of solidarity, community, and identity intact. As I indicated earlier, shared language and any shared cultural experiences prove a powerful connective force among people who might otherwise seem like a racially disparate group. David's comments illustrate how much he identifies with Latino culture, broadly speaking, and how much he finds listening to Spanish language speakers enjoyable or even evocative of nostalgic for a sense of home he continues to seek. David's comments also reveal the extent to which people can experience their identities as "home," or how much they must negotiate to establish and maintain that feeling, whether through shared language, customs, ideas, values, and so on.

When he sees those racial signifiers of culture in women, "those beautiful eyes and those nice hips," he comes to this realization:

> It's those beautiful eyes and those nice hips that represent a part of me that I'm afraid to lose because, you know, I'm biracial and I'm, I'm very aware that my partner will have a huge impact on how much of my cultural identity will develop further down the line if I have children. My sisters both married white, blue-eyed men and I'm aware of that and there's a part of me that doesn't want the white to win, that doesn't want the white to sort of block out the one Panamanian woman who married this guy from Pennsylvania.

Wrestling with his own internal conflict, David also struggled with knowing that his mother wants him "to marry a Panamanian girl." Because he was constantly border patrolled by significant others, David felt a lot was invested in his partner choice, socially and symbolically speaking. Such a decision could cement his Panamanian authenticity or compromise it. He saw this choice as potentially strengthening and/or diluting his own identities and invisible mixture. Not being "clearly mixed" complicated these choices.

> David: I remember when my cousins "accidentally" on purpose dropped some keys near me and obviously I would pick them up, and when I would pick them up, they were all excited and celebrating because they, the whole thing was a test to see if I bent my legs, bent my legs when I picked them up.
>
> Author: When you were talking earlier about the scotch and the soda—
>
> David: Same guys.

Author: I was thinking that, I wonder whether, because I thought that you were going to say that it was just sort of, more about your masculinity but that interestingly that kind of got attached to your whiteness, rather than just questioning your masculinity.

David: Right. Right. To me, it's all the same. They linked, when they said, "You gotta be a 'Gonzalez'," I knew that not every Panamanian was named "Gonzalez," so to me it turned into, "You're not really going to be Panamanian. You're going to be a [his last name]." A gringo.

In enduring various types of authenticity testing around his performance of race and gender, David felt that his preference for a Latina related to his wanting someone that seems like home, someone familiar. David acknowledged the structural barriers that limit the likelihood of him finding such a person in the institutional and social spaces he inhabits. The irony here is that, as David discussed, he appears to be a white (non-Hispanic) man, and thus is largely afforded privileges on the basis of his appearance and others' perception of him as white. His observation of the ways skin color benefits him also partially explains why he is unlikely to encounter many potential partners (Latinas) who he prefers who also have a similar higher level of education. In the matrix of domination, at the intersections of racism, sexism, and colorism, these barriers further impede his search for familiarity and similarity in potential partners; even as he stands within and simultaneously resists his positions of dominance within this matrix, David consider his white male privilege, and the cost of his invisible mixture.

David's example underscores the importance of the family as a social institution that shapes people's racial identity and sense of self. Families also shape that sense of nostalgia, an affectively rich place that colors our memories with a mix of emotions. For some multiracial people, these memories may be intensified or minimized in their movements away from home. I want to acknowledge the complexities of the racial identity development process, which may increase for multiracial people in transnational movement. As they "search for home abroad" (Lesser 2003), they must navigate new cultural norms and social expectations in new national contexts. In addition to any negotiations taking place regarding other identities (nationality, sexuality), transnational multiracial people must figure out their racial identities within and across national contexts. They may find the crossing of various borders becomes easily integrated in this sense of self, or they may struggle to blend these borders. In either case, transnational multiracial people may be trying to resolve ideological tensions produced by competing racial paradigms (of their respective national backgrounds and heritage). In these various landscapes, they must also find ways to develop a healthy self-understanding in a manner that proves effective for them.

When people tire of the process of crossing the borders of race and nation, they often choose to flatten out the complexities of their heritage. Some may have always already blended racial borders, through their invisible mixture. However, these individuals may still attempt to blur the borders between the racial and ethnic groups to which they claim membership. Sometimes, reclaiming the complexity of their heritage proves a difficult task, as it involves making mixture visible to others. Yet, for others, racial migrations and transformations facilitate racial relocations, with shifting mixture a movement into categories that add new dimensions to their identities. In the next section, I discuss how these racial migrations or relocations lead to racial reconfigurations for some multiracial individuals in interracial families.

Racial Relocations: Moving from Multiracial to "More Than Multiracial"?

Multiracial people may develop racial identities and consciousness that reflect their involvement in their interracial families of origin, procreation, and choice. As interracial families gain or lose members, they take on new forms; they may experience shifting mixture, or a changing demography that reflects the addition or inclusion of new members or the attrition of others. The changing family structure or demography intersects with the geography of race, as described above. As families change, and geographies change, race can change for the family as a unit, and/or for particular members within families. That is, the racial descriptors of families can change as their membership changes, and/or as their racial identities and consciousness shift in any way.

The mixing and remixing of families recognizes that individuals influence one another in these intimate spaces. This conveys the reality that race is relational, and people's racial identities reflect these impressions. As relationships grow, so to do people's racial consciousness, of themselves and others. Thus, as racial consciousness shifts, so too might racial identities accordingly. Twine (2011) discusses this both in terms of racial literacy and honorary memberships, while Keating (2013) and others discuss this in terms of racial consciousness.

In her book, *A White Side of Black Britain*, Twine (2011) shows how, in the intimate spaces of the everyday, couples can learn to become more than the others, as they witness and directly experience how the other is treated on a daily basis. For interracially married white mothers, they acquire racial literacy not only in loving and living with their black partners, but also in caring and nurturing for their black or biracial children. Within their interracial families, these women develop a racial literacy that facilitates their understanding of their biracial and black family members. According to Twine, these white women earn a kind of honorary blackness, or an honorary membership within categorical blackness. This occurs as these white women demonstrate an experiential knowledge and understanding of brown and black lives; they empirically illustrate how black lives matter within the context of their own families and communities. In my research, I observed similar practices of multiracial respondents expressing empathy for others, and cultivating racial literacy through their intimate family relations.

Here, I want to link Twine to Keating (2013), who argues society works to keep racial group location and consciousness congruent and consistent. Developing racial awareness that shifts consciousness may result in incongruity. This incongruence exposes the reality that people's racial consciousness may expand or take on new forms or shapes as their families do the same. Building on Twine's research, this suggests that for some interracial families, the mixture in and across family members across can be remixed to influence each person's racial consciousness, and the collective family unit. Consider the example offered by the effervescent Bobbi, a young woman with black/white parentage, wavy brown hair and very light skin color. Bobbi noted that strangers frequently mistake her for Hispanic or Hawaiian. Some even wonder if she is Asian. She explained, "Because my stepmother is Filipino(a), I've had experiences in the past where, I guess—I used to live in a small town. She didn't like anyone to know (that she was my stepmother), so people just thought I was Asian as well." Feeling more of an affinity to her stepmother, Bobbi appreciated others' mistake, or found it complimentary, not incorrect in an offensive way. She enjoyed the way (albeit fleeting) that these misperceptions of her as Asian connected her to her stepmother, who she described feeling a strong connection to and considered her mother, for all intents and purposes. Having been primarily nurtured and raised by her Filipina stepmother explains why Bobbi values the Filipina culture she has been immersed in and exposed to most of her life.

Bobbi has cultivated an honorary Asian membership in her "doubly blended family" (blended both in terms of composition of family members rearranged by separation, divorce, and remarriage, but also by race as a result of that remarriage). That is, while her family of origin was black and white, her blended family (from remarriage) is now also Asian. In this family, racial borders blend, along with culture. To Wendy Roth's (2012) point, considering "race within a cultural framework" would be useful here, given that racial layers are building the family, as are the cultures that people keep, even as they cross racial borders, or blend into new family forms.

That people know that Bobbi is "more than black" is okay with her (see Daniel 2002). Sometimes, being "more than black" means that they suspect that she is multiracial, and sometimes, it means that she is also "more than multiracial." In the latter case, this occurs if and when people grant her an "honorary Asian" membership. Because Bobbi cannot necessarily make her affinity, admiration, and appreciation for Asian culture visible, she laments when her familial connection to Asian ethnicity and culture remains invisible or illegible. She cites this connection as equally, if not more, important as her connection to whiteness and blackness. Recognizing her particular combination of races, ethnicities, and cultures remained central and significant to Bobbi. For some multiracial people, making these connections visible to others proves as arduous a task as making their own invisible mixture visible.

To her earlier point about the legibility of multiraciality, Bobbi noted that, in contrast to strangers who saw her as Latina, Asian, or Hawaiian (Pacific Islander), her racially mixed friends could tell that she, too, was mixed: "They already knew. I guess mixed people kinda can tell. They can kind of see that. But a lot of people have always said that, nobody's ever taken me saying that you're (I'm) officially black. It's always, 'You've got something in you. I just don't know what it is.' So, you know, they know I'm mixed with something. They just don't know what it is." These comments indicate that others' observation of Bobbi ostensibly affirms her multiracial identity. That others express knowledge of her racial mixture attempts that affirmation, at least discursively.

Bobbi reported many interactions with others that work to affirm some identities at the risk of negating others. In the bigger scheme of things, she can assert a multiracial identity that more broadly conveys her connection to her white, black, and/or Asian relatives. For her, this involves finding ways to affirm, that yes, she is multiracial, but that her meaning of multiracial includes her racial heritage by birth, but also by a different kind of blending. This blending makes her "more than multiracial" or an honorary Asian, when she is granted membership in a group where she so desires more permanent residence. I will return to this multiracial matter of racial and familial blending momentarily.

First, I want to connect Bobbi's experience to that of one of her siblings, Ellen, who echoed her sentiments. Ellen shared how much her Asian stepmother and biracial (black and Asian) half-sister, positively influence her and impact her racial sense of self. Ellen described her visits to the Philippines, and the various festivities and cultural practices she participated in there. Her own movement around the world and through Filipino culture facilitated her love of this culture, and her ability to create cultural fusions between American and Filipino cultures and cuisines.

> Ellen: It's a great country. I love it. And when they party, they party. I'm telling ya! When they party, they eat.
>
> Author: What do they eat?
>
> Ellen: Rice is their main thing. People laugh at me because I eat rice with almost everything.
>
> Author: From growing up with your (step)mom?
>
> Ellen: Yeah. Yes, and they put sugar and butter. We eat plain rice (but the butter and sugar is how they eat it in Filipino culture).

The above excerpt hints at how much Ellen (and Bobbi, by implication) successfully merged her multiracial and multicultural life together. This process may have been both inhibited and facilitated by the various kinds of borderism Ellen (and other multiracial respondents with black ancestry) experienced. While the experience of having their blackness policed proved painful, it also curiously worked to affirm their racial mixture. The accusations of not being "black enough" opened up the space for some, like Ellen and others, to claim both white *and* black parents, and in Ellen's case, to recognize the tremendous influence of her Asian stepmother. During our interview conversation, I said to Ellen, "So in some ways, you're black, white, *and* Asian?" She smiled at my observation, and confirmed that she feels like she is a part of the Asian community. She then shared, "In fact, I know some of the customers…at Western Union, they'll send money to the Philippines, and I'll say, 'Oh, my mom's from there.' 'Oh, you look Asian.' And I don't say anything. I don't ever say, 'Well, she's my stepmom.' So, and I guess you've heard, 'Well, you've lived so long together that you all look alike.' Well, you could say that. I tell my mom that. She don't say anything but

I know she feels good about that." I would suggest here that Ellen feels pretty good about being seen as Asian, just like her mom.

What Ellen's narrative demonstrates here is the power of connections in everyday life, connections that may not appear obvious, in the absence of any immediate resemblance among family members. These connections reflect great levels of intimacy and require deeper inspection for their detection. They may not be "obvious" to the average observer, but they exist, these connections cultivated across the borders of race, nation, and culture. They grow from the shared experiences of family members, and are cultivated by love. That people presume Ellen's stepmother is her biological mother, or that Ellen is Asian like her stepmother, speaks to the bonding and building of social ties that multiracial and multicultural families do; it also speaks to the specific bridging and shifting that happens, as I see it, in interracial families. As Keating (2013), Anzaldua (1987), and others suggest, individuals in such families develop consciousness that reflects this diversity, that enables people to develop new ways of thinking and seeing, because these intimate spaces reshape the ways people understand themselves and each other racially (among other ways). These relationships challenge our tendency to make categories cohesive, singular, and static. Instead, they invite us to imagine how we all can shift racial consciousness, to minimize borderism, to grow our collective understandings of each other, and embrace shifting mixture in individuals and in society.

This embrace can also simply include one another. As people make efforts to become aware of border-patrolling behaviors, others have already been doing the work of blending borders and breaking them down where possible. One way of dissolving these racial divides is in the blending of races, families and identities, as described above, and in a few additional examples that follow.

Another example of this racial and familial blending of borders comes from Theresa. I turn next to her example, as her narrative offered initial hints at this multiplicative mixture, or that multiracial people experience many layers of mixture. Hers was one of the first interviews where that concept started to bloom and evolve, so I want to unpack it here. Theresa lives in what I called above a "doubly blended," or alternately, a "twice blended" family. The two terms refer to racial and familial blending, or a family that shifts in racial mixture, and through cohabitation, separation, divorce, and/or remarriage or new romantic partnerships. Hers is an interracial and intercultural household with her white partner and his multiracial ("half Mexican") son, whom she lovingly refers to as her "bonus son." Her family is blended racially and structurally, and represents the many families whose lives and families are mixed on many levels (or blends borders racially, culturally, and structurally).

Theresa ostensibly benefits from her racially and ethnically ambiguous appearance, or as she describes herself, looking a "little Latina." She might even be considered, perhaps, an "honorary Hispanic or Latina," given her caring involvement in and love for her bonus son. Her ambiguous appearance facilitates this blending in both visual and familial ways, allowing for her shifting between categories and the blending of racial borders. Ambiguity potentially minimizes the family's experiences with "visual dislocation" (see Steinbugler 2005). As a form of border patrolling, visual dislocation suggests that disparate parts do not belong together. In this case, interracial families or partnerships experience fragmentation from other people's practice of visual dislocation; this dislocation occurs when others do not see the social, familial, or relational bonds between individuals who consider one another family (see Steinbugler 2012). Theresa observes:

> I think it's been good for him. He did, he did not have a close relationship with his mother and she actually passed away several years ago. And so his main relationship has been with his father and I guess for me, because I'm not just white, I feel like we kind of have something in common. And he calls me mom and he introduces me to his friends as mom and a lot of people say, "Oh, he looks just like you." And you know, he's brown. And he's actually darker than I am. He's pretty brown. So there are some similarities between he and I that we kind of look like a family that fits because he is brown. So I think that that kinda made him feel comfortable, as me being, I guess, his stepmom.

Being a "family that fits" alludes to Theresa's perception that she resembles her stepson, and her sense of relief that because her skin clor closely matches hers strangers may see her as her stepson's biological mother. Theresa suggested that this approximation in appearance gives her the ability (or luxury) to minimize the border patrolling that might arise in a more visibly mixed family. For example, if she and her husband both looked white and her "bonus son" looked brown, people might border patrol them by asking about the relationship between the three[3]. Theresa's intermediary position between her husband and bonus son allows her to serve as a bridge between the two. This bridge deflects borderism, as she visually and socially shifts and blends between white and brown. They do not experience the visual dislocation that they might otherwise; her appearance approximates that of her brown-

skinned "bonus son." This approximation meets or satisfies the
seemingly requisite "racial resemblance" required or expected of family
members. Any resemblance arguably buffers her and her family from
various kinds of borderism. The resemblance is also coincidental.
Nevertheless, Theresa's discussion shows how she attempts to protect
her bonus son from any implicit or explicit harm or danger that
borderists might provoke. This protective parental mechanism illustrates
how much she cares for her son, and works to shield him from some of
the unsavory experiences interracial families face in a racially divisive
society (see also Dalmage 2000). Theresa is likely replicating, to some
degree, any protective parental border patrolling she experienced from
her own parents and within her family of origin. This borderism can be
understood, then, as a learned self-protective response that extends from
living on color lines, intergenerationally.

Were Theresa whiter-looking than her son, and presumably less like
him in appearance, she might have to manage the gap created by their
lack of racial resemblance to one another. This point hints at the
"bridging" that multiracial people within families, to make the
relationships transparent and logical to border patrollers. Bridging, a
term I borrow from Anzalduan scholars, is another way of thinking
about racial migrations and transformations, or movement that helps
solidify social ties between people who are understood as different
based on racial group membership.

This figurative bridge is something multiracial individuals are often
expected to build, but it is one that ultimately serves Theresa and her
family well. In addition, Theresa's cultural, but not necessarily racial,
literacy has helped her in raising her Mexican bonus son (Twine 2003;
Twine and Steinbugler 2006). She observes, "I do feel like there are
some things about his culture that I want to learn more about and I, we
actually have a really close relationship with his grandmother, um, his
mother's mother. She's like my mom, and I love her to death. And so I
talk to her about that. All the traditions, um, and mostly food. We talk
about the things that they fix and that kind of thing. I get recipes from
her."

Rather than ignore or whitewash her son's Mexican heritage,
Theresa incorporates it into her family. She reported recognizing the
importance of doing so, and saw how much he enjoyed that, along with
some things that his maternal grandmother and great-grandmother
cooked for him. Theresa creates a transracial multiracial, multicultural
literacy, in learning about her stepson and husband's family as a
multiracial person of different mixture/heritage. Twine (2011) discusses
this sharing of knowledge and the ways social and cultural exchanges

impact the identities and everyday lives of interracial (as well as interethnic and intercultural) families.

Finally, Theresa and her husband ensured that their son went to school where his peers would not tease him. Having experienced her own kind of school menace, she knew the importance of "fitting in and feeling good" in school (see Phillips 2004). She noted that her bonus son's school peers would make "comments, like, 'Are you going to sit in the back of the truck on the way home?' *That* kind of stuff." This covert racism, cloaked in "racetalk" (Myers 2005), reminded her of being called names and facing more overt discrimination and differential treatment because of her mixture and her Asian identity in particular. Myers (2005:2) describes "racetalk" as "the vocabulary and conceptual frameworks that we use to denigrate different races and ethnicities in our everyday lives."

While parents may attempt to protect or shield their multiracial children from teasing, bullying, or other verbally (or physically) aggressive environments in public, they may find managing this racetalk next to impossible. Where multiracial children and adults fall into more than one group, they risk racetalk intensified by their mixture. They may be the target of racist humor about any of the groups to which they belong based on parentage, as well as on perception or misrecognition. If a multiracial child looks Latino, but is white and black, they may risk hearing unsavory racialized jokes about all three groups, if not more.

Parents may opt to simplify the racial identity of their child(ren) to minimize or manage this harm. To link back to earlier discussions, they may do so by perpetuating borderism of various kinds. They may simplify, as some respondents reported, multiracial identities, choosing a singular race for simplicity sake, not as a preferred identity. The reality of racetalk, as it relates to multiracial people, has not fully been explored but provides insight into how hostile social environments in public and private support or dissuade multiracial people from embracing and claiming the complexities of their racial identities.

Myers argues that an analysis of racetalk would strengthen our collective understanding of this racially divisive society. Theresa's examples illustrate Myers' (2005:3) point that "people have not expunged racialized thinking from their imaginations—they have simply learned to be more discreet. Formal changes have made the public expression of certain ideas politically incorrect, but their expression endures in the private realm: an unofficial classroom where the old ways can be nurtured, innovated, and passed on with little scrutiny or castigation." Identifying, naming, and confronting this racetalk remain some of the many challenges of social life today, especially given the contagion of racetalk. This work aims to contribute to that process of disrupting or curbing its spread.

As multiracial people move around discursive obstacles such as racetalk, they rely on a variety of strategies to clarify their racial locations, and to affirm themselves and their multiracial families. They may encounter racetalk that prohibits their inclusion in particular racial categories, or that guides them away from central social membership in these racial groups. They engage in this movement, potentially as members of "invisibly mixed" families or ones experiencing shifting mixture. In the final section of this chapter, I illustrate how these exclusions, when expressed through border patrolling racetalk, can curiously affirm the multiple social locations multiracial people occupy. I argue that these dislocations facilitate racial transformations, and result in racial reconfigurations in identity and racial groups. How we conceptualize the heterogeneity of racial categories in the present moment will guide how we understand multiracial identity in the future, and if/how we reconfigure the entire racial categorization system.

Consider another example of someone who has experienced racial border patrolling in ways that motivated her migration towards other racial groups. Rachel, a white and Native American-identified woman, also discussed how she felt about friends who border patrol her and "see her as white":

> Yeah, it pisses me off royally....It's not that I'm not proud to be white because I'm really proud of my mom's heritage but don't discredit my other half too just because I look white to you....People will accuse me of acting Indian. I don't know why. Because we have "time issues." Or if I talk about eating venison, people are like, "Eewww." I'm like, "Why? Deer meat's good." "That's so Indian of you," they say. "Shut up!" Or because I eat fry bread...And my music choices. Oh, I get harassed because I listen to drum music, and Native folk singers who sing about Native issues, and they're like, "Oh my...you listen to the weirdest music." "Like what? I like it."

With a good sense of humor, Rachel challenged borderism, by attempting to transform border patrolling into opportunities to expose her friends to parts of her heritage (music, food, etc.), and inform them about cultural differences. She did this in an effort to help them gain a greater understanding of her mixture and the importance of Native American culture to her. For Rachel, the contrast to white culture appears in what she viewed as the consistency of indigenous culture. That is, Native Americans participated in important cultural practices, rituals, and observations that get infused into one's upbringing. Rachel contrasted this with white American culture, which she described as observing occasions "once a year." This is a clear reference to the symbolic ethnicity that many white ethnic groups adopt in this society (Waters 1990; Doane 1997). Thus, Rachel perceives Native American culture as more meaningful and less superficial than other cultures, particularly white culture. This perception perpetuates the myth of "vanilla" whiteness (Rubin 1984; hooks 1992; Sandoval 2002), and makes the fetishism and Orientalism of "Other" cultures and/or races more likely (Said 1978).

Despite discussions of people desiring honorary white status, Rachel rejected its imposition on her life and instead did a "double border crossing" to become "black by proxy" or "honorary black." Through her friendships with black women (which included women she named in our interview as her "two best friends"), Rachel developed "a lot more comfort [around blacks]" but clarified, "It's not like I didn't hang out with them [whites]. I just felt more comfortable than with someone uber white." This admission points to the extent to which some multiracial individuals forge friendships across race(s) in ways that appear to go against the grain of racial affinity, homophily, or homogeny, terms capturing the human tendency for "like to attract like" or for people to stay in their comfort zone (Korgen 2002). Rachel gained honorary membership into blackness, while maintaining her white and Native American multiracial identity. Arguably, her honorary blackness makes her more than multiracial, or multiracial in multiple ways: as she defines it, based on racial parentage and heritage; and on the basis of meaningful connections and friendships. Rachel's racial migration shows the more productive or generative side of borderism, as she experiences shifting mixture that moves her in closer alignment to the social group with which she has great affinity and connection.

Conclusions

I ended this chapter with examples of multiracial people shifting towards groups with whom they may feel more affinity and alignment. This multidirectional multiracial movement is important because it illustrates a particular kind of racial migration that is made possible through the strength of central social ties, including friendships. Through the deep and meaningful connections made possible in their friendships and other relationships, some multiracial people reported experiences of racial kinship, loyalty, and a sense of shifting group membership in racial groups not limited to their own heritage. Instead, some experienced a more expansive or malleable sense of belonging, a feeling of racial kinship and being that I call "more than multiracial." For these individuals, being "more than multiracial" did not mean rejecting that identity, or moving away from their multiracial identity, parentage, or heritage. Instead, it offered an additional layer to this identity, and allowed them to recognize important connections to other racial groups. This recognition is reflective of their inclusion in "some other race." Being included in racial groups beyond their own extended the scope of their social networks and the groups of people with which they could feel a sense of racial kinship. That is, even in the absence of shared racial group membership, some multiracial people reportedly cultivated close ties and developed kinship to group members who might be viewed as lacking an immediate or presumed alliance.

For multiracial people who experienced this kinship, they described a kind of kinship made possible by the malleability and flexibility of their racial identity, a robust racial literacy, and frequently, their existing familiarity with multiracial movement through a variety of social settings, and across time and space. It was not always the case that multiracial people who had lived in a number of places cultivated these connections, but their experiences with these migrations seemed to enrich their ability to manage the borders of race, and facilitate multiple border crossings. This multiracial movement, or the physical and social migration of multiracial individuals, suggests that people who cross geographical borders may cultivate an ease or develop some fluency in crossing the borders of race in a variety of settings, socially, culturally, and nationally.

As multiracial individuals add layers to their racial identity, or experience this shifting mixture, they expressed a sense of affirmation and appreciation in belonging to racial groups beyond their own. They did not necessarily want to claim permanent residence in these other racial categories, but they did not want to pretend or appear to simply be passing or touring through them either. Given that many of these multiracial people faced authenticity testing about their own racial identity, they respected and enjoyed these honorary memberships because of their knowledge and understanding of the racial realities of their closest friends and allies. They did not want to be misread as "passing" into these categories for some social or economic/material gain; instead, they felt these honorary memberships captured the beauty of racially diverse social networks, in which friends strengthen one another's racial literacy by becoming familiar with each other's racial realities.

While honorary memberships arguably have a temporary quality to them, given that they will likely end when the respective friendships end, they may have more enduring or lasting impacts on both the individuals granting these memberships and on those enjoying this honorary status. My sense was that these honorary memberships ostensibly could be revoked, but were awarded and experienced as longer-lasting aspects of a person's identity. This description speaks to the dynamic of blending and blurring the borders of race, as a multiracial person, and as someone who crosses into racial categories through these honorary memberships. Once such knowledge is acquired and intimacy is cultivated, can individuals who enjoy honorary status in a group undo its effects on their racial identity? If multiracial people embrace their connections to "some other race," what do they do if these connections dissipate over time?

The above questions underscore one of the central themes of this work, of shifting mixture. For multiracial individuals, everyday experiences likely involve living on or across the color lines of their respective racial combinations (and/or the perception thereof), *and* on the fault lines of any racial groups into which they were welcomed with honorary membership status. For these individuals, and any of the existing members of the honorary status-granting racial group (friends and family), they may all be asked border-patrolling questions, or be expected to clarify the borders of race to others. How do racially mixed groups of friends explain their racial kinship, when they do not share the same racial identities? How might they explain to border-patrolling others that they share similar racial group memberships (made partially possible through honorary memberships), even as they occupy different racial locations?

As friends like these face any questions from borderists, they may experience positive effects of this borderism. This borderism might strengthen the group's social ties and connections to one another, or this borderism might break them apart, the interrogations a slow erosion or imposition to their racially diverse friendships with multiracial people. The formation and dissolution of such social networks reflects a kind of racial migration that deserves further scholarly attention. So too does the other aspect of racial migrations and relocations upon which I focus in this chapter.

Prior to my discussion of honorary memberships, I provided an in-depth look at the lives of David and Maritza, two respondents from my research whose narratives typified racial migrations and the "cultural transformations of race" (see Roth 2012). Their narratives offer interesting examples of the ways moving from one country to another or between countries changing the way one sees or conceptualizes race, and how one understands oneself in the process. I employed the terms "multiracial movement," and, "shifting mixture," to show how migrations from one part of the world to another prompt multiracial people to ask, "What am I?" In this twist, multiracial people ask themselves who they are racially, when the ways that they used to see themselves change. They may be experiencing "shifting mixture," or changes in how they understand themselves racially. These changes may be developmental ones, or social ones facilitated by their movement from one society to another, and one culture to another. Just as multiracial people explore this question on their own terms, they may continue to confront the "What are you?" question from others. As I discussed in the previous chapters, these questions convey various forms of borderism, from the benevolent to malevolent kind in strangers.

As multiracial people move between nations, they may find themselves moving between racial categories. This multiracial movement can generate borderism, as people encountering these multiracial individuals have questions about their racial locations. For multiracial individuals unfamiliar with or less fluent/racially literate, they may have social interactions with strangers who place them in any number of (correct or incorrect) racial categories. When the racial multiplicity of multiracial people or their racial migrations (from one country to another) cannot be translated, border-patrolling people likely move multiracial people into the racial category they imagine is the best fit. These racial relocations may be resisted or accommodated by the multiracial individuals themselves. Sometimes, they offer corrections, in an effort to more fully communicate and nuance border-patrolling others' understanding of them, of racial migrations, and of racial differences within a global context. However, at other times, some multiracial people may prefer or desire these racial relocations, particularly if they are placed in "better" racial categories or they can disidentify from less desirable ones. To this end, I found evidence that some multiracial people manage this movement towards and away from the term, "multiracial," in a variety of ways and for a number of reasons. As multiracial people experience their own choose migrations, they also experience involuntary ones, whereby strangers or other people move them into particular racial categories they might not otherwise claim. This multiracial movement results in racial categories being much more complex and nuanced than typically accounted for in discussions of race.

Among the research participants, some managed to disqualify their racial locations, or equivocate multiraciality with partiality or singularity. To the conversation above, some simplified their identities to strangers and others as a way of attempting to successfully navigate racial borders. Rather than seeing their respective "parts" as whole, many respondents viewed themselves in racially fragmented ways. This discourse of fragmentation thematically ran through most of the interviews I conducted with participants. Notably, however, not all respondents made racial maneuvers *away* from particular terms, including "multiracial," or singular racial group references. Sometimes, multiracial respondents had reason to make other identity claims, including complex family histories and racially diverse friendship groups or social networks. This complexity involved the blurring of racial lines, as well as ethnic and cultural ones. In borrowing Daniel's (2001) concept, "more than black," I introduced the idea that familial reconfigurations and racial migrations produced dynamics that make some multiracial people "more than multiracial." This can mean that multiracial people should be able to claim a singular race (without contestation or rejection); claim two or more races; claim "some other race(s)"; or enjoy honorary memberships by virtue of the strong friendship connections that they have fostered in their lifetime. My discussion of honorary memberships illustrates a different way of being "more than multiracial." Living on the borders of race means navigating racial lines, as well as any rearrangements to family structures. As families blend, so too might race. Thus, the borders of race shift mixture in multiracial individuals who cultivate connections with new family members who prove as important or pivotal as existing ones.

As multiracial people migrate into (and out of) nations, and into (and out of) potentially new (to them) racial classification systems, they complicate the ways in which we understand race in the United States. They expose how much they must navigate the borders of race, as well as physical spatial borders between nations. These migrations bring into relief the differences between racial classification systems across nations, and they highlight the rewards and challenges of learning new ways of seeing race in various countries and across time, space, and place. These migrations strengthen the language and literacy of new arrivals, as well as border-patrolling people who take up the charge of defending the borders of race. Through these migrations, social interactions take place that may clarify these blurred boundaries of race or make them messier, to both multiracial people and any border-patrolling inquirers.

These migrations ask us to consider why it is still so critical to clarify racial locations, even as people locate multiracial people in the wrong category(ies) much of the time. If multiracial people are taking up residence, as honorary members of "some other race" or racial categories into which border-patrolling others place them, then these racial migrations are destabilizing race by revealing the existing and persistent porosity of racial boundaries.

Notes

[1] This is a nod to Patricia Hill Collins (1993).

[2] The racial identification one makes when completing institutional forms, such as the Census.

[3] This type of border patrolling involves "visual dislocation" (see Steinbugler 2005), a topic that Dalmage (2004c) also discusses in "Mama, Are You Brown?"

7

The Shifting Mixture of Racial Identities

"What many people on the border say is that we assume a multiple repertoire of identities. We have transitional identities in the making. We are developing new cultures. Jokingly, we have talked about imaginary identities that make more sense than the ones we are offered as possibilities" (Fusco 1995: 153–4).

The above quote by Coco Fusco captures the spirit of this concluding chapter on shifting mixture, and on the entire book project as a study of racial identities in the making. Her ideas help frame the fluidity of these identities through her recognition of multiplicity. Fusco also draws attention to the powerful force that imagination plays for "people on the border." For some, "imagined identities," much like "imagined communities," offer up greater possibilities than the truths of our contemporary and collective racial realities (see Anderson 1999). They create the space where "new forms of identity…and community become imaginable," as feminist scholars Chela Sandoval (2002) and others suggest. When taken together, these thoughts thread into the notion that dreams precede reality. In a more serious way than Fusco describes, this process entails dreaming our way to a future full of real and imagined identities all envisioned as possibilities that can become realities.

Through this vision, people can build or rebuild communities to be more inclusive of individuals with identities in the making or identities in bloom. Linking Benedict Anderson (1999) concept of "imagined communities" to Fusco's "imaginary identities" illustrates the importance of imagination and ingenuity in a world that does not always embrace difference. Fusco makes this point in recognizing how many people cultivate their creativity and employ their imagination to fashion new kinds of identities and to foster connections across time and space.

Of the 60 individuals interviewed for this research, several of them addressed this idea. That is, they shared their narratives about their racial senses of self and community, in their own words and on their own terms.

Their everyday experiences of race involved them figuring out, as I discussed in the last chapter, the changing geography and demography of race. A different and more literal kind of "multiracial movement" facilitates these changes. As multiracial people move around, they carry their ways of seeing race with them; they cross racial and geographical borders and discover new ways of seeing themselves and others. In so doing, they encourage others to expand their understandings of racial borders and shifting mixture. This movement of multiracial people proves a metaphor for the borders of race. The borders of race do not move with each attendant move a multiracial person makes. However, racial borders do expand and contract, contingent on geographical location, to include or exclude multiracial people.

The expansion and contraction of these racial groups reflect a societal imperative toward social order amidst slow and steady change. Many people believe this order is best established and maintained through the racial classification system. The illusion of racially pure and distinct categories allows this sense of social order to exist, even as it remains elusive to accurately categorize anyone based on race. This is so because race is a social, rather than biological, construction. Nevertheless, people are deeply invested in maintaining the prevailing ways of seeing race and preserving the current racial categories. This includes multiracial people.

As I illustrated throughout this book, part of the process of preserving the current racial classification system is accomplished, or at least attempted, through border patrolling. Border patrolling occurs in a plethora of ways; the nuances of each scenario too great to detail here. However, I observed some general patterns and discussed three different social groups that engage in border patrolling of multiracial people: strangers, family members and friends, and multiracial people themselves. In many ways, this list reflects, in ascending order, the level of attendant surprise I felt at discovering that members of these groups police the borders of race much like strangers do. However, the latter two groups are privy to much more personal information about the multiracial person's preferred racial identity and family biography and can ostensibly use this information against them (or themselves, as the case may be).

When strangers encounter a person who lives across racial borders, those strangers tend to ask clarifying, if now cliché, questions to figure out where best *they* could place the multiracial person. This view of a singular place or racial location for a person of multiple races to belong exposes the contradictory and faulty logic of race in contemporary society; it refuses to recognize racial multiplicity in racially mixed people. Further, it suggests that strangers know best and that their perceptions matter most when it comes to clarifying the racial locations of multiracial people.

Border patrolling denies multiracial people the agency to assert their preferred racial identities publicly and without contestation. It also creates a conundrum for multiracial people who assert protean identities, or ones who name the composite parts of who they are and who they claim in terms of their parentage and heritage. I discussed this shifting mixture and the ways in which multiracial people might move into and out of racial categories intentionally, synthesizing their composite parts but experiencing the fluidity and flexibility of their racial multiplicity all the same.

Often, strangers who border patrol multiracial people have a difficult time deciphering the racial borders and locations of those considered racially and ethnically ambiguous. These border patrollers often move multiracial people who are ambiguous in appearance into racial categories different than the ones the multiracial people would claim for themselves. This explains why scholars describe the kinds of transitional identities that people form while living on the borders of race. For some multiracial people, "life at the border," as Homi Bhabha (2004, 1991) puts it, involves embracing interstitial racial and spatial locations.

As border patrollers push or pull multiracial people into and out of various racial groups, these multiracial people must figure out ways to interact with strangers who border patrol them; they must learn to navigate not only this racial terrain but also the broader social landscape informing so much of these interactions. In this post–Civil Rights Era of colorblindness and colormuteness, or rhetorical devices reflective of our collective tendencies towards reticence around discussions of race, it is important to acknowledge the everyday interactional work that multiracial people engage in with strangers in public.

Optimistically, these interactions with border-patrolling strangers have the potential to enhance shared learning and self-knowledge which strengthen the racial literacy of all involved individuals. This literacy can be sharpened to the point of becoming fluency; this newfound fluency would enhance the quality of any similar future exchanges, making them more mutually satisfying, reciprocal, and consensual. Less optimistically, these interactions simply result in multiracial people perpetually having to explain their lives on the borders of race. Further research should consider the cumulative and collective impact of these interactions, especially in cases where malevolent border patrolling in particular creates harm, injury, and trauma for multiracial people. This will become increasingly imperative as evidence gathers that both primary social groups, which includes family members and friends, and multiracial people themselves engage in the practice of border patrolling.

At the time of this research, it took me a bit by surprise that many of my respondents reported being border patrolled by the very people arguably best positioned to support and affirm them. As their narratives revealed, various family members and close friends engaged in border patrolling practices similar to any multiracial people engage in themselves; by refusing to see the preferred identity of the multiracial people, they engaged in the negation or invalidation of multiracial people's racial identity preferences. Given the number of racial identity options that multiracial people can assert, this notion of a preferred identity is not always already "multiracial." The many choices open to multiracial people might fluster or confuse others but border patrollers in the family generally did not even bother to ask the kinds of questions that might allow them access to greater insight and understanding of the racial complexities of multiplicity. Instead of exploring the contours of these choices, or asking how multiracial members of their family opted into and out of certain racial categories, border-patrolling family members frequently prioritized their own perceptions of the multiracial people. This did little to inform or educate the multiracial members of any given family and instead actually worked to negate, rather than affirm, their preferred racial identities.

Based on the narratives of some of my respondents, many parents in particular seemed to have limited racial literacy which otherwise might have allowed them to more effectively have conversations with their multiracial children about race, racial identity, and concepts like racial ambiguity, fluidity, multiplicity, and incongruity. As I discussed, these concepts speak to much of "the multiracial experience" because an increasing number of individuals have a racially and ethnically ambiguous appearance. They shift between racial categories because of this appearance and/or because of the racial groups to which they lay claim. Although they can and may claim two or more races, they also sometimes or always claim "one-and-only-one" race. In any of these examples, their appearance may or may not align with their identity or identities. My research suggests that room for improvement exists in the strategies people employ, both within their families and in the broader society, to talk about race, racism, and racial identity. This entails individual and collective efforts to learn how to effectively talk about, rather than elude, these issues and other mixed race matters.

These conversations would prove useful for everyone who polices the borders of race, including multiracial people. Much to my surprise, within the narratives of many of the multiracial respondents, I heard traces of evidence to suggest that multiracial people practice border patrolling as well. In retrospect, this should have been of little surprise since people tend to internalize patterns of behavior that are normalized in society. As a different but related example, we see this when victims of violence become violent offenders themselves (see Smith 2005). Thus, just as multiracial people report being border patrolled by strangers, and perhaps particularly by those closest to them, they, too, learn this practice. They may have their own motivations for doing so, but they border patrol all the same.

What might seem like a benign side effect of being a target of border patrolling by others arguably becomes more nefarious when multiracial people feel its negative or adverse effects. If auto- or self-border patrolling affects multiracial people's ability to affirm their preferred racial identity or to fully embrace their racial multiplicity or a chosen simplicity or racial singularity, and affects the ability to also enjoy any shifting mixture they experience, then the space exists for such border patrolling to desist. In fact, this society should create space for everyone's preferred identities to peacefully exist, without any particular groups bearing the burden of proof. Together, then, we can collectively engage in thinking about racial borders as so many people move across the color line(s) in their everyday lives.

Thinking mixture requires the kind of empathy and sympathy that facilitates a remembering and rethinking of the interstices. This rethinking of the color line (Gallagher 2003a) might move us collectively towards a society where the blurring of racial boundaries is no longer policed in color-blind ways but encouraged sincerely and wholeheartedly, for those who desire doing so. Allowing shifting mixture to shift our consciousness so that we encourage, rather than police, the blending or blurring of racial borders encourages deeper reflection on the color line. This reflection would ideally invite more people to cross the color line, if only to engage in conversations about its continuing significance, to cultivate their racial literacy, and to support complexity in identities, including but not limited to multiracial ones.

Final Reflections and New Directions for Future Research

In focusing on the migrations of multiracial people, in racial, social, and spatial terms, I explored their experiences moving between races, and sometimes nations, to understand how they navigate the borders of race. Multiracial people are experiencing racial migrations, as well as transformations, as a result of that movement across time and space. Some of the transformations occur at the level of the individual, specifically in terms of racial identity, but also more broadly in terms of their racial schemas and frameworks or ways of seeing race. This multiracial movement facilitates changes in the national population and foreshadows future social interactions, none of which have to involve much of the usual borderpatrolling behavior I describe in this book.

It is important to note that while multiracial people are experiencing racial transformations through geographic and social migrations, they are transforming the social landscape of American society. They are potentially transforming the ways in which people see race and come to recognize shifting and in/visible mixture. They challenge people's policing of racial borders because they challenge the dominant understandings of the borders of race. Just as some of my respondents are figuring out where they fit in the U.S. racial classification system and learning to see themselves among the "new faces in a changing America," they are changing the way we understand how race is lived on these borders (see Winters and DeBose 2003).

These changing demographics and social dynamics move slowly but steadily; the shifting mixture and in/visible mixture that exists in contemporary society will likely continue to dissipate and intensify. As the narratives of the respondents show, multiracial people can blend the borders of race, slipping into racial categories not their own and falling out of racial categories that they want to claim because of their parentage and heritage. Multiracial people also intensify racial borders by serving as reminders, through any racial ambiguity, incongruity, or fluidity in identity, that race matters and that racial borders still matter given the contestations around them.

This book underscores mixed race matters and foreshadows a future full of similar social interactions related to these racial negotiations. I argue this despite Jennifer Hochschild's (2014) contention that the "current American racial order will look very different by the time our children reach old age." As families mix and blend, as new immigrants arrive and return, or move between home, host, or any other countries to maintain and cultivate their transnational identities, the racial order changes to reflect these migrations and these complexities in identities. Yet, despite this mixing and blending, so many of the narratives of my respondents indicate that the borders of race remain relatively intact, even as they blur or blend at the edges to accommodate and reflect shifting mixture.

As evidenced throughout the book, racial borders are policed and protected or, at best, questioned when racial border crossings are detected or people who are living across color lines and the borders of race become perceptible. Border patrolling thus remains largely contingent on the appearance and disappearance of racial mixture; shifting mixture, and in/visible mixture complicate social interactions in part because of the optical illusion of race, and in particular, of multiraciality. Because of this situational legibility of multiraciality, that "now you see it, now you don't" effect where the racial mixture of multiracial people appears or disappears to onlookers, border patrolling practices ostensibly offer better detection of anyone crossing color lines or blending racial borders (see Bonilla Silva 2015).

For multiracial people who are "clearly mixed," clarifying these color lines can involve fielding a variety of questions designed to better locate them or determine their racial coordinates. Rather than allow them multiple locations or claims to more than one racial group and/or only one racial group of their preference, racial border patrollers generally deny or limit this possibility. Racial border patrollers prefer a sort of clarity and fixity over the ambiguity and fluidity that allows multiracial people to float between categories, to be either/or/one/both/some/all or none at all (the transcendent, human race). They fail to register the reality that racial categories are not pure but always already mixed. They also neglect to consider that their actions, the border-patrolling practices of putting multiracial people into different racial categories than they prefer or claim, perpetuate this mixture. The irony of this might be lost on border patrollers who see themselves as preserving racial categories, rather than reinforcing the very racial mixture that they otherwise seem to oppose.

Many racial border patrollers do not want to accommodate any racial fluidity or shifting mixture; they police racial borders out of ignorance, benevolence, malevolence, and/or more. Whatever their reasons or motivations may be, their actions often serve as a negation of multiracial realities and preferred racial identities. Instead of affirming the various racial combinations made possible in this historical moment, many racial border patrollers, including multiracial people themselves, cling to the notion that a multiracial individual can belong to "one-and-only-one" racial group. Others refuse to recognize that some multiracial people prefer to claim a singular racial identity. Racial border patrolling complicates the choices and experiences of multiracial people wanting to choose identities on their own terms, whether the choice points to one race or includes all of the composite parts of that person's racial heritage. Racial border patrolling also continues to impact people who are interracially married/coupled/partnered and/or anyone living or growing up in racially mixed families or forming ones of their own.

While important new research continues to examine multiracial people, more research must focus on adult multiracial children. Much of the way that multiracial people appear and disappear in society is reflected in the Census data, or they appear as a perpetually infantilized population in much of the sociological literature. Studying the growing number of children who identify or are identified as multiracial is as important as studying how growing up multiracial shapes the way those individuals enter adulthood and parenthood. More research should focus on the adult multiracial population alongside that which focuses on multiracial children. Focusing on multiracial adults might allow researchers to answer some of the following questions: How differently do adult multiracial people socialize their children around these issues of racial identity? How might their own experiences dealing with racial border patrollers shape the messages they send to their children? Will the borders of race eventually blur so much as to validate Jennifer Hochschild's (2014) contention that, in another generation, the national population will look nothing like today's population?

Research that examines the explicit and implicit messages multiracial parents disseminate to their children is needed, alongside studies that consider whether "interracial" will survive the next generation. As multiracial people increasingly partner with other multiracial people, will they and/or others consider these relationships "interracial"? Will it matter if the individuals involved have the same racial background but different appearance or have different racial backgrounds but similar physical appearances? These questions suggest that more research must be done to consider the numerous ways multiracial people manage the borders of race. This work focuses on multiracial identity, while opening the door to studies on multiracial parenting, and multiracial people in interracial relationships. Rich opportunities also exist to explore more multiracial movement at the intersections of the international, interracial, and multiracial.

Bibliography

Acker, Joan, Kate Barry, and Johanna Esseveld (1983). "Objectivity and Truth: Problems in Doing Feminist Research." *Women's Studies International Forum* 6(4): 423-35.

Ali, Suki (2003). *Mixed-Race, Post-Race: Gender, New Ethnicities, and Cultural Practices.* New York, NY: Berg.

Alonso, Karen (2000). *Loving v. Virginia: Interracial Marriage.* Landmark Supreme Court Cases Series. Berkeley Heights, NJ: Enslow Publishers, Inc.

Althusser, Louis (1971). "Ideology and Ideological State Apparatuses (Notes towards an Investigation)" in *Lenin and Philosophy and Other Essays.* Translated from the French by Ben Brewster. New York, NY: Monthly Review Press.

Alvarez, Julia (1998). "A White Woman of Color" in C.C. O'Hearn (Ed.). *Half and Half: Writers on Growing Up Biracial and Bicultural.* Pp. 139–149. New York: Pantheon Books.

Andersen, Margaret L. (2003). "Whitewashing Race: A Critical Perspective on Whiteness" in *White Out: The Continuing Significance of Racism.* Edited by Ashley W. Doane and Eduardo Bonilla-Silva. Pp. 21–34. New York: Routledge.

Anderson, Benedict (1999). *Imagined Communities: Reflections on the Origin and Spread of Nationalism.* New York: Verso.

Anzaldua, Gloria (1987/1999). *Borderlands/La Frontera: The New Mestiza.* (2nd Ed.). San Francisco, CA: Aunt Lute Books.

Anzaldua, Gloria and AnaLousie Keating (Eds.) (2002). *This Bridge We Call Home: Radical Visions for Transformation.* New York: Routledge.

Almaguer, Tomas (2008). *Racial Fault Lines: The Historical Origins of White Supremacy in California.* Berkeley, CA: University of California Press.

Appadurai, Arjun (1996). *Modernity at Large: Cultural Dimensions Of Globalization.* Minneapolis, MN: University of Minnesota Press.

Babbie, Earl (1998). *The Practice of Social Research* (8th Ed.). New York, NY: K,Wadsworth Publishing Company.

Bailey, T.K., Y.B. Chung, W.S. Williams, A.A. Singh, and H.K. Terrell (Oct 2011). "Development and Validation of the Internalized Racial Oppression Scale for Black Individuals." *Journal of Counseling Psychology* 58(4):481–93.

Baldwin, James (1995). *The Evidence of Things Not Seen."* New York: Holt.

Bhabha, Homi (2004). *The Location of Culture.* New York: Routledge.

Bhabha, Homi (1991). "The Third Space: Interview with Homi Bhabha" in *Identity: Community, Culture, Difference.* Edited by John Rutherford. London: Lawrence Wishart.

Bhavnani, Kum-Kum (Ed.) (2001). *Feminism and 'Race.'* New York, NY: Oxford University Press.

Bliss, Catherine (2012). *Race Decoded: The Genomic Fight for Social Justice.* Stanford, CA: Stanford University Press.

Blum, Linda (1999). *At the Breast: Ideologies of Breastfeeding and Motherhood in the Contemporary United States.* Boston: Beacon Press.

Blumer, Herbert (Spring 1958). "Race Prejudice as a Sense of Group Position" from *The Pacific Sociological Review* 1(1):3–7.

Bonilla-Silva, Eduardo (May 6, 2015). "Now You See It, Now You Don't! Racism in Post-Racial Times." Lecture. University of Colorado.

Bonilla-Silva, Eduardo (2004). "From Biracial to Tri-Biracial: The Emergence of a New Racial Stratification System In The United States" in *Skin Deep: How Race And Complexion Matter In The 'Color-Blind' Era.* Edited By Cedric Herring, Verna Keith, and Hayward Derrick Horton. Pp. 224–239. Urbana, IL: University of Illinois Press.

Bonilla-Silva, Eduardo (2003a). *Racism without Racists: Color-Blind Racism and the Perspectives of Racial Inequality in the United States.* New York: Rowman and Littlefield.

Bonilla-Silva, Eduardo (2003b). "'New Racism,' Color-Blind Racism, and the Future of Whiteness in America" in *White Out: The Continuing Significance of Racism.* Edited by Ashley W. Doane and Eduardo Bonilla-Silva. Pp. 271–284. New York, NY: Routledge.

Bonilla-Silva (2002). "The Linguistics of Color Blind Racism: How to Talk Nasty About Blacks without Sounding 'Racist'." *Critical Sociology* 28(1–2): 41–64.

Bonilla-Silva, Eduardo (2001). *White Supremacy And Racism in The Post-Civil Rights Era.* Boulder, CO: Lynne Rienner Publishers.

Bordo, Susan (1999). "Feminism, Foucault, and the Politics of the Body" in *Feminist Theory and the Body: A Reader.* Edited by Janet Price and Margrit Shildrick. Pp. 246–257. New York: Routledge.

Bradshaw, Carla K. (1992) "Beauty and the Beast: On Racial Ambiguity" in *Racially Mixed People in America.* Edited by Maria P.P. Root. Pp. 77–88. Thousand Oaks, CA: Sage Publications.

Bratter, Jenifer (December 2007). "Will 'Multiracial' Survive to the Next Generation?: The Racial Classification of Children of Multiracial Parents." *Social Forces* 86(2): 821–849.

Bridges, Khiara (2011). *Reproducing Race: An Ethnography of Pregnancy as a Site of Racialization.* Berkeley, CA: University of California Press.

Brown, Brene (2012). *Daring Greatly: How the Courage to Be Vulnerable Transforms the Way We Live, Love, Parent, and Lead.* New York: Penguin.

Brown, Michael K., Martin Carnoy, Elliott Currie, Troy Duster, David B. Oppenheimer, Marjorie M. Schultz, and David Wellman (2005). *Whitewashing Race: The Myth of a Color-blind Society.* Berkeley, CA: University of California Press.

Brown, Ruth Nicole (2013). *Hear Our Truths: The Creative Potential of Black Girlhood.* Urban Champaign: University of Illinois Press.

Brown, Ruth Nicole (2008). *Black Girlhood Celebration: Toward a Hip-Hop Feminist Pedagogy.* New York: Peter Lang Publishers.

Browne, Simone (2015). *Dark Matters: On the Surveillance of Blackness.* Durham, NC: Duke University Press.

Brunsma, David L. (Ed.) (2006a). *Mixed Messages: Multiracial Identities in the "Color-Blind" Era.* Boulder, CO: Lynne Rienner.

Brunsma, David L. (2006b). "Public Categories, Private Identities: Exploring Regional Differences in the Biracial Experience." *Social Science Research* 35:555–576.

Brunsma, David L. and Kerry Ann Rockquemore (January 2002). "What Does 'Black' Mean? Exploring the Epistemological Stranglehold of Racial Categorization." *Critical Sociology* 28(1–2):101–121.

Brunsma, David L. and Kerry Ann Rockquemore (2001). "The New Color Complex: Appearances and Biracial Identity" in *Identity: An International Journal of Theory and Research* 3(1): 29–52.

Buchanan, NiCole T. and Cathy A. Acevedo (2004). "When Face and Soul Collide: Therapeutic Concerns with Racially Ambiguous and Nonvisible Minority Women" in *Biracial Women in Therapy: Between a Rock and the Hard Place of Race.* Edited by Angela R. Gillem and Cathy A. Thompson. Pp. 119–132. New York, NY: The Haworth Press.

Butler, Judith (2004). *Precarious Life: The Powers of Mourning and Violence.* New York: Verso.

Campbell, Mary E. (2007). "Thinking Outside the (Black) Box: Measuring Black and Multiracial Identification on Surveys." *Social Science Research* 36:921–944.

Canclini, Nestor Garcia (2005). *Hybrid Cultures: Strategies for Entering and Leaving Modernity.* Minneapolis, Minnesota: University of Minnesota Press.

Canclini, Nestor Garcia (1992). "Cultural Reconversion" in *On Edge: The Crisis of Contemporary Latin American Culture.* Edited by George Yudice, Jean Franco, and Juan Flores. Minneapolis, Minnesota: University of Minnesota Press.

Chang, Sharon H. (2015). *Raising Mixed Race: Multiracial Asian Children in a Post-Racial World.* New York: Routledge.

Childs, Erica Chito (2005). *Navigating Interracial Borders: Black-White Couples and Their Social Worlds.* New Jersey: Rutgers University Press.

Coates, Ta-Nehisi (2015). *Between the World and Me.* New York: Spiegel and Grau.

Collins, Patricia Hill (2005). *Black Sexual Politics: African Americans, Gender, and the New Racism.* New York, NY: Routledge.

Collins, Patricia Hill (2004). "The Sexual Politics of Black Womanhood" in *Sex Matters: The Sexuality and Society Reader.* Edited by Mindy Stombler, Dawn M. Baunach, Elisabeth O. Burgess, Denise Donnelly, and Wendy Simonds. Pp. 388–402. New York, NY: Pearson Education, Inc.

Collins, Patricia Hill (2000/1991). *Black Feminist Thought: Knowledge, Consciousness, and the Politics of Empowerment.* (2nd Ed.). New York: Routledge.

Collins, Patricia Hill (Sum 1998a). "It's All in the Family: Intersections of Gender, Race, and Nationality. *Hypatia: A Journal of Feminist Philosophy* 13(3): 62–82.

Collins, Patricia Hill (1998b). *Fighting Words: Black Women and The Search for Justice.* Minneapolis, MN: Regents of the University of Minnesota.

Collins, Patricia Hill (Fall 1993). "Towards a New Vision: Race, Class and Gender as Categories of Analysis and Connection," *Race, Sex and Class* 1(1): 25–45.

Collins, Patricia Hill (Oct.–Dec. 1986). "Learning from the Outsider Within: The Sociological Significance of Black Feminist Thought." *Social Problems 33(6)*:S14–S32.

DaCosta, K. M. (2007). *Making Multiracials: State, Family, and Market in the Redrawing of the Color Line.* Stanford, CA: Stanford University Press.

Dalmage, Heather M. (Ed.) (2004a). *The Politics of Multiracialism: Challenging Racial Thinking.* Albany, NY: State University of New York Press.

Dalmage, Heather M. (2004b). "Protecting Racial Comfort, Protecting White Privilege" in *The Politics of Multiracialism: Challenging Racial Thinking.* Edited by Heather Dalmage. Pp. 203–218. Albany, NY: State University of New York Press.

Dalmage, Heather M. (2004c). "'Mama, Are You Brown? Multiracial Families and the Color Line." In *Skin Seep: How Race and Complexion Matter in the 'Color-Blind' Era.* Edited by Cedric Herring, Verna Keith, and Hayward Derrick Horton (Eds.). Pp. 82–98. Copublished by Institute for Research on Race and Public Policy, University of Illinois at Chicago and University of Illinois Press, Urbana and Chicago.

Dalmage, Heather M. (2000). *Tripping On The Color Line: Black-White Multiracial Families in a Racially Divided World.* New Brunswick, NJ: Rutgers University Press.

Daniel, G. Reginald (2002). *More Than Black? Multiracial Identity and the New Racial Order.* Philadelphia: Temple University Press.

Davis, Angela Y. (1981). *Women, Race, and Class.* New York: Vintage.

Davis, F. James (1991). *Who Is Black? One Nation's Definition.* University Park, PA: The Pennsylvania State University Press.

Dawkins, Marcia Alesan (2012). *Clearly Invisible: Racial Passing and the Color of Cultural Identity.* Waco, TX: Baylor University Press.

Debord, Guy (1995/1994). *The Society of the Spectacle.* New York: Zone Books.

DeBose, Herman L. and Loretta I. Winters (2003). "The Dilemma of Biracial People of African American Descent" in *New Faces In A Changing America: Multiracial Identity in The 21st Century.* Edited by Loretta I. Winters and Herman L. DeBose. Pp. 127–157. Thousand Oaks, CA: Sage Publications.

Delgado, Richard and Jean Stefanic (2001). *Critical Race Theory: An Introduction.* New York, NY: New York University Press.

Delgado, Richard and Jean Stefanic (Eds.) (1997). *Critical White Studies: Looking Behind the Mirror.* Philadelphia, PA: Temple University Press.

Delgado, Richard (1993). "Words That Wound: A Tort Action for Racial Insults, Epithets, and Name Calling" in *Words That Wound: Critical Race Theory, Assaultive Speech, and the First Amendment.* Edited by J.M. Matsuda, C.R. Lawrence, R. Delgado, and K. Williams Crenshaw. Pp. 89–110. Boulder, CO: Westview Press.

DeLoria Phillip (1999). *Playing Indian.* New Haven: Yale University Press.

Deters, Kathleen A (Summer 1997). "Belonging Nowhere and Everywhere: Multiracial Identity Development" in *Bulletin of the Menninger Clinic* 61(3):368–84.

Doane, Ashley W. Jr (1997). "Dominant Group Ethnicity in the United States: The Role of 'Hidden' Ethnicity in Intergroup Relations. *The Sociological Quarterly* 38(3):375–397.

Doane, Ashley and Eduardo Bonilla-Silva (2003). *White Out: The Continuing Significance of Racism.* New York: Routledge.

Douglas, Mary (2002). *Purity and Danger: An Analysis of the Concepts of Pollution and Taboo.* New York: Routledge.

Doyle, Jamie M. and Grace Kao (2007). "Are Racial Identities of Multiracials Stable: Changing Racial Self-Identification among Single and Multiple Race Individuals." *Social Psychology Quarterly.* 70(4): 405–423.

Doyle, Jamie Mihoko and Grace Kao (2004). "'Multiracial' Today, but 'What' Tomorrow? The Malleability of Racial Identification Over Time." Paper submitted to the 2005 Annual Meeting of the Population Association America.

DuBois, W.E.B. (1903). *The Souls of Black Folks.* New York: W.W. Norton.

Duneier, Mitch and Harvey Molotch (March 1999). "Talking City Trouble: Interactional Vandalism, Social Inequality, and the 'Urban Interaction Problem.'" *American Journal of Sociology 104(5):* 1263–1295.

Dyer, Richard (1997). *White: Essays on Race and Culture.* New York: Routledge.

Espiritu, Yen Le (2004). *Asian American Women and Men.* Walnut Creek, CA: AltaMira Press.

Espiritu, Yen Le (2003). *Homebound: Filipino American Lives Across Cultures, Communities, and Countries.* Los Angeles: University of California Press.

Espiritu, Yen Le (2001). "'We Don't Sleep Around Like White Girls Do': Family, Culture, and Gender in Filipina American Lives" in *Signs* 26(2): 415–440.

Espiritu, Yen Le (1992). *Asian American Panethnicity: Bridging Institutions and Identities.* Philadelphia: Temple University Press.

Farley, Reynolds (2001). *Identifying with Multiple Races.* Population Studies Center Report No. 01-491. Ann Arbor: University of Michigan.

Feagin, Joe (2009). *The White Racial Frame: Centuries of Racial Framing and Counter-Framing.* New York: Routledge.

Feagin, Joe (February 1991). "The Continuing Significance of Race: Anti-black Discrimination in Public Places." *American Sociological Review 56*:101–116.

Ferber, Abby L. (1998). *White Man Falling: Race, Gender, and White Supremacy.* Lanham, MD: Rowman and Littlefield Publishers.

Ferrante, Joan and Prince Brown, Jr. (2001). *The Social Construction of Race and Ethnicity in the United States* (2nd Ed.). Upper Saddle River, NJ: Prentice-Hall.

Fine, Michelle, Lois Weis, Linda C. Powell, and L. Mun Wong (Eds.) (1997). *Off White: Readings on Race, Power, and Society.* New York: Routledge.

Fine, Michelle (Mar 2002). "2001 Carolyn Sherif Award Address: The Presence of an Absence." *Psychology of Women Quarterly* 26(1): 9–24. Blackwell Publishing.

Fischer, Rosalind (2006). "Do White Mothers of Biracial Children Adopt Traitorous Identity Traits? Paper presented at Annual Meeting of the Association of Black Sociologists. Montreal.

Foner, Nancy (2000). *From Ellis Island to JFK: New York's Two Great Waves of Immigration.* New Haven, CT: Yale University Press.

Foucault, Michel (1977). *Discipline and Punish: The Birth of the Prison.* Translated from the French by Alan Sheridan. New York: Vintage Books.

Francia, Luis H. and Eric Gamalinda (1996). *Flippin': Filipinos on America.* New York: Asian American Writers' Workshop.

Frankenberg, Ruth (Ed.) (1997). *Displacing Whiteness: Essays In Social And Cultural Criticism.* Durham, NC: Duke University Press.

Frankenberg, Ruth (1993). *White Women, Race Matters: The Social Construction Of Whiteness.* Minneapolis: University of Minnesota Press.

Fusco, Coco (1995). *English is Broken Here: Notes on Cultural Fusion in the Americas.* New York: The New Press.

Gallagher, Charles A. (2006). "Color Blindness: An Obstacle to Racial Justice?" in *Mixed Messages: Multiracial Identities in the "Color-Blind Era."* Edited by David Brunsma. Boulder, CO: Lynne Reinner.

Gallagher, Charles A. (2004). "Racial Redistricting: Expanding the Boundaries of Whiteness" in *The Politics Of Multiracialism: Challenging Racial Thinking.* Edited by Heather Dalmage. Pp. 59–76. Albany, NY: State University of New York Press.

Gallagher, Charles A. (Ed.) (2003a). *Rethinking The Color Line: Readings In Race and Ethnicity* (2nd Ed.). New York: McGraw Hill.

Gallagher, Charles A. (2003b). "Color-Blind Privilege: The Social And Political Functions Of Erasing The Color Line In Post Race America." *Race, Gender And Class Vol 10(4)*: 22–37.

Gallagher, Charles A. (2000). "White Like Me? Methods, Meaning, And Manipulation In The Field Of White Studies" in *Racing Research, Researching Race: Methodological Dilemmas in Critical Race Studies.* Edited by France Winddance Twine and Jonathan W. Warren. Pp. 67–92. New York: New York University Press.

Gambol, Brenda (2016). "Changing Racial Boundaries and Mixed Unions: The Case of Second-Generation Filipino Americans." *Ethnic and Racial Studies 39(14)*: 2621–2640.

Gans, Herbert (1999). "The Possibility of a New Racial Hierarchy in the Twenty-First-Century United States" in *The Cultural Territories Of Race: Black And White Boundaries.* Edited and with an introduction by Michele Lamont. Pp. 371–390. Chicago, IL: University of Chicago Press.

Gaskins, Pearl Fuyo (1999). *What Are You? Voices Of Mixed-Race People.* New York: Henry Holt and Company.

Gates, Henry Louis (1986). *"Race," Writing, and Difference.* Chicago, IL: University of Chicago Press.

Geertz, Clifford (1977). *The Interpretation of Cultures.* New York: Basic Books.

Gillem, Angela R. and Cathy A. Thompson (2004). *Biracial Women in Therapy: Between a Rock and the Hard Place of Race.* New York, NY: The Haworth Press.

Goar, Carla (2008). "Experiments in Black and White: Power and Privilege in Experimental Methodology" in *White Logic, White Methods: Racism and*

Methodology. Edited by Tukufu Zuberi and Eduardo Bonilla-Silva. Pp. 153–162. Lanham, MD: Rowman and Littlefield Publishers.

Goffman, Erving (1967). *Interaction Ritual: Essays on Face-to-Face Behavior*. New York: Pantheon Books.

Goffman, Erving (1963). *Behavior in Public Places: Notes on the Social Organization of Gatherings*. New York, NY: The Free Press.

Goldberg, David Theo (1997). *Racial Subjects: Writing on Race in America*. New York: Routledge.

Golden, Marita (2005). *Don't Play in the Sun: One Woman's Journey Through the Color Complex*. New York: Anchor.

Gonzalez, Belisa (2016). "How Can I Trust You If You Don't Know Who You Are? The Consequences of a Fluid Identity on Cross-Racial Organizing between African American Women and Latinas in Atlanta." *Societies* 6(13): 1–24.

Gramsci, Antonio (1971). *Selections from the Prison Notebooks*. New York: International Publishers Co.

Gray-Rosendale (2013). *College Girl*. Albany, NY: SUNY Press.

Hacker, Andrew (1992/2003). *Two Nations: Black and White, Separate, Hostile, Unequal*. New York, NY: Scribner.

Hall, Stuart (1999). "Cultural Studies and Its Theoretical Legacies" in *Cultural Studies Reader* (2nd Ed). Edited by Simon During. Pp. 97–112. New York, NY: Routledge.

Hall, Stuart (1997). *Representation: Cultural Representations and Signifying Practices*. London: Open University Press.

Hansen, Marcus (1952). "The Third Generation in America." *Commentary* 14(Nov.): 492–500.

Harding, Sandra (Ed.) (2003). *The Feminist Standpoint Theory Reader: Intellectual and Political Controversies*. New York: Routledge.

Harper, Phillip Brian (2000). "The Evidence of Felt Intuition: Minority Experience, Everyday Life, and Critical Speculative Knowledge." *GLQ: A Journal of Lesbian and Gay Studies* 6.4:641–657.

Harris, Cheryl (1993). "Whiteness as Property." *Harvard Law Review* 106(8):1707–1791.

Harris-Perry, Melissa (2011). *Sister Citizen: Shame, Stereotypes, and Black Women in America*. New Haven, CT: Yale University Press.

Hartsock, Nancy (1983). "The Feminist Standpoint: Developing the Ground for a Specifically Feminist Historical Materialism" in *Discovering Reality: Feminist Perspectives on Epistemology*. Edited by Sandra Harding and Merrill Hintikka. Dordecht: Reidel.

Herring, Cedric, Verna Keith, and Hayward Derrick Horton (Eds.) (2004). *Skin Deep: How Race And Complexion Matter In The 'Color-Blind' Era*. Copublished by Institute for Research on Race and Public Policy, University of Illinois at Chicago and University of Illinois Press, Urbana and Chicago.

Hintzen, Percy Claude and Jean Muteba Rahier (2003). *Problematizing Blackness: Self-Ethnographies by Black Immigrants to the United States*. New York: Routledge.

Hobson, Janell (2012). *Body as Evidence: Mediating Race, Globalizing Gender*. New York: SUNY Press.

Hochschild, Jennifer L. (2014). *Creating a New Racial Order: How Immigration, Multiracialism, Genomics, and the Young Can Remake Race in America*. Princeton, NJ: Princeton University Press.

Hooks, bell (2003). "Selling Hot Pussy: Representations of Black Female Sexuality in the Cultural Marketplace" in *The Politics of Women's Bodies: Sexuality, Appearance, and Behavior* (2nd Ed). Edited by Rose Weitz. Pp. 122–132. New York, NY: Oxford University Press.

Hooks, bell (1992). *Black Looks: Race and Representation*. Boston, MA: South End Press.

Horton, Hayward Derrick (2006). "Racism, Whitespace, and the Rise of the Neo-Mulattoes" in *Mixed Messages: Multiracial Identities in the "Color-Blind" Era*. Edited by David L. Brunsma. Pp. 117–124. Boulder, CO: Lynne Rienner.

Houts Picca, Leslie and Joe R. Feagin (2007). *Two-Faced Racism: Whites in the Backstage and Frontstage*. New York: Routledge.

Houze, Yalonda and Weberman, David (July 2001). "On Racial Kinship." *Social Theory and Practice 27*(3):419–436.

Hunter, Margaret L. (2005). *Race, Gender, and the Politics of Skin Tone*. New York: Routledge.

Ifekwuniwe, Jayne O. (Ed.) (2004). *'Mixed Race' Studies: A Reader*. New Routledge.

Johnson-Bailey, Juanita (1999). "The Ties That Bind and the Shackles That Separate: Race, Gender, Class, and Color in a Research Process." In *International Journal of Qualitative Studies in Education 12(6)*: 659–670.

Johnson, Mat (2015). *Loving Day*. New York: Spiegel and Grau.

Jones, Nicholas A. and Amy Symens Smith (2003). "Who Is Multiracial?" Exploring the Complexities and Challenges Associated with Identifying the Two or More Races Population in Census 2000. Unpublished paper presented at the Annual Meeting of the Population Association of America, Minneapolis MN. May 2003.

Jones, Nicholas A., and Amy Symens Smith (2001). "The Two or More Races Population: 2000." Census 2000 Brief. U.S. Census Bureau #C2KBR/01-6.

Jones, Nicholas A. and Jungmiwha Bullock (2012). "The Two or More Races Population: 2010. 2010 Census Briefs.

Joseph, Ralina L. (2013). Transcending Blackness: From the New Millennium Mulatta to the Exceptional Multiracial. Durham: Duke University Press.

Joyner, Kara and Grace Kao (2005). "Interracial Relationships and the Transition to Adulthood" in *American Sociological Review 70(4)*: 563–581.

Kaw, Eugenia (2003). "Medicalization of Racial Features: Asian-American Women and Cosmetic Surgery." In *The Politics of Women's Bodies: Sexuality, Appearance, and Behavior*. Edited by Rose Weitz. Pp.184–200. New York: Oxford University Press.

Keating, AnaLouise (2013). *Transformation Now!: Toward a Post-Oppositional Politics of Change*. Chicago, IL: University of Illinois Press.

Keating, AnaLouise and Gloria Gonzales-Lopez (2012). *Bridging: How Gloria Anzaldua's Life and Work Transformed Our Own*. Austin: University of Texas Press.

Keenan, Sarah (March 6, 2014). "Inheriting Entitlement: Property, Whiteness, and Rape." Talk Delivered at School of Law, University of London.

Kenney, Mark and Kelley Kenney (June 2012). "Contemporary U.S. Multiple Heritage Couples, Individuals, and Families: Issues, Concerns, and Counseling Implications." *Counseling Psychology Quarterly* 25(2):99-112. Special Issue: Race, Culture, and Mental Health: Mestizaje, Mixed 'Race', and Beyond.

Khanna, Nikki and Cherise A. Harris (Jan 2014). "Discovering Race in a 'Post-Racial' World." *Teaching Sociology 43(1)*:39–45.

Khanna, Nikki (2011). Biracial in America: Forming and Performing Racial Identity. Lanham, MD: Lexington Books.

Khanna, Nikki (2010). "'If You're Half Black, You're Just Black': Reflected Appraisals and the Persistence of the One Drop Rule in the South." *The Sociological Quarterly 51*(1): 96–121.

Kibria, Nazli (2002). *Becoming Asian American: Second-Generation Chinese and Korean American Identities.* Baltimore, MD: Johns Hopkins University Press.

Kibria, Nazli (1995). *Family Tightrope: The Changing Lives of Vietnamese Americans.* Princeton, NJ: Princeton University Press.

King-O'Riain, Rebecca, Stephen Small, Minelle Mahtani, Miri Song, and Paul Spickard (Eds.) (2014). *Global Mixed Race.* New York: New York University Press.

Kivel, Paul (1996). *Uprooting Racism: How White People Can Work For Racial Justice.* Gabriola Island, BC: New Society Publishers.

Korgen, Kathleen (2002). *Crossing The Racial Divide: Close Friendships Between Black and White Americans.* Westport, CT: Praeger.

Korgen, Kathleen Odell (1998). *From Black To Biracial: Transforming Racial Identity Among Americans.* Westport, CT: Praeger.

LaFerla, Ruth (December 28, 2003). "Generation E.A.: Ethnically Ambiguous." *New York Times.* New York.

Lamphere, Louise, Helena Ragone, and Patricia Zavella (Eds.) (1997). *Situated Lives: Gender and Culture in Everyday Life.* New York: Routledge.

Landale, Nancy S. and R.S. Oropesa (2002). "White, Black, or Puerto Rican? Racial Self-Identification Among Mainland and Island Puerto Ricans." *Social Forces* 81:231–254.

LaRossa, Ralph (2005). "Grounded Theory Methods and Qualitative Family Research." *Journal of Marriage and Family* 67:837–857.

Lazarre, Jane (1996). *Beyond The Whiteness of Whiteness: Memoirs of a White Mother of Black Sons.* Durham, NC: Duke University Press.

Lee, Jennifer and Frank D. Bean (2007). "Reinventing the Color Line: Immigration and America's New Racial/Ethnic Divide" in *Social Forces* 86(2): 561–586.

Lee, Jennifer and Frank D. Bean (2004). "America's Changing Color Lines: Immigration, Race/Ethnicity, and Multiracial Identification" in *Annual Review of Sociology* 30: 221–42.

Lesser, Jeffrey (2003). *Searching for Home Abroad: Japanese Brazilians and Transnationalism.* Durham, NC: Duke University Press.

Lewis, Elliott (2006). *Fade: My Journeys in Multiracial America.* New York: Carroll and Graf.

Lipsitz, George (2006). *The Possessive Investment in Whiteness: How White People Profit From Identity Politics.* Philadelphia, PA: Temple University Press.

Lorber, Judith (December 1993). "Believing is Seeing: Biology is Ideology." *Gender and Society 7(4):*568–581.

Lorde, Audre (1984). *Sister Outsider: Essays and Speeches*. Berkeley, CA: The Crossing Press.

Loury, Glenn (2002). *The Anatomy of Racial Inequality*. Cambridge, MA: Harvard University Press.

Lucal, Betsy (1999). "What It Means to be Gendered Me: Life on the Boundaries of a Dichotomous Gender System. *Gender and Society 13(6)*:781–797.

McIntosh, Peggy (1998). "White Privilege and Male Privilege: A Personal Account of Coming to See Correspondences Through Work in Women's Studies." Working Paper 189. Wellesley, MA: Wellesley College Center for Research on Women.

Mahtani, Minelle (2001). "'I'm a Blonde-Haired, Blue-eyed Black Girl': Mapping Mobile Paradoxical Spaces among Multiethnic Women in Toronto, Canada" in *Rethinking 'Mixed Race.'* Edited by David Parker and Miri Song. Pp. 173–190. Sterling, VA: Pluto Press.

Manganelli, Kimberly Snyder (2012). *Transatlantic Spectacles of Race: The Tragic Mulatta and the Tragic Muse*. Piscataway, NJ: Rutgers University Press.

Markovitz, Jonathan (2011). *Racial Spectacles: Explorations in Media, Race, and Justice*. New York: Routledge.

Matsuda, Mari (1993). *Words That Wounds: Critical Race Theory, Assaultive Speech, and the First Amendment*. Boulder, CO: Westview Press.

Maxwell, Audrey (1998). "Not All Issues are Black or White: Some Voices from the Offspring of Cross-Cultural Marriages in *Cross-Cultural Marriage: Identity and Choice.* Edited by Rosemary Breger and Rosanna Hill. Pp. 209–228. New York, NY: Berg Publishers.

Mirzoeff, Nicholas (2011). *The Right to Look: A Counterhistory of Visuality*. Durham, NC: Duke University Press.

Moore, Wes (2015). *The Work: Searching For a Life That Matters*. New York: Spiegel and Grau.

Mora, G. Cristina (2014). *Making Hispanics: How Activists, Bureaucrats, and Media Constructed a New American*. Chicago, IL: University of Chicago.

Moraga, Cherri (2002). "La Guera." *This Bridge Called My Back: Writings of Radical Women of Color* (2ⁿᵈ Ed.). Edited by Cherrie Moraga and Gloria Anzaldua. Pp. 22–29. New York: Kitchen Table: Women of Color Press.

Moraga, Cherri and Gloria Anzaldua (1983). *This Bridge Called My Back: Writings of Radical Women of Color*. New York: Kitchen Table: Women of Color Press.

Morning, Ann (2011). *The Nature of Race: How Scientists Think and Teach About Human Difference*. Oakland, CA: University of California Press.

Morning, Ann (2003). "New Faces, Old Faces: Counting the Multiracial Population Past and Present" in *New Faces in a Changing America: Multiracial Identity in the 21ˢᵗ Century*. Edited by Loretta I. Winters and Herman L. DeBose. Thousand Oaks, CA: Sage Publications.

Morning, Ann (2000). "Who Is Multiracial? Definitions and Decisions." *Sociological Imagination* 37(4): 209–229.

Muñoz , Jose (1999). *Disidentifications: Queers of Color and the Performance of Politics*. Minneapolis, MN: University of Minnesota Press.

Myers, Kristen (2005). *Racetalk: Racism Hiding in Plain Sight*. New York: Rowman and Littlefield Publishers, Inc.

Myers, Kristen (2003). "White Fright" Reproducing White Supremacy through Casual Discourse" in *White Out: The Continuing Significance of Racism*. Edited by Ashley W. Doane and Eduardo Bonilla-Silva. Pp. 129–144. New York: Routledge.

Nakazawa, Donna Jackson (2003). *Does Anybody Else Look Like Me? A Parent's Guide To Raising Multiracial Children*. Cambridge, MA: Perseus Publishing.

Nash, Robert J. and Sydnee Viray (2014). *How Stories Heal: Writing our Way to Meaning and Wholeness in the Academy*. New York: Peter Lang Publishers.

Nash, Robert J. and Sydnee Viray (2013). *Our Stories Matter: Liberating the Voices of Marginalized Students Through Scholarly Personal Narrative Writing*. New York: Peter Lang Publishers.

Neal, Mark Anthony (2013). *Looking for Leroy: Illegible Black Masculinities.* New York: New York University Press.

Nemoto, Kumiko (2009). *Racing Romance: Love, Power, and Desire Among Asian American/White Couples*. New Brunswick, NJ: Rutgers University Press.

Noble Maillard, Kevin (2008). "The Multiracial Epiphany of *Loving*," 76 Fordham Law Review, 2709.

Noble Maillard, Kevin and Rose Cuison Villazor (Eds.) (2012). *Loving v. Virginia in a Post-Racial World: Rethinking Race, Sex, and Marriage.* Cambridge, England: Cambridge University Press.

O'Hearn, Claudine Chiawei (Ed.) (1998). *Half-and-Half: Writers On Growing Up Biracial And Bicultural*. New York: Pantheon.

Ocampo, Anthony Christian (2016). *The Latinos of Asia: How Filipino Americans Break the Rules of Race*. Redwood City, CA: Stanford University Press.

Omi, Michael and Howard Winant (2014). *Racial Formation in the United States: From the 1960s to the 1990s* (3rd Ed.). New York, NY: Routledge.

Oliver, Melvin (2003). "Interview" in *Race: The Power of an Illusion.* Written by Christine Herbes-Sommers, Tracy Heather Strain, and Llewellyn M. Smith. Produced by California Newsreel.

Phillips, Layli (2004). "Fitting In and Feeling Good: Patterns of Self-Evaluation and Psychological Stress Among Biracial Adolescent Girls" in *Biracial Women in Therapy: Between A Rock and the Hard Place of Race*. Edited by Angela R. Gillem and Cathy A. Thompson (2004). Pp. 217–236. New York, NY: The Haworth Press.

Phoenix, Ann (2001). "Practising Feminist Research: The Intersection of Gender and 'Race' in the Research Process" in *Feminism and 'Race.'* Edited by Kum-Kum Bhavnani. Pp.203–219. New York, NY: Oxford University Press.

Pollock, Mica (2005). *Colormute: Race Talk Dilemmas in an American School.* Princeton, NJ: Princeton University Press.

Protean (2016). In *Merrian-Webster.com.* Retrieved May 10, 2016, from https://www.merriam-webster.com/dictionary/protean

Reddy, Maureen T. (1997). *Crossing the Color Line: Race, Parenting, and Culture.* New Brunswick, NJ: Rutgers University Press.

Reinharz, Shulamit (1992). *Feminist Methods in Social Research*. New York: Oxford University Press.

Roberts-Clarke, Ivory, Angie C. Roberts, and Patricia Morokoff (2004). "Dating Practices, Racial Identity, and Psychotherapeutic Needs of Biracial Women" in *Biracial Women in Therapy: Between a Rock and the Hard Place of Race*. Edited by Angela R. Gillem and Cathy A. Thompson (2004). Pp. 103–118. New York, NY: The Haworth Press.

Rockquemore, Kerry Ann (2005). "Forced to Pass and Other Sins Against Authenticity." *Women and Performance: A Journal of Feminist Theory* 29(15:1):17–31.

Rockquemore, Kerry Ann (2002). "Negotiating the Color Line: The Gendered Process of Racial Identity Construction among Black/White Biracial Women." *Gender and Society* 16(4):485–503.

Rockquemore, Kerry Ann (1998). "Between Black and White: Exploring the 'Biracial' Experience" in *Race and Society* 1(2): 197–212.

Rockquemore, Kerry Ann and Patricia Arend (2002). "Opting for White: Choice, Fluidity and Racial Identity Construction in Post Civil-Rights America." *Race and Society* 5(1):49–54.

Rockquemore, Kerry Ann, David L. Brunsma, and Daniel Delgado (2009). "Racing to Theory or Re-Theorizing Race? Understanding the Struggle to Build a Multiracial Identity Theory." *Journal of Social Issues* 65(1): 13–34.

Rockquemore, Kerry Ann and David L. Brunsma (2004). "Negotiating Racial Identity: Biracial Women and Interactional Validation" in *Biracial Women in Therapy: Between A Rock and the Hard Place of Race*. Edited by Angela R. Gillem and Cathy A Thompson (2004). Pp. 85–102. New York, NY: The Haworth Press.

Rockquemore, Kerry Ann and David L. Brunsma (2002). *Beyond Black: Biracial Identity in America* (2nd Ed.). Thousand Oaks, CA: Sage Publications.

Rockquemore, Kerry Ann and Tracey Laszloffy (2005). *Raising Biracial Children*. New York: AltaMira Press.

Roediger, David R. (2003). *Colored White: Transcending the Racial Past*. Berkeley, CA: University of California Press.

Rodriguez, Clara (2000). *Changing Race: Latinos, The Census, and the History of Ethnicity in the United States*. New York: New York University Press.

Rodriguez, Clara and Hector Cordero-Guzman (1992). "Placing Race in Context." *Ethnic and Racial Studies* 15:523–542.

Rodriguez, Juana Maria (2003). *Queer Latinidad: Identity Practices, Discursive Practices (Sexual Cultures)*. New York: New York University.

Rodriguez, Richard (2002). *Brown: The Last Discovery of America*. New York, NY: Penguin Books.

Roithmayr, Daria (2014). *Reproducing Racism: How Everyday Choices Lock in White Advantage*. New York: New York University Press.

Rondilla, Joanne and Paul Spickard (2007). *Is Lighter Better? Skin-Tone Discrimination Among Asian Americans*. Lanham, MD: Rowman and Littlefield Publishers.

Root, Maria P.P. and Matt Kelley (Eds.) (2003). *Multiracial Child Resource Book: Living Complex Identities*. Seattle: MAVIN Foundation.

Root, Maria P.P. (2001). *Love's Revolution: Interracial Marriage*. Philadelphia, PA: Temple University Press.

Root, Maria, P.P. (1999). "Resolving 'Other' Status: Identity Development of Biracial Individuals" in *American Families: A Multicultural Reader.* Edited by Stephanie Coontz. Pp. 439–454. New York: Routledge.

Root, Maria P.P. (1997). *Filipino American: Transformation and Identity.* Thousand Oaks, CA: Sage Publications.

Root, Maria P.P. (Ed.) (1996). *The Multiracial Experience: Racial Borders as the New Frontier.* Thousand Oaks, CA: Sage Publications.

Root, Maria P.P. (Ed.) (1992). *Racially Mixed People in America.* Thousand Oaks, CA: Sage Publications.

Rosenberg, Morris (1979). *Conceiving the Self.* New York: Basic Books.

Rosenblatt, Paul C., Terri A. Karis, & Richard D. Powell (1995). *Multiracial Couples: Black and White Voices.* Thousand Oaks, CA: Sage Publications.

Roth, Wendy (2012). *Race Migrations: Latinos and the Cultural Transformations of Race.* Stanford, CA: Stanford University Press.

Rothenberg, Paula (Ed.) (2005). *White Privilege: Essential Readings On The Other Side of Racism* (2nd Ed.). New York: Worth Publishers.

Rothman, Barbara Katz (2006). *Weaving a Family: Untangling Race and Adoption.* Beacon, MA: Beacon Press.

Rothman, Barbara Katz (2001). *The Book of Life: A Personal and Ethical Guide to Race, Normality and the Human Gene Study.* Boston, MA: Beacon Hill.

Row, Jess (2015). *Your Face in Mine: A Novel.* New York: Riverhead Books.

Rubin, Gayle (1984). "Thinking Sex: Notes for a Radical Theory of the Politics of Sexuality." In *Pleasure and Danger: Exploring Female Sexuality.* Edited by C. Vance. London: Routledge.

Russell, Kathy, Midge Wilson, and Ronald Hall (1992). *The Color Complex: The Politics of Skin Color Among African Americans.* New York, NY: Harcourt Brace Jovanovich Publishers.

Said, Edward W. (1978). *Orientalism.* New York: Vintage Books.

Sanchez, Diana T., and Courtney M. Bonam (2009). "To Disclose or Not to Disclose Biracial Identity: The Effect of Biracial Disclosure on Perceiver Evaluations and Target Responses." *Journal of Social Issues* 65(1): 129–149.

Sandoval, Chela (2002). "Dissident Globalizations, Emancipatory Methods, Social-Erotics" in *Queer Globalizations: Citizenship and the Afterlife of Colonialism.* Edited by Arnaldo Cruz-Malave and Martin F. Manalansan IV. Pp. 20–32. New York: New York University.

Sandoval, Chela (2000). *Methodology of The Oppressed: Theory Out of Bounds.* Minneapolis: University of Minnesota Press.

Santiago, Roberto (Ed.) (1995). *Boricuas: Influential Puerto Rican Writings-An Anthology.* New York: Ballantine Books.

Scales-Trent, Judy (1995). *Notes of a White Black Woman: Race, Color, Community.* University Park, PA: Pennsylvania State University Press.

Schuman, Howard, Charlotte Steeh, Lawrence Bobo, and Maria Krysan (1997). *Racial Attitudes in America: Trends and Interpretations.* Cambridge: Harvard University Press.

Segrest, Mab (1994). *Memoir of a Race Traitor.* Boston: South End.

Senna, Danzy (2004). "The Mulatto Millennium" in *'Mixed Race' Studies: A Reader.* Edited by Jayne O. Ifekwuniwe (2004). Pp. 205–208. New York: Routledge.

Seshadri-Crooks, Kalpana (2000). *Desiring Whiteness: A Lacanian Analysis of Race.* New York: Routledge.

Smith, Abbe (2005). "The 'Monster' in All of Us: When Victims Become Perpetrators. Georgetown Law Faculty Publications. *Suffolk University Law Review* Vol. 38:367-394.

Smith, Linda Tuhiwai (1999). *Decolonizing Methodologies: Research and Indigenous Peoples.* New York, NY: Zed Books Limited.

Somerville, Siobhan (2000). *Queering The Color Line: Race and The Invention of Homosexuality In American Culture* (Series Q). Durham, NC: Duke University Press.

Spelman, Elizabeth (2001). "Gender and Race: The Ampersand Problem in Feminist Thought" in *Feminism and 'Race.'* Edited by Kum-Kum Bhavnani. Pp. 74–88. New York, NY: Oxford University Press.

Spencer, Rainier (2010). *Reproducing Race: The Paradox of Generation Mix.* Boulder, CO: Lynne Reinner Publishers.

Spencer, Rainier (2006). *Challenging Multiracial Identity.* Boulder, CO: Lynne Rienner Publishers.

Spencer, Rainier (2004). "Beyond Pathology and Cheerleading: Insurgency, Dissolution, and Complicity in the Multiracial Idea" in *The Politics of Multiracialism: Challenging Racial Thinking.* Edited by Heather Dalmage. Pp. 101–124. Albany, NY: State University of New York Press.

Spickard, Paul (1989). *Mixed Blood: Intermarriage and Ethnic Identity in Twentieth-Century America.* Madison, WI: University of Wisconsin Press.

Stanley, Christine A. and Patrick Slattery (2003). "Who Reveals What to Whom? Critical Reflections on Conducting Qualitative Inquiry as an Interdisciplinary Biracial, Male/Female Research Team." *Qualitative Inquiry* 9(5): 705–728.

Steele, Claude (2011). *Whistling Vivaldi: How Stereotypes Affect Us and What We Can Do.* New York: W.W. Norton.

Steinbugler, Amy C. (2012). *Beyond Loving: Intimate Racework in Lesbian, Gay, and Straight Interracial Relationships.* New York: Oxford University Press.

Steinbugler, Amy (2009). "Hiding in Plain Sight: Why Queer Interraciality is Unrecognizable to Strangers and Sociologists," in *Interracial Relationships in the 21st Century.* Angela J. Hattery and Earl Smith (Eds.). 89-114. Durham, NC: Carolina Academic Press.

Steinbugler, Amy (2007). "RaceWork." Paper Presentation at ASA Annual Meeting.

Steinbugler, Amy (2005). "Visibility as Privilege and Danger: Heterosexual and Same-Sex Interracial Intimacy in the 21st Century. *Sexualities* 8:425–443.

Stombler, Mindy, Dawn M. Baunach, Elisabeth O. Burgess, Denise Donnelly, and Wendy Simonds. (2007). *Sex Matters: The Sexuality and Society Reader (2nd Ed.).* New York, NY: Pearson Education, Inc.

Stone, D. J. (2009). "Parent and Child Influences on the Development of Black-White Biracial Identity." Doctoral Dissertation.

Strauss, Anselm and Juliet Corbin. (1998). *Basics of Qualitative Research: Techniques And Procedures For Developing Grounded Theory* (2nd ed). Newbury Park, CA: Sage Publications.

Strauss, Anselm and Juliet Corbin. (Eds.) (1997). *Grounded Theory in Practice.* Thousand Oaks, CA: Sage Publications.

Streeter, Caroline A. (2003). "The Hazards of Visibility: "Biracial" Women, Media Images, and Narratives of Identity" in *New Faces in a Changing America: Multiracial Identity in the 21ˢᵗ Century.* Edited by Loretta I. Winters and Herman L. DeBose. Pp. 301–322. Thousand Oaks, CA: Sage Publications.

Streeter, Caroline A. (1996) "Ambiguous Bodies: Locating Black/White in Cultural Representations" in *The Multiracial Experience: Racial Borders as the New Frontier.* Edited by Maria P.P. Root. Pp. 305–320. Thousand Oaks, CA: Sage Publications.

Stryker, Sheldon (1991). "Identity Theory." Pp. 871–76 in *Encyclopedia of Sociology*, Vol. 2. Edited by Edgar F. Borgatta and Marie L. Borgatta. New York: MacMillan.

Stryker, Sheldon (1989). "Further Developments in Identity Theory: Singularity versus Multiplicity of Self." Pp. 35–57 in *Sociological Theories in Progress: New Formulations.* Edited by Joseph Berger, Morris Zelditch, Jr. and Bo Anderson. Newbury Park, CA: Sage.

Stryker, Sheldon (1980). *Symbolic Interactionism: A Social Structural Version.* Menlo Park, CA: Benjamin/Cummings.

Stryker, Sheldon and Richard T. Serpe (1994). "Identity Salience and Psychological Centrality: Equivalent, Overlapping, or Complementary Concepts?" in *Social Psychological Quarterly* 5(1):16–35.

Sue, Derald Wing (2010). Microaggressions in Everyday Life: Race, Gender, and Sexual Orientation. Hoboken, New Jersey: Wiley.

Takaki, Ronald (1993). *A Different Mirror: A History of Multicultural America.* Boston, MA: Back Bay Press.

Telles, Edward (2014). *Pigmentocracies: Ethnicity, Race, and Color in Latin America.* Chapel Hill: The University of North Carolina Press.

Thompson, Becky (2001). *A Promise and a Way of Life: White Antiracist Activism.* Minneapolis, MN: University of Minnesota Press.

Thompson, Becky and Sangeeta Tyagi (1996). *Names We Call Home: Autobiography on Racial Identity.* New York: Routledge.

Thompson, Maxine C. and Verna M. Keith (2004). "Copper Brown and Blue Black: Colorism and Self-Evaluation" in *Skin Deep: How Race and Complexion Matter in The 'Color-Blind' Era.* Edited By Cedric Herring, Verna Keith, and Hayward Derrick Horton (Eds.). Pp. 45–64. Urbana, IL: University of Illinois Press.

Thompson, V. L.S. (1994). "Socialization to Race and Its Relationship to Racial Identification among African Americans." *Journal of Black Psychology* 20:175–188.

Thornton, M.C. (1997). "Strategies of Racial Socialization Among Black Parents: Mainstream, Minority, And Cultural Messages" in *Family Life in Black America.* Edited by R. Taylor, J.S. Jackson, and L.M. Chatters. Pp. 201–215. Thousand Oaks, CA: Sage.

Thornton, M.C., Chatters, L.M., Taylor, R.J., and Allen, W.R. (1990). "Sociodemographic And Environmental Correlates of Racial Socialization By Black Parents." *Child Development* 61:401–409.

Turner, Jessie (2013). "Retheorizing the Relationship Between New *Mestizaje* and New Multiraciality as Mixed Race Identity Models." *Journal of Critical Mixed Race Studies.*

Tunstall, KT (2006). "Suddenly I See." U.S. Single Radio Version. *Eye to the Telescope.*

Twine, France Winddance (2011). *A White Side of Black Britain: Interracial Intimacy and Racial Literacy.* Durham, NC: Duke University Press.

Twine, France Winddance (2003). "Racial Literacy in Britain: Antiracist Projects, Black Children, and White Parents." *A Journal of the African Diaspora* 1(2):129–153.

Twine, France Winddance (2000). "Racial Ideologies and Racial Methodologies" in *Racing Research, Researching Race: Methodological Dilemmas in Critical Race Studies.* Edited by France Winddance Twine and Jonathan W. Warren. Pp. 1–33. New York: New York University Press.

Twine, France Winddance (1997). "Brown-skinned White Girls: Class, Culture, and the Construction of White Identity in Suburban Community" in *Displacing Whiteness: Essays in Social And Cultural Criticism.* Edited by Ruth Frankenberg. Pp. 214–243. Durham, NC: Duke University Press.

Twine, Frances Winddance (1996). "Heterosexual Alliances: The Romantic Management of Racial Identity" in *The Multiracial Experience: Racial Borders as The New Frontier.* Edited by Maria P.P. Root. Pp. 291–304. Thousand Oaks, CA: Sage Publications.

Twine, France Winddance and Amy Steinbugler (Fall 2006). "The Gap Between *Whites* and *Whiteness*: Interracial Intimacy and Racial Literacy." *DuBois Review: Social Science Research on Race* 3:341–363.

Twine, France Winddance and Jonathan W. Warren (Eds.) (2000). *Racing Research, Researching Race: Methodological Dilemmas In Critical Race Studies.* New York: New York University Press.

U.S. Census Bureau (2012). "2010 Census Shows Interracial and Interethnic Married Couples Grew by 28 Percent over Decade." http://www.census .gov/newsroom/releases/archives/2010_census/cb12-68.html

U.S. Census Bureau (2011). U.S. Census Bureau Releases 2010 Census Population Counts for the U.S. Virgin Islands [Website]. Available at: www.census.gov.

U.S. Census Bureau (2000). Racial Classification Definitions [Website]. Available at: www.census.gov.

Vaca, Nicholas (2004). *Presumed Alliance: The Unspoken Conflict Between Latinos and Blacks and What It Means for America.* New York: HarperCollins.

Van Ausdale, Debra and Joe Feagin (2001). *The First R: How Children Learn Race and Racism.* Lanham, MD: Rowman and Littlefield.

Vidal-Ortiz, Salvador (2004). "On Being a White Person of Color: Using Autoethnography to Understand Puerto Ricans' Racialization." *Qualitative Sociology* 27(2):179–203.

Wade-Gayles, Gloria (1997). *Rooted Against the Wind.* New York: Beacon Press.

Wallenstein, Peter (2002). *Tell the Court I Love My Wife: Race, Marriage, and Law—An American History.* New York: Palgrave Macmillan.

Walters, Karina, Selina A. Mohammed, Teresa Evans-Campbell, Ramona Beltran, David H. Chae, and Bonnie Duran (2011). "Bodies Don't Just Tell Stories, They Tell Histories." *DuBois Review 8(1):* 179–189.

Warren, Jonathan W. and France Winddance Twine (1997). "Whites, the New Minority? Non-Blacks and the Ever-Expanding Boundaries of Whiteness." *Journal of Black Studies* 28(2): 200–218.

Washington Post (August 25, 2008). "Three Quarters of Whites Don't Have Any Non-White Friends." http://www.washingtonpost.com/blogs /wonkblog/wp/2014/08/25/three-quarters-of-whites-dont-have-any-non-white-friends/

Waring, Chandra D. L. (2013). "Beyond 'Code-Switching': The Racial Capital of Black/White Biracial Americans." *Doctoral Dissertation.* Paper 81.

Waters, Mary (1999). Black Identities: West Indian Immigrant Dreams and American Realities. Cambridge, MA: Harvard University Press.

Waters, Mary (1994). "Ethnic and Racial Identities of Second Generation Black Immigrants in New York City." *International Migration Review* 28: 795–820.

Waters, Mary C. (1990). *Ethnic Options: Choosing Identities in America.* Berkeley, CA: The Regents of the University of California.

Weitz, Rose (Ed.) (2003). *The Politics of Women's Bodies: Sexuality, Appearance, And Behavior.* New York, NY: Oxford University Press.

Williams-Leon, Teresa and Cynthia Nakashima (Ed.) (2001). *The Sum of Our Parts: Mixed Heritage Asian Americans.* Temple, PA. Temple University Press.

Williamson, Joel (1980/1995). *New People: Miscegenation and Mulattos In The United States.* Baton Rouge, LA: Louisiana State University Press.

Winters, Loretta I. and Herman L. DeBose (2003). *New Faces in a Changing America: Multiracial Identity in the 21ˢᵗ Century.* Thousand Oaks, CA: Sage Publications.

Wise, Tim (2008). *Speaking Treason Fluently: Anti-Racist Reflections from an Angry White Male.* Berkeley, CA: Soft Skull Press.

Wise, Tim (1999/2004). *White Like Me: Reflections on Race from a Privileged Son.* Berkeley, CA: Soft Skull Press.

Woodfork, Joshua Carter (2005). *Shifting Whiteness: A Life History Approach to US White Parents of "Biracial" or "Black" Children.* A Doctoral Dissertation. College Park, MD: University of Maryland.

Wu, Frank (2003). "The Changing Face of America: Intermarriage and the Mixed Race Movement" in *Rethinking The Color Line: Readings In Race And Ethnicity* (2ⁿᵈ Ed.). Edited by Charles A. Gallagher. Pp. 546–564. New York: McGraw Hill.

Wu, Frank (2002). *Yellow: Race in America Beyond Black and White.* New York, NY: Basic Books.

Wynter, Leon (2002). American Skin: Pop Culture, Big Business, and The End Of White America. New York, NY: Crown Publishers.

Xie, Yu and Kimberly Goyette (December 1997). "The Racial Identification of Biracial Children with One Asian Parent: Evidence from the 1990 Census." *Social Forces* 76(2): 547–570.

Yancey, George A. (2003). *Who is White? Latinos, Asians, and the New Black/Nonblack Divide.* Boulder, CO: Lynne Rienner Publishers.

Yudice, George, Jean Franco, and Juan Flores (Eds.) (1992). *On Edge: The Crisis of Contemporary Latin American Culture.* Minneapolis, Minnesota: University of Minnesota Press.

Zack, Naomi (Ed.) (1997). *Race/Sex: Their Sameness, Difference, and Interplay*. New York: Routledge.

Zerubavel, Eviatar (1997). *Social Mindscapes: An Invitation to Cognitive Sociology*. Cambridge, MA: Harvard University Press.

Zerubavel, Eviatar (1991). *The Fine Line: Making Distinctions in Everyday Life*. Chicago, IL: University of Chicago Press.

Zhou, Min (2003). "The Changing Face of America: Immigration, Race/Ethnicity, and Social Mobility" in *Rethinking the Color Line: Readings in Race and Ethnicity* (2nd Ed.). Edited by Charles A. Gallagher. Pp. 441–462. New York: McGraw Hill.

Zuberi, Tukufu and Eduardo Bonilla-Silva (2008). *White Logic, White Methods: Racism and Methodology*. Lanham, MD: Rowman and Littlefield Publishers.

Index

228, 231, 252; single-parent
households, 128; stepfamily,
stepparents, 3-4, 17, 30, 231, 233-
4; "twice blended," 234
"family love story," 78. See also
storytelling.
"family that fits," 235. See also
racial resemblance.
"felt intuition," 70-1, 73, 75, 85, 154
feminism, 51
feminist praxis, 60
feminist research(er), xi, 50, 61
"first-generation" multiracial, 8, 35,
62, 64, 173
Fischer, Rosalind, 204
friends, friendships, x, xii, xiii, 24,
26, 34, 51, 57, 63, 68, 88-90, 92,
101-2, 107-9, 113-4, 117-9, 124,
126-8, 143, 145, 147-8, 150, 153,
158-9, 161, 181-2, 186, 196, 200-
2, 204, 215-6, 232, 235, 238-41,
243, 246, 248
Fusco, Coco, 245

Gallagher, Charles, 12, 13, 67, 133,
183
Gambol, Brenda, 17, 84, 218
Gans, Herbert, 21, 27
Geertz, Clifford, 35
gender binary, 57
Generation E.A. (Ethnically
Ambiguous), xi, 41, 77
genes, genomic matter, 170
geographies of race, global, 5, 38, 39,
45, 48, 97, 166, 207, 225
global, 45, 48, 62, 81, 97, 206, 208,
211, 242
Global Mixed Race, 208
"global mixed race," 208, 211
Grounded Theory Method, 56
Guess My Ethnicity game, 85
Guess My Race game, 85

Hansen, Marcus 57
Harper, Phillip Brian, 70, 154
hegemonic whiteness, 222
heritage, parentage, 1, 9, 10-3, 16, 19,
22, 25, 26, 30-4, 36, 38-42, 44,
50, 52, 54, 59, 61, 63-4, 68-9, 72,
74, 82-3, 87-8, 95, 98-9, 103,

107-112, 114, 116, 119-20, 122,
124, 128-31, 134-5, 137-9, 141-6,
150-2, 155-57, 161, 164-5, 170-5,
177-9, 181, 183, 186, 188, 197,
204, 211, 213, 218, 220-22, 226-
7, 230, 232, 236, 238-40, 247,
250, 252
hiding in plain sight, 8, 20, 34, 38-40,
87, 110, 132, 172
hierarchy, racial, 12, 14-7, 19, 26-7,
29, 32-3, 46, 49, 55, 61, 81, 89,
90, 92, 104, 115, 123 128, 134,
159, 161, 163, 169, 170 ,172,
175, 180, 182-4, 191, 195, 203,
217-8, 220
Hispanic, x, 30, 63, 83, 97-100, 104-
5, 142, 144-5, 167, 182, 191-2,
195, 200-2, 206, 218-20, 223-5,
229, 231, 235
Historically Black Colleges and
Universities (HBCU), 197
Hochschild, Jennifer, 250, 252
homogeny, 239
homophily, 90, 239
honorary memberships, Asian, 4, 6,
17, 231-2; Black(ness), 17, 43,
133, 148, 231, 239; Hispanic or
Latino, 202, 235; white(ness), 12,
14-7, 27, 92, 135, 137-40, 146,
169, 181-2, 191, 198, 200-2, 218,
239
hybridity, 169
hyperbolic blackness, 199
hyperbolic whiteness, 193-4

idealizing whiteness, 215
identity
"a different kind of black," 151;
"a different kind of mixed," 156;
"a different kind of white," 192;
"Anglo-Indian," 78, 104;
blended, 11, 146, 213, 216;
border, 11; fluidity of, 10-1, 14,
19, 25-7, 29-30, 38-40, 43, 45,
47, 63, 65, 68-9, 82, 86, 109-110,
112, 117, 119, 158, 220, 224,
227, 245, 247-8, 250; formal, 2,
5-8, 10, 19-21, 74, 109, 132, 137,
175, 223, 237; fragmented or
fractional, 11, 31, 243; freedom

206, 212-3, 215-7, 219-20, 222-3, 228, 237
Latinos of Asia (Ocampo), 17-8, 83, 148
"learning to be mixed," 118, 120, 122
Lee, Jennifer, 13-6, 19, 27, 31, 81
liminality, racial and spatial, 11, 24, 26, 43, 49, 53, 55, 65, 68, 112, 211, 222. See also liminality in identity.
"Linguistics of Color Blind Racism" (Bonilla-Silva), 198
literacy, cultural, 236; multicultural, 236; racial, 6, 19, 67, 71-2, 75-6, 81, 85, 88, 98, 102, 111, 113, 115, 117, 119, 121-2, 133, 136-7, 144-5, 147-50, 158, 176, 178, 180, 187, 209, 211, 214, 225, 230-1, 236, 240, 247-9
Lorde, Audre, 71, 77, 79, 171
Loury, Glenn, 13
Loving v. Virginia, 125, 162
Lucal, Betsy, 63

male privilege, 58, 127, 217, 229
"many faces of multiraciality," 47-8, 208
masculinity, 58, 126, 229
Matsuda, Mari, 92
McIntosh, Peggy, 14, 189
McNeal, Reanae, 223
merengue, 195
methodological challenges, 35, 38-9, 42-5
methods, research, 39
microaggressions, 85-7, 114, 116, 123
microassaults, 86
microinsults, 86
microinvalidations, 86
"mixed like me," 41, 47, 60
mixed race matters, 37-9, 43, 46, 60, 63, 91, 249-50
mixture, contemporary, 2, 37-8, 40, 164-5; familial, 167; historical, 37-8, 83, 167; shifting, 9-12, 24, 26, 29, 35, 38, 42-45, 47-9, 63, 74, 82, 95, 103, 112-3, 121, 128, 131, 134, 137, 142, 145, 183,

203, 207, 218, 220, 230, 234, 238-42, 245-7, 249-51
Mohammed, Selina A., 122
Moraga, Cherrie, 135
Mora, G. Cristina, 206
"more than black," 134, 173, 211, 232, 243
"more than multiracial," 3, 40, 81, 111, 230, 232, 239-40, 243
Morning, Ann, 98
multidimensionality of multiracial identity, 9, 24, 47, 65, 75, 224
multidirectionality of multiracial identity, 239. See also multiracial migrations.
"multifacial," 44, 47, 70
multiracial, blackness, 211; different racial cominations of, 52-4, 60, 156; epiphany, 47; experience ("the multiracial experience"), 51, 60, 70, 75, 85, 103, 248; heritage, 1, 31, 42, 64, 107, 112, 129, 137, 141, 146, 171, 174, 178-9; movement, see also migrations, 43, 81, 203, 210, 239-40, 242, 246, 250, 252; parentage, 6, 11, 52, 59, 111, 186, 199; whiteness, 211. See also Identity.
Multiracial Movement, ix, 7, 8, 162, 167
Muñoz, Jose, 221
Myers, Kristen, 136, 197, 203, 237
"mysteries of histories," 35, 120, 122-3, 155, 166, 177-8

Nash, Robert, 120
Native American, 12, 18, 44, 52, 63-4, 72, 84, 95, 105, 107, 123, 154, 156, 159, 163-7, 170, 172, 175, 177-80, 184, 187-8, 197, 204, 238-9
Native Hawaiian or Other Pacific Islander, 7, 8, 63. See also U.S. Census.
nepantla, 49
"not quite white," 133

Ocampo, Anthony, 17-9, 83-4
Office of Management and Budget, 6, 110

About the Book

Who is "multiracial"? And who decides? Addressing these two fundamental questions, Melinda Mills builds on the work of Heather Dalmage to explore the phenomenon—and consequences—of racial border patrolling by strangers, family members, friends, and even multiracial people themselves.

Melinda Mills is assistant professor of gender and women's studies, sociology, and anthropology at Castleton University.